MW00905536

Racing Fuel For The Spirit

Inspirational Devotions and Stories for Motorcycle Riders

By
Roy Jenkins

authorHOUSE™

1663 LIBERTY DRIVE, SUITE 200
BLOOMINGTON, INDIANA 47403
(800) 839-8640
WWW.AUTHORHOUSE.COM

© 2005 Roy Jenkins. All Rights Reserved.

No part of this book may be reproduced, stored in a retrieval system, or transmitted by any means without the written permission of the author.

First published by AuthorHouse 08/19/05

ISBN: 1-4208-4480-6 (sc)

Printed in the United States of America
Bloomington, Indiana

This book is printed on acid-free paper.

Roy's first published book:

Devotions for Racers, and Other People in a Hurry

Copyright 2000
http://2wheelcommunications.com

All pictures taken by Roy Jenkins unless otherwise noted.

All scripture quotations, unless otherwise indicated, are taken from the HOLY BIBLE, NEW INTERNATIONAL VERSION. 1973, 1978, 1984, by the International Bible Society. Bible quotations are italicized.

Cover

Bottom picture: The author surveys Mount Shasta while on a motorcycle trek through Northern California with his son Kyle in July, 1998. (photo by Kyle Jenkins)

Right Top: #1 Chris Pursell, #1x Monroe Voyles and #321 Hunter Broullette during a race at Down South Motocross in New Iberia in 2005. (photo by Kyle Jenkins)

Left Top: Pro Motocross racer Kevin Windham gets a jump on the 250 expert class at Wildwood Motocross in Kentwood in 2003. #51 is Coy "Boogeyshoes" Hobgood.

Back Cover: The author interviews Seth Savell after his win at Down South Motocross in 2005. (photo by Kyle Jenkins)

This book is dedicated to Kyle Chaney, who puts a face on courage and perseverance for the southern racing community.

Acknowledgements

This book would not have happened without my lovely wife, Linda. Her love has persevered beyond all my ADHD behavior. She is the steadying force in my life, 24 years and counting. My daughter Lacey and son Kyle are an inspiration to me and have helped me with this book. My Mom and Dad continue to offer their guidance and support. Most of all, I owe everything to my Lord and Savior Jesus Christ, who died that I may live. Now He lives in my heart, giving me guidance and purpose.

Also, thanks to all those people in the racing community. Many of you are in this book. Thanks for tolerating me. I have learned so much from you. May God richly bless you and your families.

My old friend, Robbie Burgess helped start all this. He talked me into announcing while I was trying (unsuccessfully) to make a racing comeback. Then He allowed me to start the devotions during the riders meetings at his races in Liberty and Fernwood, Ms.

Finally, thanks to all the track owners for paying me to announce and allowing me to bring the devotions at their races. God is using you to bring His good news to the racers and their families. Their tracks and locations are listed below, even though some are no longer in business. Thanks for the memories.

Down South Motocross Track – New Iberia, La.
Extreme Motocross Track – Kentwood, La.
Fernwood Motocross Track – Fernwood, Ms.
Gravity Alley Motocross Track – Breaux Bridge, La.
High Rollers Motocross Track – Gonzales, La.
Holeshot Motocross Track – Loranger, La.
LA Supercross – Avondale, La.
River's Edge Motocross Track – Geismar, La.
Tuff-E-Nuff Motocross Track – Oak Grove, La.
Wildwood Motocross Track – Kentwood, La.

The Arenacross Promoters in La. and Ms.
The American Historic Racing Motorcycle Association

Table of Contents

Introduction

In our fast-paced, over-worked, over-stressed, adrenaline-laced lives we need fuel to run on. Just like our body needs a healthy, balanced diet to grow strong, our minds need to be fed with the proper knowledge to function well. Likewise, deep inside where our emotions, feelings, consciences, desires and wills stir, reside our souls. In order for our souls to be strong they need healthy food; food recommended by our manufacturer. We need the good stuff, not just the candy of entertainment. We need fuel from our creator, God Himself.

He left this fuel in a book called the Bible. It is the most beloved, scrutinized, popular, oldest story in history and has stood the test of time and criticism. It is God's love letter to us. In it is the Who and Why of our creation and creator. He knows us each personally and loves us anyway. He wants relationship with us and knew we would need Him, along with regular doses of His wisdom, knowledge and encouragement.

Even before my call into ministry back in 1989, I had given my life to Him and to the study of His Word. After several years of jail ministry, Sunday School teaching and personal study courses, I answered God's call into Christian ministry. When I went to Seminary I took 6 years of intensive study under godly professors at New Orleans Baptist Theological Seminary. I finished my Bachelor's of Science degree and spent the next 5 years earning an Associate of Divinity and a Master's of Divinity degree with a major in Biblical studies with languages (Greek and Hebrew). I started pastoring a little country church while in seminary (Grace Baptist Church in Folsom, La.) But after three years I realized that pastoring a traditional church was not my calling.

I went on to teach Bible to 7th through 10th grade students at a Christian school for seven years. While I was doing that I found my way back to the motocross racing scene. Soon I was announcing and leading prayers and devotions. I found my calling was to bring the church to the motorcycle racing community. I did this by working as a race chaplain and leading devotions at riders meeting before each race. My first book, *Devotions for Racers* is a collection of many of those devotions as daily readings for inspiration, Bible study and personal spiritual growth. *Racing Fuel for the Spirit* is basically a sequel to that first book, with a few differences. Besides containing new devotions, and more personal stories about the people of the racing community, it also contains pictures. More importantly perhaps, the lessons in *Racing Fuel* reflect my own maturity and spiritual growth to date. I also expanded the stories to include street riding, Touring, cruising, road racing and vintage racing. This book is for anyone who struggles with life. It's a way to help you read the Bible.

I start with the assumption that we all have some things in common. We have the need for love and respect, to feel significant. We wonder about the world around us, how it works and how to conquer it. We yearn for relationship with at least one other person we can trust, who'll accept us as we are. We have a hole in our soul that only God can fill. We have fears, especially of pain, death and the afterlife. We have to deal with unmet expectations, getting mis-understood, knocked down, mis-treated and we become weary – soul weary. We make mistakes and suffer consequences, then have to deal with the guilt. We struggle with emotions of anger, sadness, and yes, even depression. We go through stages of life, learning about who we are, changing and growing.

We need hope, inspiration, strength and a vision for our own future; not someone else's, ours. We need to find our place in life, even after we have lost time chasing the wrong things, going down the wrong roads and suffering from bad decisions. We want to know there is a reason why things happen, and sometimes God allows us to see the answer. We need to be able to put our mistakes behind us - completely. We need help forgiving others and ourselves.

Our creator knew this. He knew about evil and temptation and the struggles we would face. That's why He inspired prophets, priests and kings long ago to shine the light of truth through the veil that separates this world from the heavenly one. At just the right time in history He sent His Son to fulfill prophecy, reveal His character and show us the depth of His love. Jesus Christ confronted empty religion, self-righteousness and hypocrisy. On the other hand He offered forgiveness to those who had sinned, acceptance to the outcast, hope to the hopeless, power to the powerless and gave the poor a new inheritance. He afflicted the comfortable and comforted the afflicted. Then Jesus surprised humanity by laying down His life when He died on the cross. He paid for our sins so we could be forgiven and have an open door to God the Father. Three days later He confirmed His promises by rising from the grave and ascending into heaven.

The good news is that anyone who responds by faith to God's invitation of salvation will receive His free gift of, – well, Himself. This includes: forgiveness of sins, a new start, a new life, new power and new peace. He sends us the gift of the Holy Spirit to live inside us, empowering, illuminating, guiding and encouraging us. Then we are capable of having an intimate relationship with our creator that starts here in this world and goes past the grave into eternity. The love we receive literally spills over into our earthly relationships, giving new life and hope to others. He reveals His purpose and direction for our lives, the reason for our existence..

My prayer is that you would come to know the living Lord Jesus Christ and have a personal relationship with Him as He comes to live in you. When you begin to see the light of truth and walk in the light, your chains will be broken. It will not be me that has rescued you, but Jesus and the truth that has flowed through God's Word. I am only the farmer who sows godly seeds. God sends water and "Sonshine" and brings forth new life.

Will you take a few minutes a day to allow God's seed to be sown into your life?

Roy Jenkins
September, 2004

How to Read This Book

This book is a series of devotional thoughts about life and God. I used some of these devotions at races during riders' meetings or church services. Some are based on articles I've published in magazines, newspapers and the internet. Others are just stories, usually true from events that happened to me or someone else. I use stories to illustrate Bible truths. Most are about motorcycle racing, touring, vintage bikes or cruising. I threw in a few commercial diving, hunting and everyday life stories for variety. But I directed this book to men and boys, to help them read the Bible.

I suggest you read one devotion a day, along with the Bible. Look up the scriptures in your Bible and read for yourself. My goal is for you to accept the Lord Jesus Christ and receive the Holy Spirit so you can read and understand the Bible for yourself. Some of these devotions will have special meaning to you and some you will not relate to at this time. That's ok, as those may be for someone else. I have resisted the temptation to include all those "feel good" stories that come through the internet (with a couple of exceptions).

So here you go, use the pictures to visualize the situation, read the story and absorb God's truth, one devotion at a time. Think of them as spiritual vitamins to take every day for good health. Wash the vitamins down with prayer, meditating on God and His wonderful qualities. Then ask Him to make you into the person you were meant to be. I promise that if you will invest at least 5 minutes a day in God's Word (using either this devotional book or another one) your life WILL CHANGE for the better.

Lastly, daily see yourself as He sees you, an individual like no other in creation, made in love for a purpose; endowed with a combination of gifts and abilities to serve Him and enjoy Him all your life on this earth as He prepares you for eternity.

Jackson Arenacross, Jamie Dishon drops the gate on the 250 Novice class, but Brock Hollis jumped too early. Also shown #48 David Hutchins, #977 Alex Raynor, #1 Chris Pursell, and #118 Scotty Allen in his last race.

Dillon Dufrene at Holeshot MX in Loranger.

1. Getting Back Up

It was Sunday April 27, 2003. The race was an Arenacross in Houma's Civic Auditorium. I was announcing the 125 beginner class. This is usually a dangerous and crowded class in the sport of motocross racing. This race proved to be a true reflection of that pattern. Fourteen powerful motocross racing bikes were lined up at the gate. Nervous riders revved their engines, watching the starter, Jamie Dishon. All eyes in the arena were on this veteran starter as he pointed down the line and got the nods of readiness from each racer. After he was convinced that all were ready, he quickly made his way to the release bar hidden at the end of the line. The crescendo of horsepower reached its peak as he dropped the gate. Clutches engaged, knobbies spun, dirt flew, and bikes broke loose and gained momentum to the fearful first turn where the high speed bullying and jockeying for position began.

One rider became a victim in the chaotic action. Chris St. Pierre, a local rider was taken down. Usually the riders bounce back up and get back into the race. But Chris was motionless. Since the injury looked so serious and he was right in the middle of the track, the red flag came out to abort the race. Medics came running. Flagmen were flagging. Women screamed. Then the crowd fell into a hushed anticipation. The other riders made their way back to the line cautiously killing their motors to wait. An eerie silence had fallen upon the smoky arena like a dark mood. As announcer, I dared not try to fill the time with more prize give-a-ways or witty remarks. I just announced his name. "Chris St. Pierre is down."

I hung my head to pray as he was being attended to. The three minutes seemed like thirty. Finally, the crowd began to applaud. I look up to see that Chris was being helped to his feet. "He's getting up - Chris St. Pierre from Houma," I cheerily announced. As he was helped off the track I turned to grab a ticket out of the box for another prize give-a-way as the entertainment resumed. A voice crackled on my headset. "He's getting back on his bike." It was Charlie Pausina, the race referee. A glance over to the gate confirmed this surprising news as Chris was swinging a leg over his bike which was now at the line. "He's gonna race again," Charlie said in an unbelieving tone. Even before I could announce it, the crowd erupted into a roar of approval as they watched the teenager put his goggles back on.

The gate dropped for the restart. My co-announcer in the tower relayed the news first, "Chris St. Pierre into the turn first!" Sure enough,

2

this young man got the holeshot and held on to win. I called for the officials to grab him and send him back into the arena for an on-track interview. When he finally returned, I stuck the microphone in his face and asked him, "What happened?" He said, "I got a calf injury, but it must have just been a 'charlie horse'. I just HAD to get back up." Again the crowd roared its approval.

A few races later, in the 50cc open class, a 6 year old rider from Westwego charged up to the front of the pack and won his race. Right as he crossed the finish line jump he crashed. Flagmen scrambled over to assist. Dillon Dufrene slowly began to crawl off the track. His Dad, Blue Dufrene had come running onto the track to pick him up. He checked him out, and then put him up on his shoulder for a victory ride back to the pits. I stopped them and asked Dillon what happened and placed the microphone under Dillon's helmet for the reply. "I just had to get up." I asked a smiling Dad, "How do you feel?" He answered smiling, "It's great. He did it."

Blue Dufrene had a heart attack at a race in Fernwood, Mississippi a year ago. He said they lost him on the operating table. But prayers were answered. He came back to us. He got back up. This night he enjoyed watching his son win an Arenacross race. How things can change. They looked bad, there was pain, but they turned out good. We all were reminded again about the value of human life and relationships.

It's not "if" you will go down in life, but "when." We all live in this world, and we will all face trials, setbacks and suffering. Whether we caused it or were just an innocent bystander. It's part of life. If we will accept this fact and be mentally and spiritually prepared, it won't seem so bad when it comes. Life's knockdowns don't have to be fatal. We CAN get back up. What's the secret?

Read Matthew 14:25-31 and look for Peter's mistake. He took his eyes off Jesus and focused on the problem. As soon as he did that, he started to sink. Then Jesus had to rescue him.

When life deals you the "dirty blows", here are some answers from God's Word:

1. Ask God for help. Don't try to rescue yourself.
2. Keep your focus on Jesus. They don't call Him "Savior" for nothing.
3. Look at life from God's perspective. This is a "long distance race," not a sprint. Just because you fall behind, or crash doesn't mean it's all over.

4. Read the Bible. In it is story after story of people who struggled and failed, but got back up. (David, Peter, Paul, Timothy, John, James, Abraham, Joseph, Moses, Joshua, etc.)

Quote for the day: "Real champions are not judged on how they handle winning, but how they handle defeat." (R.J.)

Lindsey Escoyne picks her bike back up during a race at Down South MX in 2005.
(photo by Kyle Jenkins)

Jacob Heintze goes down in the first turn at Down South MX in 2005.
(photo by Kyle Jenkins)

2. The Answer is already there

Michael Lewis tells about a man who visited New College in Oxford, England. When he walked into the Commons building he was amazed at the architecture. He asked when it had been built. "1386," the administrator replied. As he scanned the inside of the building, his eyes were drawn to the majestic old beams that crossed the open ceiling, holding it up. He had never seen anything like them. They were huge, massive, and magnificent. He asked if they were original.

No, they're not. They were replaced in the late 1890's. Those are new beams. When it became apparent, in the 1890's that the original beams were in need of replacement, a small crisis developed. No one knew where they would ever be able to find giant oaks of the size that could work. The college forester had the answer to the problem.

Hidden away in the back hills of the college property, is a great stand of giant oaks. Those oaks are over 550 years old. They were all planted by the same man who fashioned and installed the original beams back in 1386.

The provision was made hundreds of years earlier when the builder planted those trees for replacement timber. Isn't that how God works with us? He is timeless, not bound by current thoughts, trends or fads. He knows the truths that will last. He sees the beginning and the end. He has our provision ready at each station of life. He knows what challenges you and I will face, and He has the resources standing by at the right time and place.

When you face your crisis, you need look no further than the God who is only a prayer away. He may speak the answer through a godly friend, a circumstance or His written word. He may speak through your conscience.

Listen to one of my favorite verses. I inserted the underlined words because the word for "temptation" is *periasmos* in the original Greek language of the Bible. It can be translated as trial or test as well. Many of our struggles are combinations of trial/test/temptation. It just depends on what point of view the struggle is coming from. If it is from God, it is not a temptation, but a test. From the world, or Satan or our own evil desires' point of view, it is probably a temptation. What's the difference? God tests us to reveal and build our faith. Temptation is to invite us to sin, which God never does. (James 1:13-14)

No temptation (<u>trial/test</u>) *has seized you except what is common to man. And God is faithful; he will not let you be tempted* (<u>tried/tested</u>) *beyond what you can bear. But when you are tempted, he will also provide a way out so that you can stand up under it.* (1 Corinthians 10:13)

Notice from this verse that:
1. We are not the only ones facing this problem.
2. God is faithful, we can always trust Him.
3. He will not allow more on you than you can take. (One of my favorite promises of scripture)
4. He will PROVIDE an answer/solution/way out/strength to bear up under it.
5. It is only TEMPORARY. This, too shall pass.

Quote for the day: *"For your Father knows what you need before you ask Him."* (Jesus in Matthew 6:8)

Race Referee Charlie Pausina holds his daughter Molly before a race.

Potts Thomas (left) relaxing in his pits near one of his vintage bikes.
This is a 1977 Wheelsmith Maico

3. Respect

We all want it. Many will do almost anything for it. It's the foundation upon which love is built. It must be present for friendships to prosper. There are many names in the motocross racing fraternity that are respected. Racers who are respected have some things in common. First, they have won their share of races. Second, they have been around a while. Third, they try to help other racers become better. Fourth, they possess a lot of knowledge about the sport. Fifth, they are dependable people with a good reputation. Sixth, they really care about the sport.

Mr. I.W. Simmons and his sons, Wendell and Wayne are one such family. They have owned and operated tracks and shops and still volunteer time at racing events. Those two guys and their sons, Kevin and Jeffrey still race.

Charlie and Mike Pausina are another example. These guys own and operate a string of 4 wheel drive shops in Louisiana (and used to operate tracks as well). They have been racing since they were about 3 years old. Mike still drag races and Charlie officiates at big motocross and arenacross events (when they're not racing).

The Burgess family helped bring competition dirt bikes into the state back in the sixties. Mike Sr. was on the first American team (along with John Penton) who competed at the many of the biggest Enduro, Scrambles and Trials in the world, and has won hundreds of races. His son Robbie has been operating tracks for almost 30 years with his wife, Sue. Robbie and his son Nicolas were extremely fast money riders.

Peanut Brown has been around a long time and is still supporting motocross racing. Peanut and his wife Staci, both still race and now own a shop in Covington. They load up their camper and trailer with bikes, parts, accessories and gear and bring it all to the tracks on race day for sale. They are known for having just about anything you need, helping kids, and giving good advice.

Glen Guidry has been around since the early 70's when he raced Hodakas. His wife Dana runs D & G Cycles in Gonzales while he does shift work. His son Chase has won his share of money in the expert class.

One racer who is still racing at the tender age of 51 is Potts Thomas. He stands about six foot six and weighs over 270. He is as tough as nails. He'll tell you that he's been around, "longer than dirt." In 1986 he won a seniors National Championship at Glen Helen Raceway. Don't whine about the track around Potts. Like many of the other old school riders

9

(like me), we remember when we raced against the natural conditions and didn't complain about ruts, bumps and puddles.

One day Potts crashed hard at Kentwood. The rider behind him ran into his head with his steel foot peg while he was on the ground, breaking his helmet apart and cutting open his skull. By the time the ambulance got him to the hospital in McComb, he had lost a lot of blood and was almost dead. (If I had lost that much blood, I would have died, twice). When I got to the hospital to visit, it was the usual routine, family and friends in the waiting room, only a few family members in intensive care.

As I walked into the room, my eyes were drawn to dried blood all over the floor. Potts' wife was standing next to him with a worried look. Potts face was swollen and bandaged. He had received over 400 stitches in his face. When he saw me he smiled and gave me that familiar greeting, "Brother Roy, glad you could come." We prayed for healing and thanked God for his life.

Today Potts is healthy, still racing, still building tracks with his heavy equipment and still sharing his "trackside wisdom" with others. He loves to find old vintage motocross bikes, restore them and race them at events around the country. When he speaks, riders listen.

Who do you respect? What does it take to earn your respect? Who does God respect? What earns His respect? Oh, He loves everyone, and you don't have to earn His love. But respect is different. It is earned.

Here is a verse for today that will show you how to please God. Isaiah 66:2b has God speaking. This is what He said, and still says to us today: *"This is the one I esteem: he who is humble and contrite in spirit, and trembles at my word."*

Quote for the Day: Brains and beauty are nature's gifts; character is your own achievement. (unknown)

Peanut Brown of Champion Cycles about to congratulate Tyler Hancock after winning a race at Down South MX in 2005. (photo by Kyle Jenkins)

Jay Michon wins a helmet at the Champion Cycles Easter Egg hunt at Holeshot MX in 2004.

Peanut's wife Stacey (left), and Dawn Cortez show off new hats in the pits at Holeshot MX.

11

4. Being in Position

You never can tell what's going to happen during a race. Oh you can guess who MAY win, who is the fastest, who's been riding the best, who has the most skill, etc. But that doesn't mean they will automatically win.

In the 2003 Pro Supercross season, Honda mounted rider Ricky Carmichael was the favorite. He set a record the year before by winning EVERY moto. (A moto is a single race, and in the outdoor format of motocross usually consists of 2 to settle the overall winner) He had been on fire. With Kevin Windham out with an injury, and the retirement of Jeremey McGrath, it seemed as though Ricky was unchallenged. But a newcomer from Australia, Chad Reed was not intimidated. He stayed behind Ricky in overall points, even winning on occasion. Several times while Reed was just racing his race, Carmichael fell allowing Reed to garner the win. Toward the end of the season, Reed got to the checkered flag before Ricky five times. He placed himself in position to take advantage of any mishap on Ricky's part. Reed went on to win the Pro Supercross championship in 2004.

We've seen this many times at the local level. The fastest rider doesn't always win. But to take advantage of any problem he may have, whether it is a broken bike, crash, injury, or mistakes, the second place rider must be in position. Besides being close to the leader, he must be ready with an alternative line, be going fast enough to get by and determined enough to make it stick.

How can you place yourself in position to receive God's blessings and promises? You must first come into relationship with Him. *"Repent, then, and turn to God, so that your sins may be wiped out, that times of refreshing may come from the Lord."* (Acts 3:19)) Jesus said in John 3:3, *"No one can see the kingdom of God unless he is born again."*

How do we come into relationship with Him? How can we position ourselves to receive God in our lives? Recognize that we need forgiveness from God because we are sinners. *"All have sinned and fallen short of the glory of God."* (Romans 3:23)

Jesus frequently got in trouble with the religious leaders of his day. They wanted Him to be a rule-keeper according to their set of religious beliefs. But those leaders had made some mis-calculations about God, which is one reason God sent Jesus to show them the right way to interpret His Word. Those leaders were NOT in position to benefit from God's grace and forgiveness. Why? They didn't see their need. They had declared themselves right based on their own rules, but were really spiritually blind.

In Luke 5:30, they were condemning Jesus for hanging out with "sinners". (People who hadn't bought into THIER religious program). Jesus said, *"It's not the healthy who need a doctor, but the sick. I have not come to call the righteous, but sinners to repentance."*

In other words, only those who recognized their weakness (sin), their need (forgiveness) and are willing to turn God's way (repentance) can receive it. And whoever positions themselves that way and call upon Him are saved. How about you? Are you depending on your own "goodness" to get into heaven? Or will you put away pride, admit you are a sinner and cast yourself upon His mercy?

Romans 3:23: *"For ALL have sinned and fall short of the glory of God."*
Romans 6:23: *"For the wages of sin is death, but the gift of God is eternal life in Christ Jesus our Lord."*
Romans 5:8: *"But God demonstrates his own love for us in this: While we were still sinners, Christ died for us."*
Romans 10:9-10: *"That if you confess with your mouth, "Jesus is Lord," and believe in your heart that God raised him from the dead, you will be saved."*

Dillon Toups positions himself to win the 2004 Winter Series in the beginner class by winning the first race at New Iberia.

J.D. Kirby and his wife Kay prepare Jenna Schillage's bikes on race day at High Rollers MX in 2002.

(from left) Taylor Watts, Kaci Simon, and Jenna Schillage wait their turn to qualify at Gravity Alley MX for the AMA National Amateur Championship.

5. Preparation

Have you ever prayed for something, only to have something go wrong? Have you then wondered, "Did God send that?" Perhaps He did. Why? Because sometimes God must remove something old from your life to make room for something new. Maybe the loss is a friend, an opportunity, a job, some health, loss of money, a move away, a possession, a pre-conceived notion or belief, a hobby, or even a family member.

I remember making a new commitment in my relationship to God back in the mid-80's. When I did that, my boss didn't like it, and he fired me for wanting to go to church. It wasn't that good of a job anyway, I was just driving a truck, delivering produce from Independence, La. to grocery warehouses in New Orleans. But the issue became working on Sundays. I wanted to go to church on Sunday, and my boss wouldn't let me off. So I chose God over the job. Later, God brought me to a better job. It's been my experience, that if you trust God and act in faith, when you leave one station of life, He'll bring you to a higher station.

I often describe it this way: It's like wanting new furniture. You ask God for it. When the time is right these movers show up at your door, unannounced and start taking your old furniture out. You complain, "No, no. That's my favorite chair. And leave that table, I made that. No, not the sofa. It's so comfortable." But they don't listen. You look outside and see "God's Moving Company" on the truck. So you help them. You trust what God is doing.

Later, when you are ready for it, they start moving some new furniture in that is WAY better than the old. You couldn't even have imagined how much nicer it is until it all gets arranged in the proper order. Looking back you thank and praise God. Good thing you didn't argue and insist that He do it your way. Good thing you trusted Him to take all that old stuff out, even though you were robbed of your comfort zone.

God never promised us comfort. He promised us peace in the middle of the storms, and that He would give us new life, an abundant life. And He will never leave us. He will meet our Needs.

Back in Jesus' day, they put wine in animal skins or bladders, not bottles. (Although they did have clay and metal pitchers and cups). Jesus told a parable to the religious leaders when they criticized the disciples for not keeping all the religious rules.

No one tears a patch from a new garment and sews it on an old one. If he does, he will have torn the new garment, and the patch from the new will not match the old.

And no one pours new wine into old wineskins. If he does, the new wine will burst the skins, the wine will run out and the wineskins will be ruined. (Luke 5:36-39)

You know that new thing you're asking God for? Maybe he can't put that in your old lifestyle. He may require you to change something before it can work. But if you act in faith, and trust God, you'll be glad you did.

Quotes for the day: "Nothing leaves heaven unless - first, something leaves earth." (Mike Murdock)

"Everything that has happened before is preparation for today." (unknown)

6. Blessings

What are blessings? According to my desktop reference a blessing is: a desirable state; or the formal act of giving approval.

We ask God to "bless" our food, "bless" our day, "bless" the game, "bless" our home, "bless" our children, and "bless" our lives. Blessing is something good, something you want, especially from God. If I give you a Psalm, would you read it? Come on, go get your Bible. I'll wait.

Hey! Don't forget a pencil or pen.
Why? You'll see.

What's takin' so long?
Well, where's the last place you left it?

Yep, I'm still here. I'm not goin' anywhere. But you have a busy day, so hurry up and find it.

Ok. Open to the middle of your Bible. That's the Psalms. Turn to the 37th Psalm. (These were songs the ancient Hebrews sang for worship. They are filled with truths about God.)

Now carefully read that Psalm and jot down the blessings/promises of God on one side of this page, and what He requires you to do for them on the other side. Sure it's ok to write in this book. It's yours isn't it? Besides, you'll remember the truths better, and have a record for when you come back browsing for treasure.

Promises/Blessings from God   **What God requires from me**

Jason Manuel glances over at his Dad for instruction as he struggles in the money class during the Mid-South Shoot Out at Holeshot MX.

Bad news for the Orazio race team at an AHRMA Vintage race; Shannon Silva is out of the race after the transmission locked up and he crashed at over 100mph. Notice the ice-pack on his arm. To his right Billy Orazio inspects his CB72 Honda Hawk, while his mechanic George Carter holds it up and surveys the damage.

7. The Blues

There is a whole genre of music dedicated to it. The blues, feeling puny, discouraged, depressed. Did you know that sometimes it's good to feel depressed? Sure - when we suffer loss. Emotion is a part of being human. God made us that way for a reason. A negative emotion tells us something is wrong and helps motivate us to action, grief, rest or prayer.

There may be times in our lives when we go through a whole season of depression. We can't always be happy. If we were always happy, how would we know what happiness was? How could you enjoy a sunny day without having been through the storms? Besides, the storms bring change to the environment, like much needed water to replenish the earth for life.

There are reasons for seasons. However, it's not healthy to be stuck in one season, either. If you have been feeling depressed for two years or more, you probably have "clinical depression" and should see a doctor right away. You should get counseling to help regain proper perspective. Depressions can be caused by what happens to us (or doesn't happen when expected). It can also be caused by hormone imbalance (especially if you're over 30). It may be other chemical problems in your body that aren't working together properly. Stress and adrenaline recovery is an old problem that is just now being talked about in the counseling community. Depression could also be caused by "stinkin thinkin." You know what I mean, wrong attitude. Did you know it's not a sin for a Christian to be depressed? Many Christian leaders and high profile celebrities share testimonies about going through depression and finally getting help: Sheila Walsh, Abraham Lincoln, C. S. Lewis, Winston Churchill, John Wesley, Martin Luther, Nelson Mandela and Elijah, to name a few. I have experience in this area and the odds are, you do, too.

Even one of the greatest statesmen and warriors, King David suffered under its debilitating effects. He was kicked out of Jerusalem by King Saul because of jealousy. David's twin crimes were: being too successful in battle and becoming too popular with the people. The pain of rejection by the king he loved was made even worse when 85 innocent priests of God were murdered for giving him food. You can read the story starting in 1 Samuel 20.

There are other times when David caused his own pain and suffering because of mistakes he made. One was the sin of adultery and murder with Bathsheba. You can read that story starting in 2 Samuel 11. Here is an example of disaster coming upon David and his men:

When David and his men came to Ziklag, they found it destroyed by fire and their wives and sons and daughters taken captive. So David and his men wept aloud until they had no strength left to weep. David's two wives had been captured—Ahinoam of Jezreel and Abigail, the widow of Nabal of Carmel. David was greatly distressed because the men were talking of stoning him; each one was bitter in spirit because of his sons and daughters. But David found strength in the LORD his God. (1 Sam. 30:3-6)

Notice how David survived - he found strength in God. Here are some Psalms he wrote where he expresses his anguish and pain. If you read closely, you will see where his healing and joy comes from as well: Psalms 3; 4:1; 31:1-2; 32:3-4; 40:1-3; 22

Don't ever forget that the Lord hasn't forgotten you. He is with you and knows what you're going through. When the season of trouble/testing/trial is over, you can rise to a new place of maturity, strength, understanding and wisdom.

Quote for the day: *"Weeping may remain for a night, but rejoicing comes in the morning."* (Psalm 30:5)

8. Fear Factor

Mac Edmonston is a motocross racer and has the coolest piece of property in Galvez, Louisiana. He, along with help from his brother Brady, who also races, has turned it into a technical motocross track, complete with sprinklers, RV hook-ups and other camping facilities. Old moss-draped oak trees shade the camp with a pond in the center. Each year he holds a Motocross/Bible camp. It's called G2G (Glory to God) camp. Campers compete on teams for points through the six station obstacle course as they learn such lessons as faith, sacrifice, teamwork, courage, humility, trust and priorities.

Later the campers are given small group racing instruction. Such topics include cornering, jumping, starting gate and bike set-up. Then the riders get to ride the track all afternoon before the bonfire and worship service.

Once there was a 13-year old boy who was afraid of heights. When it was his turn to scale the wall he was petrified. His teammates yelled encouragement. Counselors reasoned with him that he could do it. His friends gave their votes of confidence. But balancing at the top of the wooden wall ten feet in the air was a different perspective.

He knew he could drop into the sand pit at the bottom, but he just couldn't let go. Teammates could yell all they wanted, but in the end, he would have to choose to drop. He battled fear for fifteen minutes. Even the other teams came over to encourage him.

Finally he launched his big body over the side and landed with a thud on his feet. The crowd cheered and this young man was relieved to be on the ground. But most of all he was filled with the joy of overcoming a fear, and found that it wasn't as bad as he had built it up to be in his mind.

Is there something looming on your horizon that has you worried? Is there an enemy plane on your radar? If you turn and face it you may find that what you thought was a jet fighter was just a bird. If you face your fear and let God have control, you will gain His courage. You will find that facing a fear in faith brings you to a new place of confidence.

What's the reason for not fearing? The fact that God is with you. Just talk to Him, read His Word, wait on Him, then go. If you have trusted Him, then it's His battle.

Scripture for the Day: *"So do not fear, for I am with you; do not dismayed, for I am your God. I will strengthen you and help you; I will uphold you with my righteous right hand. All who rage against you will* *surely be ashamed and disgraced; those who oppose you will be as nothing and perish. Though you search for your enemies, you will not find them. Those who wage war against you will be as nothing at all. For I am the LORD, your God, who takes hold of your right hand and says to you, Do not fear; I will help you."* (Isaiah 41:10-13)

Quote for the Day: "Fear knocked, Faith answered, there was no one there." (Unknown)

Mitch Gourney at the finish line jump of River's Edge MX, 2005

Red Team gets over the wall on the obstacle course at G2G, 2004

9. Vision

Without this, you die. Without this, nations die. Without this companies go bankrupt. Without this, your family will fall apart. "This" is vision. Where are you going? What direction will you take? How do you know what decisions to make, who to hang out with, how to spend your time, how to respond to people? It all starts with your vision.

In June of 2002 I took a solo sail in my little 23 foot sailboat. School had just ended and I was tired of teaching, tired of students (I love em' but...hey, all teachers feel this way in June). For weeks I had planned and loaded the boat with camping gear, fishing gear, non-perishable food, propane stove, etc. The day before I filled the ice chest, bought the fruit and breads and charged the batteries. Weeks before I had invested in something VERY important. Guess what it was? Charts, compass and a GPS (global positioning sensor).

I planned to sail out from the mouth of the Tchefuncte River in Madisonville, through Lake Pontchartrain, through Rigolets Pass, along the Gulf Coast to Cat Island. A vicious storm turned me back the first day and I spent my first night anchored in the mouth of the Tchefuncte river. But early the next morning, I repaired the rigging and set out. I spent my second night anchored in the Rigolets near Slidell. I sailed the next 17 hours straight to Cat Island. Hey, don't laugh, I was just learning and besides I was sailing directly against the wind.

What kept me from going around in circles? (All right - besides the view of the coastline). At night especially, I used the compass and the hand-held GPS. At 2:00am under a heavy fog (after running aground twice on the south side of the island), I anchored in Smuggler's Cove. How did I make it right into that cove, at night, in the fog? I had never been there before and I was basically a beginner sailor. That's right - the GPS. It takes a reading from at least three satellites and pinpoints exactly where you are. It also displays the shoreline.

I had VISION in the darkness. Not eyesight, not just feelings, or intuition, but true direction from a higher source according to the truth. Sometimes it didn't seem right. Sometimes I doubted a little. Sometimes I felt a little insecure, but I trusted the GPS and it led me right into the small harbor in the protected cove just as I had planned weeks earlier.

Do you know where you are going? Do you have a map? Or are you just living from crisis to crisis, paycheck to paycheck, following other people - going nowhere? Maybe you should get a vision for the future. Based on what? Other people's expectations? The crowd? Hollywood? What feels ok? The path of least resistance? The selfish pursuit of pleasure?

How about trusting your creator? He made you for a reason and has a purpose for your life. He can see past the storms around you, the sharks below you, the other vessels near you, the dangerous bottoms nearby, the false readings of feelings, etc. He can see through the fog of uncertainty, the darkness of fear and doubt, and keep you safe in the rough waters of problems. If you'll just trust Him and His word, He'll lead you to your own exciting destinations, important discoveries, gratifying moments of victory, and rest in safe harbor. He'll provide your daily rations, protect you from peril, and deliver you from thieves and pirates. But you have to TRUST Him.

Some of you are still tied to your dock. You're afraid to cut loose from the ordinary, the familiar. Or you may be in the paralysis of analysis. You'll never reach your dream if you don't have the courage to leave the shoreline of your comfort zone.

Get a map (the Bible) and read it. Make your plans prayerfully for where He is leading you. Get a GPS (Holy Spirit). Don't be distracted by critics or blind guides, however well-intentioned they are. Sail into the possibilities of your dreams with the right captain, the Lord Jesus Christ.

If you live in the past you are a prisoner. If you have only the present, you are going nowhere. If you have a vision, you are set for the future and on your way to victory.

Scriptures for the Day:
Habakkuk 2:3: *"...wait for it."*
Hebrews 11:27: *"he endured as seeing Him who is invisible."*
Proverbs 29:18: *"Where there is no vision, the people perish."*

Johnny Moore ignores his fear and accelerates down a blind down-hill section at Wildwood MX with the lead in 2004.

Adam Hancock tries to see through the dust at Wildwood MX while racing in the money class in 2004.

10. The Butterfly

I was having my devotion on the river when I looked up and saw a dark blue butterfly working his way across the river into the wind. He was unsteady in his steering as he flitted northeast then southeast every two seconds. He made for easy prey if any butterfly-eating bird was watching the river. But there was no bird of prey. He negotiated the gusts of wind and finally made his way toward the far river bank. He seemed to be careless, aimless in his movements, but by consistently correcting his direction he made it to his destination. I realized in that moment how much my life is like that butterfly.

I go from one direction to another in life, being buffeted by the prevailing winds. There are so many lies, traps and temptations in our culture today, and sometimes I am drawn to them. First here, then there, "am I making any real progress?" I ask myself. Three steps forward, one step back. Two steps forward one step back. Sometimes I am driven back much too far. But the butterfly will never go back to the cocoon. He will never go back to being an ugly worm. Thank God I'm not the ugly worm I used to be. God is transforming me day by day and He is taking me somewhere.

Like the butterfly I feel vulnerable to wrongful desires and thoughts. Is there a trap ahead? Are there predators? Sometimes I am attacked. But God protects me. His power and word comfort me. As the year goes by I gradually see the scenery changing, things I can be gratified about like: my children maturing, my relationships strengthening, power struggles with my wife decreasing, a deeper love developing, my finances stabilizing and I'm starting to like who I am.

God has put a homing device in the butterfly and in me. If I would but follow it, He will direct me to safe harbor and a rest from the wind. He will lead me to food and away from danger. He knows I am sometimes as dumb as a sheep and need His guidance. I also require His discipline. But He will guide me safely over the river where one day I will live with Him forever in paradise. Instead of getting bogged down in the view from the ground, maybe I should take a trip up and see things from God's point of view.

Read Psalm 23 and Romans 12:2.

Vintage Road Racers choose different lines at the American Historic Racing Motorcycle Association's National (AHRMA) series race at Mid-Ohio in 2004.

Parent/helper Todd Blair points out a line to a student at the fall 2003 G2G camp in Prairieville.

11. Choosing Lines

I was announcing an Arenacross race a few years ago in Houma, Louisiana. During practice I was standing next to a whoop section (series of bumps), watching the riders bounce their way through. The center of this section of track had a groove through it, so the flagman, who was also one of the track designers (Skipper Thibodaux from New Iberia), put a few hay bales down the center to force the riders to use other lines.

It was interesting to watch the riders come around the turn and discover the hay bale in the center of the track. It wasn't there before. They had to make a choice in a split second where to direct their bike as they attacked this straight-a-way. Some over-corrected and almost hit me near the outside. Some turned their bike directly to the inside and almost went off the other side. Some riders braked too hard, forcing the riders behind them to bump and correct. The faster riders made a decision and got back on the throttle - hard. They tended to choose the best line.

Just like on a street motorcycle, I sometimes must make an instantaneous decision about choosing a line on the highway. At 60-80 mph I better make it quick! Sometimes there is debris in the road. If I am following too close to the car in front of me I may not have enough reaction time to avoid it. I noticed that if I look directly AT the obstacle, I'll hit it. If I look at the line AROUND it, nine times out of ten, my bike will go around it. Sometimes my guardian angel was saving me. (Thank you Father!)

Today you will have to choose lines. Pray and ask God in advance to lead you to choose well. If your faith gets weak at the moment of choice, pray again, then do what you believe He is leading you to do. There's a word for choosing right – wisdom.

Scripture for the Day: *"If any of you lacks wisdom, he should ask God, who gives generously to all without finding fault, and it will be given to Him."* (James 1:5)

Quote for the Day: "Choose your rut carefully, you'll be in it for the next ten miles." (Road sign in upstate New York)

125A Pro Sport class at the 2004 AMA Championship Qualifier at Gravity Alley MX chooses their ruts. Leading is Brett Delcambre.

The author's 1993 candy apple red 750 Nighthawk.

12. You Just Never Know

One night I was touring on a motorcycle with my son Kyle on the back. We had camping gear strapped to a red, 1993 Honda 750 Nighthawk. My riding partner was Michael Brown on his 750 Kawasaki Vulcan. We were going from Covington, La. to Pensacola, Fla. It was about 7:30pm and we were eastbound on the I-10 where I- 65 joins I-10, a few miles west of Mobile, Alabama.

It was dark, the traffic was pretty heavy, and I was leading. I had just changed into the middle lane where the two Interstates merged together. I was about 3 car lengths behind the car in front of me. I should have been more like 7 car lengths at 70 mph. I saw a flash in the corner of my eye on the road. I didn't have time to change my course. I passed within 2 inches to the right side. It was an aluminum ladder lying diagonally in my lane! If I had been over on the left side or center of the lane, Kyle and I would have struck the ladder and gone down. I usually follow in the car tire grooves for this very reason. I glanced back into my rear-view and saw the constancy of Michael's headlight. Thank God he missed it, too.

You just never know what's coming around the bend. There are some things in life you just can't prepare for, like: getting fired, sickness, disease, children in trouble, being mis-understood, natural disasters, car wrecks, being a victim of a crime, mechanical breakdowns, disappointments in relationships, etc. You know what I'm talking about. You've been through some already. You know the feeling. It's as if someone has punched you in the gut. At first you can't believe it. Then you may get angry or sad. Then you have to accept, adjust and deal with the loss. That's when healing really begins.

How can we prepare for life's nasty surprises? You can start by preparing yourself spiritually at the beginning of the day. The best way is to get up a little earlier, get alone with God and His word (maybe a devotion book like this one) and pray. But you may be thinking, "I don't know what to say." Here's a little formula I learned from a tract a long time ago: A-C-T-S

A: **Adoration**: Adore God; love Him, Praise Him, Worship Him.
C: **Confession**: Confess any known sins to Him and ask for forgiveness.
T: **Thanksgiving**: Thank Him for rest, food, shelter, family, work, health, etc.
S: **Supplication**: Ask Him for whatever requests you have, especially for guidance for the day.

13. The Greedy Bird

When Lynn Harrington was a child his family was given a baby raven (which are rare in south Texas). They nursed it until it was old enough to fly outside. It hung around on the kitchen window sill until one of the family came outside. Then it would fly to their shoulder and massage their hair and ears. One day Lynn played a trick on the intelligent bird. He cupped his hands together as if he were holding a treasure of some kind that might get away. He would let his brother peek between his fingers. The raven wanted it, flapping its wings to protest. When it didn't get a peek, it flew away only to return with some treasure it had found, first a twig, then a brass casing to a 22, etc.

Each time Lynn would inspect the raven's treasure, look inside his hands, and make the comparison, then swat away the bird's treasure. Finally the raven came back with its prized possession, a cat's eye marble. After the inspection process, Lynn finally took the marble and opened his hands for the raven to see what he was hiding - nothing! The raven exploded with anger, squawking and flapping his wings at him.

This is how many of us are with life. We are trading everything we can find of value: time, money, effort, relationships and opportunities for what we think will satisfy. Meanwhile the devil holds his hands out with sin, building the suspense, making it look more and more inviting, trying to get his best deal. When the negotiation is complete, and we have traded our highest bid, we discover that what we have been making payments on is empty, and fails to satisfy.

The Apostle Paul found the secret of happiness:

I have learned to be content whatever the circumstances. I know what it is to be in need, and I know what it is to have plenty. I have learned the secret of being content in any and every situation, whether well fed or hungry, whether living in plenty or in want. I can do everything through him who gives me strength. (Philippians 4:12-13)

Quotes for the Day:
"Always take plenty of time to make a snap decision." (unknown)
"It's pretty hard for the Lord to guide a man if he hasn't made up his mind which way he wants to go." (unknown)
"Learn to say no; it will be of more use to you than to be able to read Latin." (Charles H. Spurgeon, *Sermons*)

14. The Fat Gator

My good friend Mark Graham and I were paddling down Cane Bayou near Lacombe one beautiful warm spring morning. He was paddling and bird-watching, and I was fishing in the bow of his canoe. We passed a six foot alligator that was laying at the water's edge of the bayou on a sandy bank. He was lying in the sun, asleep. He must have crawled out of the marsh and stopped at the water's edge and just took a nap in the sun, facing the bayou.

We snuck right up to him and he never moved. I even cast my lure near his mouth, and he never even opened his eyes. He was sooooo content. As we paddled on by we noticed how fat he was. He must have just eaten and was digesting while warming his cold-blooded reptile body in the sun. What a picture of contentment. Take a look at Psalm 23.

- *"The Lord is MY shepherd"* I submit to His authority and trust His leadership. We have personal relationship.
- *"I will not want"* Because I have a shepherd (protector, guide, provider) I don't have to worry. He'll take care of everything I need.
- *"He makes me lie down in green pastures"* He gives me rest in a place of plenty.
- *"He leads me beside quiet waters"* A sheep would be afraid of moving water, so he leads me to a place where I can drink in peace, without fear.
- *"He restores my soul"* I have painful burdens and scars deep within that rob my faith and separate me from my shepherd. He gives deep healing and re-connects me to Himself.
- *"He guides me in the paths of righteousness for His name's sake"* He doesn't force me, but lights the path in front of me that is true, calling me to follow. He wants to keep me out of trouble and painful mistakes that would damage my reputation and His name.

Quote for the Day: "When we cannot find contentment in ourselves, it is useless to seek it elsewhere." (unknown)

15. It Ain't So Bad

It was back in the early 70's. My racing team went to a Thanksgiving race at Turkey Creek in Louisiana. My bike was broke, so my friend Joey Johanssen loaned me his Yamaha YZ 125 with the "hop-up" kit. It had a new pipe that protruded far out to the right side (I still have a burn scar on my right calf).

It had rained the night before and the track was a mess. As I was walking the track before practice I discovered a secret. The first turn had water covering it all the way to the far outside. I walked into the water and found that it was shallow and the bottom hard. I told my team members this discovery. Later, when the gate dropped for my race, the competitors all drifted to the outside to avoid the water. I cut right through the water, getting superior traction and spraying their faces with muddy water. I pulled a major hole shot and won that moto. They were left to pull their goggles while trying to keep up. (That was before the days of "tear offs," which are plastic see-through strips over goggles)

Unfortunately, the Yamaha broke down in the 2nd moto, so I couldn't win the overall. But I'll never forget that little secret.

Many times things aren't as bad as they look. For me, the water in the first turn was a BLESSING IN DISGUISE. It allowed me good traction and a short cut to turn 2 that the others couldn't see. Let's look at the 23rd Psalm:

"Even though I walk through the valley of the shadow of death..." Notice I don't live in the shadow of death. I sometimes must walk through it. Whatever trial or problem you are struggling with, it will pass. It usually looks worse than it is. Also notice that it is not "the valley of death", but the "shadow" of the "valley of death." In other words, it is just the shadow. The shadow cannot hurt you. Death cannot hurt the believer. Jesus has removed the sting of death when He conquered it at the cross. In John 11, He said, *"He who believes in me will never die."*

"I will fear NO evil, for you are with me." I have no fear because my bodyguard is with me and will protect me. *"Greater is He that is in me, than he that is in the world."* (1 John 4:4) *"There is NOTHING that can separate us from the love of God."* (Romans 8:38-39) Whatever you are dealing with, compared to eternity, it's not as bad as it looks. Read God's great promise in 1 Corinthians 10:13: *"And God is faithful; He will not let you be tempted beyond what you can bear. But when you are tempted, he will also provide a way out so that you can stand up under it."*

Quote for the Day: "We fear man so much because we fear God so little." (unknown)

List problems that God turned into blessings:

(from left) Robby and T-Don Lerille,   Vince Hayward, his son Mason, Chad
Jay Michon, Sr. and Jr. Michon   Pattison. Down South MX

Chad McNemar at Holeshot MX   Jon-murry Barr at Holeshot MX

16. My Butt Hurts!

It's interesting to watch Dads teaching their sons to race. When they are very young they have to be taught when to let off on the throttle. After they've gone down a few times, they may need Dad to tell them to get back on the throttle (you see a lot of that during the race). But sometimes these young riders get lazy and just sit on their bike all the way around the track. In motocross, you must stand a lot. This allows you to quickly re-distribute the weight, front to back or side to side. It also allows your legs (your strongest muscles) to act as shock absorbers for a lot of the rough sections. You can even see the track ahead better by standing up.

Sometimes the Dad will remove the seat from the motorcycle so the young racer will have to stand up. If he sits down on those hard metal tubes, he won't stay down long! This DISCIPLINES (trains) the racer to stand up more. Even though it is uncomfortable at first, it will pay off later in the long run.

Psalm 23:4b says, *"Your rod and staff, they comfort me."* A staff is the stick with the hook in the end. The shepherd used that hook to gently pull a straying sheep back into line with the others. The rod was heavier and was used for defense as a weapon. A shepherd often used it to defend the flock from stray dogs, bears, lions or even other shepherds who intended to steal the sheep.

In extreme cases, a shepherd would use the rod of correction to break a sheep's legs. This was to keep the disobedient sheep from wandering off into mortal danger, away from the protection of the shepherd. The shepherd would then hand-feed that sheep until its legs healed. The sheep may not eat for a season (in anger or fear of the shepherd), but eventually, when it got hungry enough, would begin to trust the shepherd and eat from his hand. It is said that this sheep would grow to be one of the most obedient and trusting sheep of the flock. So when a sheep has been around the flock for a while, it would begin to gain confidence and security from the rod and staff of the shepherd. These tools were instruments of protection and safety.

How much more strength does God have? How many more tools of discipline and weapons against evil does He have? Won't He use everything at His disposal to train us and protect us? Take comfort in the power of the God of the Universe who loves you.

Moreover, we have all had human fathers who disciplined us and we respected them for it. How much more should we submit to the

Father of our spirits and live! Our fathers disciplined us for a little while as they thought best; but God disciplines us for our good, that we may share in his holiness. No discipline seems pleasant at the time, but painful. Later on, however, it produces a harvest of righteousness and peace for those who have been trained by it. (Hebrews 12:9-11)

Quote for the Day: "Some patients, though conscious that their condition is perilous recover their health simply through their contentment with the goodness of the physician." (Hippocrates, Precepts, VI)

#225 Brandon Hubbard had a royal battle with Dillon Dufrene at Wildwood MX in 2005.

Is Greg Steinbeck, last years AHRMA 125 champ trying to get into Shannon Silva's head before their vintage race? Mid-Ohio race course, 2004.

17. Enemies

We all seem to have them. Whether it's the neighbor you're feuding with or the co-worker who wants your job, sometimes people want to do us harm. It could be another school-mate who is jealous or wants to earn "cool points" at your expense. Maybe it's someone who has misunderstood you along the way. They may be openly hostile or could be doing sneaky things behind your back.

Some of us collect more enemies than others by virtue of our personalities and the conflicts we engage. The Bible says we have an enemy (Satan) that *"seeks to steal, kill and destroy ..."* (John 10:10a). We need not be afraid because Jesus promised *"never to leave us or forsake us."* (Hebrews 13:5). Who is more powerful than God? We can't be distracted by our critics. They are a dime a dozen. Some people make themselves feel better by putting others down. You usually become a target when you start following God or try to do something great. Someone once wrote, "If you stick your head above the crowd, you'll be hit by tomatoes." That's part of the price of trying to step forward and do something bold. Every leader knows this from experience. Jesus said: *"Do not be afraid of those who kill the body but cannot kill the soul. Rather, be afraid of the One who can destroy both soul and body in hell."* (Matt. 10:28)

The dark forces and wicked leaders of Jesus' day thought they had won when they crucified and buried Him; but they were in for a rude surprise. After the 3 days of death Jesus predicted, God raised Him from the dead. God didn't have to move the burial stone. But He did. You know why? So people could go in and see He was gone. Then an angel sat on top of the stone as if to say, "FEAR THIS! WHAT YA GONNA DO ABOUT ME?" The hardened Roman guards were so afraid, they fainted like little girls. It was as if God were doing a little taunting of His own.

Don't live in fear today. Trust God and be bold, no matter what the critics are doing or saying. Remember that, from a spiritual perspective, people are not really our enemies anyway. It's the evil spirits behind them; their wrong attitudes, ideas, motives, desires, pain or fears.

Scripture for the Day: *"For our struggle is not against flesh and blood, but against the rulers, against the authorities, against the powers of this dark world and against the spiritual forces of evil in the heavenly realms."* (Ephesians 6:12)

Quotes for the day: "If you fear God, you fear no one. If you fear man, you fear everyone." (unknown)

18. Building Your Spiritual Life

I was riding through St. Rose, Louisiana one Sunday evening and noticed a big boat being constructed right off the highway in someone's side yard. It looked to be at least a 40 foot long trawler. It had a big hand-painted sign on it that read, "We don't need any more advice on building this boat." I had to smile. I could just picture in my mind every self-proclaimed boat expert coming by and offering advice. Apparently the builder had enough unwanted advice.

About two weeks later I heard about a man who was building a boat in his yard who tired of people coming by and giving unwanted advice. He started another boat across his yard and left it barely begun. The next time someone stopped to offer advice he pointed to the other boat and said, "Leave me alone. That one's for you guys."

There are as many opinions for living your life as there are people. Who will you listen to? If you want to please God, then you will want to find out what He wants. He has left His instructions in His Word. He has spoken to us in these last days through His Son, Jesus Christ. (Hebrews 1:1-3). Jesus said *"Which of you, intending to build a tower, does not sit down first and count the cost, whether he has enough to finish it."* (Luke 14:28) If you want to follow Jesus, if you want to be his disciple (learner), you must be willing to exchange the world's path (opinions, expectations, views) for God's.

> *Large crowds were traveling with Jesus, and turning to them he said: "If anyone comes to me and does not hate his father and mother, his wife and children, his brothers and sisters—yes, even his own life—he cannot be my disciple. And anyone who does not carry his cross and follow me cannot be my disciple."* (Luke 14:25-27)

I know this is a hard saying, it is a narrow road and only a few can travel it. (Matthew 7:13-14). Notice when Jesus made his statement, when "large crowds where following Him." Many were following and didn't really get it. Many were coming along with the wrong motives: curiosity, free food, sensationalism, entertainment or to get something for free. Maybe some were just following the crowd. Jesus had to weed out the pretenders. You know people today that say they are Christians, but are really not.

It's only when you give your life up for Him, that you make room for Him. It's only when you abandon the world that you receive heaven. (1

John 2:15-16). It's only when you die to yourself that you live. (take up your cross)

This is why there is so much religion and not much power. Few have really made it to their own cross. This place of death is where you meet the risen, Lord Jesus Christ. (1 Corinthians 1:18); and you must die with Him to gain His resurrection power. (Philippians 3:10-11)

Don't be a religious wannabe, a false disciple, a blind guide. Put aside your selfish ambitions and sell out to the Lord Jesus Christ. Then you will know His wonder-working power to change your life. One day the judge of the Universe is going to call us to stand before Him. He will examine us, our decisions, words, actions and even motives. He'll want to know what we did with His provision – Jesus Christ. A Christ-led life will hold up under any scrutiny. What's more is Jesus will be our defense attorney to speak on our behalf as He faces His own Father – the Judge.

Like the boat-builders, we are responsible for how we built our own boats. Did we get distracted by all the different opinions? Or did we remain true to God's truth? Will your boat float? Will it withstand the storms? Will it stand the test of time? Will it carry its precious cargo to the destination? Listen to the Apostle Paul's words to a church he planted in Corinth:

> *By the grace God has given me, I laid a foundation as an expert builder, and someone else is building on it. But each one should be careful how he builds. For no one can lay any foundation other than the one already laid, which is Jesus Christ. If any man builds on this foundation using gold, silver, costly stones, wood, hay or straw, his work will be shown for what it is, because the Day will bring it to light. It will be revealed with fire, and the fire will test the quality of each man's work. If what he has built survives, he will receive his reward. If it is burned up, he will suffer loss; he himself will be saved, but only as one escaping through the flames.* (1 Corinthians 3:10-15)

19. Rock in the Sandal

Today when I went outside to take out the garbage I got a rock in my sandal. I was too busy to stop, take off the sandal and shake it out. So I kept going. While carrying the garbage, I would take a few steps, hesitate and shake my right foot. It looked like I was playing that game with the song, "you put your right foot in and you shake it all about." If any neighbors were watching they must have thought I was crazy. But all that the shaking managed to do was allow the rock to slip further under my foot.

After two trips out to the street I'd had enough. I reached down, took off the sandal and saw the culprit. It was a small rock, no bigger than a button. "You're kidding," I thought to myself. It felt much larger than that. I tossed it back into the gravel driveway. What a relief to get rid of that rock.

Do you have something in your life that's stuck in your craw? Are you carrying a problem that is irritating you? Maybe it's something you said to someone, or they said to you. Maybe its something you did or didn't do. Maybe it's something that was done to you or not done for you. Whatever it is, if it's burdensome to you (causing you pain) then you are carrying a burden.

One of the benefits of being a follower of Jesus Christ is you don't have to carry it alone. Listen to some of these great promises:

"Ignoring what they said, Jesus told the synagogue ruler, 'Don't be afraid; just believe.'" (Mark 5:36)

"Do not let your hearts be troubled. Trust in God; trust also in me." (Jesus in John 14:1)

"I have told you these things, so that in me you may have peace. In this world you will have trouble. But take heart! I have overcome the world." (Jesus in John 16:33)

"Do not be anxious about anything, but in everything, by prayer and petition, with thanksgiving, present your requests to God. And the peace of God, which transcends all understanding, will guard your hearts and your minds in Christ Jesus." (Phil. 4:6-7)

"Cast all your anxiety on him because he cares for you." (1 Peter 5:7)

Why not stop right now, bow your head and get the rock out?

20. Clawing My Way Out of Bed

Have you ever had some circumstances in your life that are so painful, you just can't get out of bed in the morning? I believe it happens to all of us from time to time. You just don't want to face the world. You just put the pillow over your head and ask God to take the world away.

There are some situations where it's best to stay in bed and claim a sick day. Even if you're not physically sick, you might be emotionally or mentally sick. You may need more rest. Take it.

There are other times where you just have to claw your way out of bed. This morning I prayed for longer than usual, then tried to justify staying in bed. I finally realized God had a plan for me this day, and in order for Him to use me, I had to get up. I moaned and groaned and got going. I wasn't as efficient as yesterday, but I was determined to get in motion. I thought of a rudder on a ship. The ship cannot be directed by the rudder when it is sitting still. The rudder only directs the ship when it is under way.

I started with my habits: Bible study and prayer, breakfast, work, exercise, communications on the phone and internet, practicing guitar, etc. I worked on Linda's Mother's day present. I got most of my jobs done. Did I feel like it? No. Was I glad I got out of bed? Yes.

Sometimes you just have to DO the right thing until the feelings come. No matter what circumstances caused me pain, I can't let my laziness take over. This scripture kept going through my head: *"A little sleep, a little slumber, a little folding of the hands to rest—and poverty will come on you like a bandit and scarcity like an armed man."* (Proverbs 6:10-12)

While we may need to take a day off from time to time (and God commands it once a week), we are as successful as our habits. Are there any habits you should re-evaluate? Jesus can help you break the habit if you will turn it over to Him and obey His word.

Scripture for the Day: *"You shall know the truth and the truth shall set you free... So if the Son sets you free, you will be free indeed."* (Jesus in John 8:32,36)

Quote for the Day: "I wonder what wonderful surprise God has for me today?" (R.J.)

Parents and kids dance at the Winter Series Banquet. "Porkchop" Baye at Baton Rouge
Arenacross

60 Open class preparing to enter the Parker Coliseum on LSU's campus for an
Arenacross race in Baton Rouge.

21. Persevering as a Parent

Some years ago I got back into motocross racing. I wanted my son Kyle to experience racing and I guess also wanted him to see how fast his old man was. Well he got to experience racing. One out of two ain't bad.

One of the differences between racing in the 70's and racing today are the steep jumps. We had more natural terrain and gentle slopes on the jump faces in the old days. Today's jumps are designed to throw the riders almost straight up in the air. So you ride the modern bikes different to compensate. I fell quite a few times before I started learning the new techniques on the newer bike. Modern riders are used to it. The young guys love jumping. Most older guys have backed off the throttle some, or retired due to injuries. Also, the young guys don't break bones as easily and they heal faster.

It's the same way in modern-day parenting. In the old days when parents were growing up, we never had to contend with the temptations our kids are dealing with. I attended a pretty bad high school where there were fights several times a week (all boy school). But guns? Never. Drugs? Very rarely. Open disrespect to the teacher? Few. Frivolous lawsuits? Ridiculous. Single parent families? Not that many. Distraction of video games? Yeah right, maybe Pac Man or Pong. Internet? No. TV sitcoms where the kids run the home and insult their Dads? Not at my house.

Our kids face a whole new set of distractions and temptations. We as parents are more busy and tired than ever. But there are some things that never change. At least kids are pretty resilient. We survived our parent's mistakes. If we don't make extreme mistakes with our kids, they should survive them. But God never changes. He still commands us to love our kids. That's not difficult. He built it into us. The difficult part is continuing to show this love on a consistent basis while earning a living.

My wife and I have raised two of our own (we're still trying to raise them even though they are in college). We also had three foreign exchange students who lived with us for a year. Want to hear some good news? They will grow up. They will pass through the stage you're struggling with. You're not alone in raising them. There are coaches, teachers, ministers, counselors, friend's parents, books and other influences and resources. Your main ally remains, God. He gave them to you. He answers prayer. He loves them more than you. He works when you're not around.

Entrust your kids into God's hands. Pray for them daily. Bring them to church. Believe that God hears your prayers and will answer.

Scripture for the Day: *"Children, obey your parents in the Lord, for this is right. 'Honor your father and mother' – which is the first commandment with a promise – 'that it may go well with you and that you may enjoy long life on the earth.' Father, do not exasperate your children; instead, bring them up in the training and instruction of the Lord."* (Ephesians 6:1-4)

Quote for the Day: "But at three, four, five, and even six years the childish nature will require sports; now is the time to get rid of self-will in him, punishing him, but not so as to disgrace him." (Plato, Laws, VII)

50 Oil Injector class at Holeshot MX. Blake Lagarde #5 and Donnie Lerille

Joey Gonsoulin and his son Joseph

22. Where's the White Flag?

As I stated before, I got back into racing in my forties when my son Kyle was old enough to learn to ride. One of the many things I could not get used to again was the physical punishment of the track. It didn't seem so bad when I was 17. I did remember getting serious and jogging as a teenager when I moved into the money class. But at the age of 45, no amount of bicycle riding or weightlifting seemed to help. Since I couldn't practice on the track every day or even twice a week, I could not get in racing shape.

So here is what would happen. At the races, I would get our bikes unloaded and prepped. Then I would walk the track. Whew! Next would be getting dressed. First the bike shorts, then the knee braces, then the pants and socks, boots, jersey, chest protector, gloves, helmet and hang the goggles on the handlebars until the last minute. Whew! I was tired already. Take a few practice laps, work up a sweat. Come back to the pits, take off some gear, refuel and drink lots of water. Adjust the chain, check the tires, bolts, maybe adjust the brakes, and knock the mud off. Whew!

Get to the starting gate for the race. Gate drops, intense adrenaline blast, through the first turn safely. Get in the groove. Make some passes. Get passed. After two laps of physical abuse, start looking for that white flag. Where is it? Each time I passed the scoring area I'm looking at the flagman. Has he forgotten? Is he distracted? Doesn't he know we're still out here working our tails off? Yeah, it was fun, but now I'm tired. Where's the white flag? I glance at other parts of the track and riders are still racing so I'm not alone. Here comes someone behind me. No you don't, this is my spot. Oh well, fine then pass me. Here comes the tower again. The flagman does not have the white flag in his hand. He is drinking water! How dare him, in front of us! I feel like yelling at him, "check with the scorers!" My chest is hurting, my arms are pumped up, and it's getting harder to stay on this bike.

Finally the white flag comes out and I feel a new surge of strength to make one more lap to the checkers. Since the end is now in sight I find the strength to finish the race.

In life we can become weary. "Is this going to last forever? When will this be over?" That's where faith comes in. We keep plugging away at what we know is right, even when we can't hear God or have no encouragement from others. We keep running even though we hit "the wall." We keep trying even though we are hurting.

Job was an extreme example of perseverance. He lost everything, but still continued to trust God. In Job 13:15, he said about God, *"Though He slay me, yet will I trust Him."* God rewarded his perseverance handsomely.

When life gets too tough (and if you are raising kids, it will sometimes seem that way for sure), re-focus on God. He will give you the strength and perseverance you need to hang on until the end.

Let me remind you that there is a reward at the end. Check out these scriptures:

"Because you have kept my command to persevere." (Rev. 3:10)

"And this is the will of him who sent me, that I shall lose none of all that he has given me, but raise them up at the last day." (Jesus in John 6:39)

"The LORD will fulfill his purpose for me; your love, O LORD, endures forever— do not abandon the works of your hands." (Psalm 138:8)

"though he stumble, he will not fall, for the LORD upholds him with his hand." (Psalm 37:24)

"He will keep you strong to the end, so that you will be blameless on the day of our Lord Jesus Christ. God, who has called you into fellowship with his Son Jesus Christ our Lord, is faithful." (1 Corinthians 1:8-9)

Scorekeepers (from left) Taylor Watts, Kaci Simon and Tamara Tullier mercifully allow the white flag at Wildwood MX during a race.

Chris Cotton leads Tyler Hancock during a race at Wildwood MX in 2004.

23. The String of the Bow

Years ago I used to bow hunt. I don't know if it's my Indian heritage (Choctaw from both sides of my family), or just the love of the outdoors and playing with gear. Whatever it is I am fascinated by the modern bow and arrow.

I had a Browning Explorer compound bow. It had two pulleys that gave it enough mechanical advantage to alleviate the torque needed to fully draw it. It was adjustable from 55 pounds to 75 pounds. I had it set on 70. It had a peep sight with adjustable needles for distances. It had a nock stay for the mechanical release and the arrow nock. Silencers on the strings, quiver mounted to the bow, surgical tube to the sight to keep it straight and I was ready to go.

I used aluminum shaft arrows with plastic vanes. I shot field points for practice and broad heads for hunting. I used to enjoy target shooting in the backyard. I would routinely put all six arrows in a paper pie plate up to 50 yards. But I never brought home any deer with it (I did with my rifle). Yet I enjoyed the hunts.

When I drew that bow, it pulled 70 pounds. I don't know exactly how it worked, but once I got past a certain point it get easier to hold. I could hold it to my eye for about a minute if need be. The strings would be taunt, the wooden limbs of the bow tensed, my muscles complained. But they would have to just wait until I was ready with the right moment to let the arrow fly. Once I touched the thumb trigger on the mechanical release, the string would launch the arrow and the energy from the limbs of the bow would explode with power. It was the tension that created the launch.

Sometimes God, the great archer, draws us. We get pulled into a tense situation. We may complain, but in His wisdom He doesn't give in to our whining. He continues to pull us to the launch point. Like the muscles we may get tired. Like the bow limbs we may be tensed. Like the arrow we may be impatient and want answers, but we must wait. We must trust Him to point and hold until the exact right moment when release comes.

Once He executes His shot, we finally discover His direction. We may even get to see His plan. He uses us just as we were designed if we wait on Him and endure the tension. We are released in sweet exhilaration to the target and feel the gratitude of accomplishment - For Him.

Be patient today as the great archer draws you, holds you and aims you for His glory!

"Look to the LORD and his strength; seek his face always." (1 Chronicles 16:11)

"Let us not become weary in doing good, for at the proper time we will reap a harvest if we do not give up." (Galatians 6:9)

"being confident of this, that he who began a good work in you will carry it on to completion until the day of Christ Jesus." (Philippians 1:6)

"And as for you, brothers, never tire of doing what is right." (2 Thess. 3:13)

24. "Ain't Skeered"

One of my best friends in the Motocross racing community is Mac Edmonston. He is kind of new to the scene. He used to race three-wheelers back in the day, but got bitten by the dirt bike bug a few years ago. He might be small in physical stature but he's got the biggest heart you can imagine. He used to be a brawling, spittin', short-tempered truck driver. Now that the Lord Jesus Christ lives in his heart, he is a loving husband, devoted father, fair and hard-working business owner and a developing race chaplain and mentor to teenage boys. He's still tough, and is not scared of anything. In fact, one of his famous quotes before we try something new is, "Ain't skeered."

He built a nice, technical practice track behind his business in Galvez, La. He started racing bikes, and after about three races moved out of the beginner class. At 36 years old he moved out of the Senior C class and now competes in the B class. Recently he raced his 73 Yamaha in the Vintage Pro class and took a 5th overall.

He is a man of vision. He wants to help kids. That's his major motivator besides loving God and his wife Connie. He has already put on several, first of its kind - Bible/Racing camps. People drive from all over to camp out under his shady trees, swim in his pond, and practice on his track. The camp has obstacle courses to teach Bible truths about leadership. Campers got to play paint ball, eat jambalaya, have team competitions and learn more about God.

If you watched the SRMA Winter Series, he was the rider in the Senior class who had the spectacular crash the last race at Kentwood. It was coming down to the last lap and he was in third place. He was about to pass Wayne Simmons. On the main straight-a-way right in front of the crowd, he hit a hole landing a jump. He started doing a tank-slapper at high speed (bike going back & forth sideways). He held on all the way to the next jump. First the bike popped him off to one side, then the bike bounced him to the other; but he continued to hold on. He looked like those Hollywood stunt men on horseback. When the bike finally went down, he did, too. But he popped right back up, ran to his bike (in traffic) and jumped back on. Before the leaders were back around for another lap he had worked his way back into fourth place.

You can see this spectacle on the SRMA Winter Series video produced my Motoshots studios. It is THE featured video bite on the tape. I predict, barring injury, that Mac will have a podium finish at the National Amateur Championship in the next two years.

Why do I tell you this? Cause I'm bragging' about my friend? Well, yeah, but to show the greatest miracle God still performs. Do you know what it is? The changed life. Go ask one of Mac's brothers or other people who knew him in the past how he's changed. No, he's not perfect, just different; for the better; more like Jesus. Also here's his address if your interested in his "Glory to God" MX camps. Glory to God Motocross 17551 Simpson Road Prairieville, La. 70769.

"Once you were not a people, but now you are the people of God; once you had not received mercy, but now you have received mercy." (1 Peter 2:10)

"Once you were alienated from God and were enemies in your minds because of your evil behavior. But now he has reconciled you by Christ's physical body through death to present you holy in his sight..." (Colossians 1:21)

"Yet to all who received him, to those who believed in his name, he gave the right to become children of God—13children born not of natural descent, nor of human decision or a husband's will, but born of God." (John 1:12)

"Therefore, if anyone is in Christ, he is a new creation; the old has gone, the new has come! All this is from God, who reconciled us to himself through Christ and gave us the ministry of reconciliation." (2 Corinthians 5:17)

25. Motivation to Do Right

Sometimes I wonder what motivates people. I know it can be complex, as there are a lot of different motivators - some the person may not even be aware of. What kind of fuel is the businessman running on? Is it a solution mixed with desire for money, desire for recognition, desire to move up in the company, desire to feel needed, desire to gain respect, a spirit of competition? Maybe he's stuck in that job and is just looking for his paycheck? Could it be that most of his motivation comes from home? Is it to pay for his home, car, boat or other toys? It could be love expressed in the desire to provide for his family. Maybe He just wants respect, to impress his wife, or others. Maybe he's being driven by the fear of failure, a mountain of debt, or saving for a future purchase? There is usually a mixture of motives within us that drive us.

What motivates us to do good? What is at the heart of driving us to tell the truth; restrain from retaliation, show love, go the extra mile for someone? What motivates you to read the Bible, read this book, go to church? What motivates us to pray?

What should it be? I submit that the best motivation is a vision from God and a response of love for Him. When I come to meet God, He gives me a vision; a vision of who I really am; a vision of His holiness and "set-a-part-ness." He gives me a purpose for life, a task to do for Him. The fuel to do this is His love that now drives my love – for Him and others. Now this task may be as simple as living for Him at work and at home, or He may put a specific calling on my life to serve a certain group of people. That is what YOU must work out with God. If your motive is weak or blurry, maybe you should go back to the last place you encountered God and seek Him.

"Where there is no revelation (prophetic vision), *the people cast off restraint."* (Proverbs 29:18) In other words, without God's vision we start playing fast and loose with God and begin to act on our selfish, impure motives more and more. Are you working off of a vision from God? The vision from God will keep us on the upward path of His truth, purpose and freedom.

Read what happened to Isaiah when He encountered God in the temple in Isaiah 6:1-9:

In the year that King Uzziah died, I saw the Lord seated on a throne, high and exalted, and the train of his robe filled the temple. Above him were seraphs, each with six wings: With two wings they

covered their faces, with two they covered their feet, and with two they were flying. And they were calling to one another:
"Holy, holy, holy is the LORD Almighty; the whole earth is full of his glory." At the sound of their voices the doorposts and thresholds shook and the temple was filled with smoke. "Woe to me!" I cried. "I am ruined! For I am a man of unclean lips, and I live among a people of unclean lips, and my eyes have seen the King, the LORD Almighty." Then one of the seraphs flew to me with a live coal in his hand, which he had taken with tongs from the altar. With it he touched my mouth and said, "See, this has touched your lips; your guilt is taken away and your sin atoned for."
Then I heard the voice of the Lord saying, "Whom shall I send? And who will go for us?"
And I said, "Here am I. Send me!"

Notice where Isaiah got his vision - at church (the temple). Notice when - during a time of tragedy (when good King Uzziah died). Do you see that once Isaiah saw God for who He really was, he got a vision of his own sinfulness? Then God cleansed his sin and gave him a vision, a calling. Isaiah responded with the right answer. Now Isaiah has a purpose in life beyond just surviving. He's now a servant of His creator. Since God called Him, He empowered Him.

Quotes of the day:
"Faith is the daring of the soul to go farther than it can see." (unknown)
"Maybe we need more vision and less television." (Unknown)
"To help me with right thinking, I put a sign on my desk that reads 'What is my motive?'" (Chuck Swindoll)

26. Keeping a Clear Conscience

A conscience is that voice inside that guides us to what we perceive to be right. We may have different ideas or standards for what is right. Nevertheless, most all human conscience goes in the same general direction (otherwise how would a society of people ever agree on their laws?) The highest standard comes from our creator. He has set forth His principles in His Word. When the nation of Israel made their famous transition from slaves in Egypt to free people moving toward their promised land in Canaan, the first thing God wanted to give them was a law by which to govern themselves.

As I right this, the United States, has just conquered the Iraqi army and has overthrown Saddam Hussein. Our government is now involved in a very difficult task - rebuilding the government of the Iraqi people. The move from dictatorship to freedom and rule of law is a tricky maneuver. It puts the responsibility from the dictator (Pharaoh or Saddam) to the people (Israel or Iraq). We in America know that if our leaders are going in the wrong direction, we have voted in the wrong leaders. We, the people must make a change based on our conscience.

What are our modern rules built upon? God gave the new nation of Israel a set of ten commands.

1. Have no other gods before me.
2. Don't worship idols.
3. Don't mis-use my name.
4. Remember the Sabbath day to keep it holy.
5. Honor your father and mother.
6. Don't murder.
7. Don't commit adultery.
8. Don't steal.
9. Don't lie.
10. Don't covet what your neighbor has.

A few thousand years later, when Jesus Christ walked the earth, some religious leaders tried to trick Him. They asked Him which was the greatest commandment. He replied:

1. Love the Lord your God with all your heart, soul and strength. (Commandments 1-4)
2. Love your neighbor as yourself. (Commandments 5-10)

So Jesus emphasized a vital and living relationship with God, then a resulting good relationship with other people. Both commands are based on love.

This is the highest standard. If you hold to God's standard and OBEY it, you can expect a good night's sleep, favor with God and other people and a clear conscience. (Acts 24:16; Eph. 4:30)

A Vintage era BSA motocross racing at Mid-Ohio in 2004.

A 60's era Penton 125, exactly like the first competition dirt bike I ever owned; on display at the Motorcycle Hall of Fame in Ohio.

The next generation of Pentons, and the first bike I ever raced. The 125 "6 Days" is in the foreground next to the blue 175 "Jackpiner" model.

27. Power for Today

I have to be careful how much I talk about the "good ole days" of motocross racing around this present generation of racers. Yes, there were good times, great racing, sincere camaraderie, an atmosphere of fun, interesting motorcycles, challenging tracks and a general love for the sport. There are only a few old warriors from those days that I can talk with about the old Pentons, Huskies, Maicos, DKWs and the old tracks like Waggaman, Slidell, Lake Whitney, Grangeville, etc. Carl Langley is one. He runs Racing Innovations out of his shop and box van, and is one of those guys that took the long, hard road as a teenager, and survived to pass on wisdom to the younger riders. Once we start bench racing, it gets dark before we're done.

But if we talk too much about the "old school" we will bore our listeners (unless they are from the old school). I did live and learn in the early days of MX racing in the late 60's and early 70's. I got my fair share of trophies, dirt bikes, travel, trail riding, racing, late night race-motor building, losses, crashes and broken bones. But I can't live in the past. While I can carry the lessons and the memories of the old days into today, I can't stay there. Then I would truly be a "washed-up" "has-been" that is of no use for today.

Wise grandparents know what I'm trying to say. Last night, Kyle and I spent several hours pulling a fuel tank from a Honda Civic so we could replace the fuel pump inside. It was a long, dirty grueling job. His friend's grandfather was helping us. He knew just when to get what we needed from the garage and when to keep silent. When we needed a hand holding up the tank to re-install it, he was right under the car with us. He knew when to step in and kept his suggestions to himself while we were working. That was a display of wisdom and self-control.

My point is this. There are many people who live their spiritual lives in the past. They are still depending on what God did for them back in 1975. They are still living on an experience they had with God at a church service in 1982. Some are still living on their Momma's faith. Their relationship with God is stuck in a Sunday School classroom back in 1959. Yes, God is the god of the past. He IS the God of Abraham, Isaac and Jacob. But He is also the God of the PRESENT. He is the God of the FUTURE. He is alive and present and ready to walk with you through TODAY... NOW!

When Moses was being called to go back to Egypt to lead the Israelites out of slavery, he was scared. He knew what he was up against. He had grown up with Pharaoh in his royal court. He knew how hard-headed he was and how he depended on the slaves for building projects and knew how to deal with his major ego (like many of our wives today). He knew how hard-headed the slaves were. So when God encountered Moses at the burning bush, Moses said,

> *Suppose I go to the Israelites and say to them, "The God of your fathers has sent me to you," and they ask me, "What is his name?" Then what shall I tell them? God said to Moses, "I AM WHO I AM. That is what you are to say to the Israelites: I AM has sent me to you."* (Exodus 3:13-14)

What was God saying? The Hebrew word God used was *Yahweh*, the divine personal name of God. Orthodox Jews won't even say this name aloud out of reverence for God. In the Hebrew tongue it literally means, "I was, I am, I will be." All 3 verb tenses are in the same word of personal identification. So what does this mean to you and I? The God you encountered back in 1978 is the same God who is ready to encounter you again. He has the past covered. He has the present in His hand. He has already taken care of the future. And He has the same power available to you today!

Scripture for the Day: *"Jesus Christ is the same yesterday, today and forever."* (Hebrews 13:8)

Quote for the Day: "You think about people, but God thinks about you." (Leo Tolstoy, Diaries)

28. The Open Arms of Love

There once was a wealthy businessman who had two sons. One day the younger came to him and said, "Dad, I want to go out west and live my own life. Give me my inheritance now." The Dad tried to reason with his son to wait until he was mature enough, but the son wouldn't listen. So he took his shares in the company stock, his company car, sold his remaining interest in the other joint ventures to his elder brother, cleaned out his college savings account and left.

He ended up in Vegas living large. Having become an easy target for scam artists, gold-diggers and fair-weather friends, he soon lost all his money. Since he had dropped out of school and had no real work experience, he couldn't find a job. He soon ended up on the street, living in a cardboard box. His only "fun" was reduced to getting high and drunk when he could scrape together the money from hand-outs.

One day he picked up an old newspaper to wipe his greasy face and his eye was drawn to a name in a caption. It was his father's name. A faint memory, something stirred. It was his name, too. He looked closer and read that his father's company had opened a cooperate office nearby. The young man said to himself, "Even my father's janitors live better than me. I'm getting up and going to that office and I will say, 'Dad, I am so sorry. I was wrong. Please let me have a job wherever you can fit me in. I will even work as your gardener or courier."

So he got up and went to the address of the new office. He planned to ask the receptionist to call his Dad, even if he was not in town. But when he got to the entrance, his Dad saw him from the window. He was in a meeting with a Senator, a hotel chain owner and the mayor. Without a word he jumped up and left the meeting. On the way out he told his executive secretary to call the lobby receptionist to hold his son. He was down in less than a minute.

As soon as their eyes met, the relationship picked up where it left off. The love flowed through the air as the father ran and embraced his dirty, beaten down son. With tears flowing down all four cheeks, the son started his speech. "Dad I'm so sorry..." That was as far as he got. The father shook his head, pulled out his handkerchief and wiped away his son's dirty tears. "No, no, it's ok. I understand. Oh, my son, my son." More hugs and crying. "I've been waiting for you to return for seven long years. It's about time this ordeal is over." He stepped back to look, as if making sure it was him, then hugged him again.

He turned to the receptionist and gave orders, "Call Macy's, get a complete set of clothes, including a tux. Have my tailor come by for a measuring. Get a company car for him. Reserve a room at the best hotel, so he can get cleaned up. Get my wife on the phone and tell her he returned today. Set up a party for tonight with complete catering, live music, and a dance floor. Tonight we celebrate. For my son was lost and now is found!"

Meanwhile the elder son came down. When he overheard all that was going on, he pulled his Dad aside. "Dad, what are you doing? He took a third of our money and blew it on who knows what! He wasn't here to help rebuild. I've been here working my tail off. You've never thrown a party for me. Now he gets one after what he's done? That's not fair!"

The father looked his elder son in the eyes with compassion and said slowly, "Son, you have been with me the whole time. And one day this company will be yours. But today we must celebrate. Don't you see? Your brother has returned. He was dead and now is alive!"

Ok, I made this story up. It is a modern-day parable. Jesus told parables back in the day. A parable is an earthly story with a heavenly meaning. In fact he told this very parable. But he told it better and he told it dressed in the 1st century culture that his listeners would understand. He told it in the context of how God feels about lost sinners who return to Him. (Luke 15:11-32) He told it to some self-righteous religious leaders who couldn't stand to see Jesus hanging out with the worst people of the day (in their eyes). He told the sinners they could be made right with God, if they would turn back to God. That made the religious leaders mad. Jesus set them up as the elder son in his parable.

The good news for you? Here is a picture of how God loves you, no matter what you've done or where you've been. But you say, "you don't know what I've done." It doesn't matter, God's grace and forgiveness is greater than anything bad you've done.

If you are ready to turn to God and seek His forgiveness, He will deliver. He'll accept you and give you full status as a son in His kingdom if you are willing to drop your sin and come home. You may not have the power to stay away from that sin on your own, but He has the power to cleanse, forgive and start you on your new course, with new passion and purpose.

Scripture for the Day: *"For God did not send His son into the world to condemn the world, but to save the world through Him."* (John 3:17)

Quote for the Day: " The Bible was not given to increase our knowledge, but to change our lives." (Dwight L. Moody)

29. Purpose and Contentment

Someone once said, "The purpose of life is life with a purpose." What is our purpose? Why are we here? If we look at the big, big picture of our lives, it is to glorify our creator and enjoy fellowship with Him. That's why He created man. If we narrow the focus of our lives, God has given us certain abilities and opportunities that we can fill. He designed us for a place and career. (Ephesians 2:8-10; 2 Cor. 4:10)

Note that places and careers are dynamic, not static. In other words they can change as we grow. But whether you are a housewife, nurse, policeman, carpenter, businessman, plumber, artist, teacher, scientist, etc., God has a purpose for you to glorify Him where He has planted you. He spreads His people in all parts of the world in all walks of life, in all levels of society to fill the earth with His glory.

There is no greater contentedness than finding God's will for your life and living it successfully. He has given us His salvation, but we are to "work out our own salvation." (Philippians 2:12)

Let Jesus in you work through your hands in what you do, your eyes in what you gaze upon, your ears in what you listen to, your feet in where they take you, your mind in what you think about. As you influence those that God has put around you, the big picture of your purpose in life will begin to come into focus. Then, you will find contentedness with who you are and with life itself.

The God who made the world and everything in it is the Lord of heaven and earth and does not live in temples built by hands. And he is not served by human hands, as if he needed anything, because he himself gives all men life and breath and everything else. From one man he made every nation of men, that they should inhabit the whole earth; and he determined the times set for them and the exact places where they should live. God did this so that men would seek him and perhaps reach out for him and find him, though he is not far from each one of us. "For in him we live and move and have our being." (Acts 17:24-28)

Scripture readings: 1 Corinthians 7:17; 1 Cor. 7:24; Philippians 4:11-12; 1Timothy 6:6, Hebrews 13:5

Quote for the day: "We need to learn to set our course by the stars and not by every passing ship." (General Omar Bradley)

30. "It's Always Something"

Why is it that there is always something difficult we are dealing with? Whether it is financial, relational, professional, medical, spiritual, recreational, mental or emotional, it is always something. Why can't we just have smooth sailing all the time? I submit to you today that the trials of life are what make us who we are. If a metal is not heated, it wouldn't become hard enough for good use. If we aren't "put through the oven," we wouldn't be of much use to God, our family, our friends, our job or even ourselves. Can you imagine a body-builder that never wants to lift a weight because he says it's "too heavy" or "hurts my muscles?"

It's the storms that bring growth to the vegetation. Without it there would be no leaves, no flowers and no fruit. Without the heat of the sun there would be no photosynthesis, no growth.

It is human to want to avoid pain. God built that aversion to pain to protect us from hurting ourselves and preserve our health and our lives. But a life that is consecrated to Him, obedient to His plan and purpose will enter the trial head-up, eyes open, mind alert for what God wants to teach us, and on our knees to rely on His power. If you are a believer, you are experiencing some kind of trial right now in some area of your life. Instead of whining, focus on winning. Instead of rebellion - attack it! Instead of crying to God, "why me?" Cry to Him, "Help me. Help me safely through and help me learn what you want to teach me so I won't have to go through this again!"

God's promise is: *"I will never leave you; never will I forsake you."* (Hebrews 13:5b)

Here are a few verses with some advice from God on dealing with trials. Take some time to educate yourself on His plan.

The next time a trial comes your way, don't worry (Matthew 6:33; Philippians 4:6-7); don't run (Psalm 46:10; Luke 21:19); don't hide (Isaiah 52:10); submit to His will (Matthew 26:39); keep your head (2 Timothy 4:5); drink your medicine (John 18:11); watch God's power come through your weakness (2 Corinthians 12:9-10)!

Remember that as children of the King, we have destinies that include the pain of training for royalty (1 Thessalonians 3:3); we are soldiers (2 Timothy 2:3); expect it, don't be surprised (1 Peter 4:12).

Waggaman MX, early 70's. Miss. River in background. The author landing a 73'
Elsinore, coming out of the ravine, the same site where he would crush his ankle months
later in a career-ending crash.

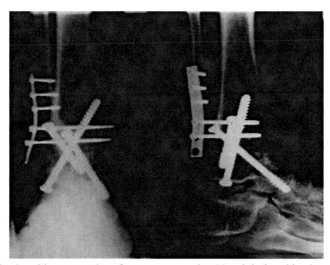

The author's ankle present day after many surgeries. Now it is fused in place to avoid
the pain of 30 years of bone deterioration and acute osteoathritis.

31. Fighting Unseen Forces

Part I

I was talking with a racer yesterday and he illustrates the battle we face. He has experienced success in racing at the highest level, has a beautiful home and family, a high paying job, has enjoyed many successes in life, and yet has tremendous internal struggles. He, like me sometimes struggles with himself. My own worst enemy is myself. I must conquer myself and the way I think. But there are other unseen enemies that would seek to destroy our lives. Who are they?

I. Satan and his demons:
For our struggle is not against flesh and blood, but against the rulers, against the authorities, against the powers of this dark world and against the spiritual forces of evil in the heavenly realms. Therefore put on the full armor of God, so that when the day of evil comes, you may be able to stand your ground, and after you have done everything, to stand. (Ephesians 6:12-13)

Related Scriptures: Gen. 3:15; 2 Cor. 2:11; James 4:7; 1 Peter 5:8; Rev. 12:17

II. The world system that goes against God's principles.
Remember when Satan tempted Jesus?
The devil led him up to a high place and showed him in an instant all the kingdoms of the world. And he said to him, "I will give you all their authority and splendor, for it has been given to me, and I can give it to anyone I want to.
(Luke 4:5-7)

"The world and its desires pass away, but the man who does the will of God lives forever." (1 John 2:17)

Related Scriptures: John 16:33; 1 John 5:4-5

III. Our own selfish desires. (Flesh)
"The righteousness of the upright delivers them, but the unfaithful are trapped by evil desires." (Proverbs 11:6)

"What causes fights and quarrels among you? Don't they come from your desires that battle within you?" (James 4:1)

Related Scriptures: Rom. 7:23; 1 Cor. 9:25-27; 2 Cor. 12:7; Gal. 5:17; 1 Peter 2:11

When we battle the dangerous unseen forces we must remember that, we cannot stand against them in our own strength.

"For though we live in the world, we do not wage war as the world does. The weapons we fight with are not the weapons of the world. On the contrary, they have divine power to demolish strongholds." (2 Cor. 10:3-4)

Notice that we (followers of Jesus Christ) don't use standard weapons in this battle of the invisible. We use God's divine weapons that have POWER to demolish strongholds. What are strongholds? Simply put, any area of your life (individual, family, or group) where there are godless or evil ideas, powers, habits, assumptions, patterns, addictions, etc.

Jesus has come to reveal the truth and light, and set us free. *"Where the Spirit of the Lord is, there is freedom."* (2 Cor. 3:17)

So since we belong to Him, it is HIS battle. Therefore we ask Him to fight for us. *"For the LORD your God is the one who goes with you to fight for you against your enemies to give you victory."* (Deut. 20:2)

32. Weapons for Invisible Warfare

Part II

So what kind of weapons do you use to fight these invisible battles? It doesn't matter if you are dealing with gossip, harassment, bad habits, bitterness, envy, pride, anger, fear, depression, addictions, etc. There is a spiritual dimension behind the actual point of pain. So you must battle against the cause of the enemy, not just the enemy himself. It's like battling poison ivy in your yard. You can't just take a rake and tear up the leaves and vines. You must go down to the roots, or it will be right back.

It's the same thing with the invisible battles we have in life. Whatever the source, we must use divine weapons to destroy the roots. Then we play a part as well when we: resist the temptation to return to the vice, confront the person causing the problem, avoid a person or place, etc. Listen how God tells us to do battle.

> *For our struggle is not against flesh and blood, but against the rulers, against the authorities, against the powers of this dark world and against the spiritual forces of evil in the heavenly realms. Therefore put on the full armor of God, so that when the day of evil comes, you may be able to stand your ground, and after you have done everything, to stand. Stand firm then, with the belt of truth buckled around your waist, with the breastplate of righteousness in place, and with your feet fitted with the readiness that comes from the gospel of peace. In addition to all this, take up the shield of faith, with which you can extinguish all the flaming arrows of the evil one. Take the helmet of salvation and the sword of the Spirit, which is the word of God. And pray in the Spirit on all occasions with all kinds of prayers and requests. (Ephesians 6:12-18)*

Ok, now that basic training is over, take this quiz before you head out into battle: (Put your hand over the answers.)

How many offensive weapons are listed? One - God's Word.

Is our struggle against people are forces behind them? Forces and powers of this world

Will this day of evil and struggle come to believers? Yes

Will there be a battle? Yes

Are you defending something? Yes, standing your ground

What part does truth play? It holds everything up as a belt.

Is living right part of the weaponry? Yes, the breastplate of righteousness protects your vital organs from attack.

Do you have to face the enemy alone, empty-handed? No.

33. Ronald Reagan Overcoming Obstacles

Former President Ronald Reagan's letters were just made public in preparation for the book, *Reagan: A Life in Letters*. Here is an excerpt taken from the September 29, 2003 issue of Time Magazine. Reagan was asked how he overcame obstacles. 1979:

Dear Miss Kellner:

... I was taught from the very beginning and accepted the idea that when all else fails, you then turn to God and put it in His hands... Let me give one example that was not a great tragedy but, at my particular age and at that particular time seemed so: I got out of college in the depths of the Depression in 1932. The government was putting announcements on the radio urging people not to leave home looking for work because there was none. I had decided that I wanted to get into radio, and I had decided that what I wanted to be in radio was a sports announcer. I didn't listen to the government announcements. I went hitchhiking around the Midwest simply asking at radio stations for a job, a job of any kind so that I could get in the studio and then would take my chances with working up to sports announcer. Finally, after weeks of this, I hitchhiked my way home, arriving in a downpour of rain.

My mother told me that a new Montgomery Ward store had opened in our small home town and was looking for someone known to the people in town for having had athletic experience to manage the sporting goods department. Wet and bedraggled as I was, I went right down and was interviewed for the manager. I must have looked like a bum, and I realized I wasn't going over very well. The next day I found that a local high school athlete of more recent vintage had been given the job. It was a very low moment, but ... that faith that my mother had given me was sustaining.

The next day, I hitchhiked out again ... where there was another radio station, walked in, stated my case and was told they had just hired a young man to break in as an announcer the day before. This was a little too much for me, and on the way out the door, I mumbled, "how does a guy ever get to be a sports announcer if he can't get a job in a radio station?" I reached the elevator. But before it arrived at the floor, the program director I'd been talking to, a wonderful old Scotsman, crippled with arthritis hobbling on canes, caught up with me, and said, "what is that you said about being a sports announcer?" And I told him of my ambition. He asked me if I knew anything about football. Well, I'd played the game for eight years-through high school and college. The upshot of it was I was given a tryout. I broadcast a Big Ten football game ... and that began my career in radio. As you can see, I look back on that Montgomery Ward job and understand very well why I didn't get it ...

Sincerely, Ronald Reagan

Scripture for the Day: *"In his heart a man plans his course, but the LORD determines his steps."* (Proverbs 16:9)

34. Check the Price Tag

Here's another letter from former President Ronald Reagan. This one is from 1972, when he saw his son's report card from Webb School in his sophomore year. Here is his advice about making sacrifices.

Dear Son:

... Some fathers get so uptight in their concern they wind up trying to relive their own youth by stage-directing their son's life. I hope by now I've convinced you this is not my intention or desire. Some fathers cop out and, under the pretense of being a 'pal,' don't set any ground rules at all, and thus avoid having to make any tough decisions. This I have no intention of doing.

These concerns have been on my mind for some time, and so has this letter. Now it has been triggered by your report card [which included a C- in French and a D in algebra] ... Everything in life has a price and our biggest mistakes are when we don't really ask the price before we make our choice. Do you remember our Christmas shopping and the jolt you had when you had the gift wrapped and then heard the price?

The "trouble" the algebra teacher mentioned is the price you pay for not forcing yourself to work at something that is less interesting than other things you'd rather do. For example, the price can be ineligibility for outside activities, including athletics. It can be cancellation of summer plans because you have to make up credits in summer school. It can be limitation of your choice of colleges because you don't meet the requirements of the ones you'd really like

This period of the school year, whether it be high school or college, is the toughest. Don't ask me why, but it's always been true. This is when the excitement of fall and starting the new year seems a long way back and the summer an even longer way ahead. It's easy to get bored, to complain about everything and to think the school and everyone connected with it are out to ruin your life. This is when you have to remember the price for giving up and copping out ... We don't know what turns our life will take or what doors will open and there is nothing worse than to have such a door open and then learn you gave away your admittance ticket back in your school days.

The other day when we were talking about the POW's we spoke of self-discipline and how it saved their lives. There is an inner man within all of us we have to call on once in a while. Having the guts to do the nasty little boring tasks, sticking to them when we'd rather goof off, decides whether that inner man has enough muscle to be of any help when we need him ...

Well, if you've read this far let me just wrap it up by telling you your mother and I have known many moments of great pride in you. We've also known moments of doubt in ourselves; times when we've worried as to whether we've made that inner man as strong as he'll need to be sometime later in life when you call on him for help.

Keep an eye on the price tag; some things are very expensive and you pay for the rest of your life.

Love, Dad

Scripture for the Day: *"Better a patient man than a warrior; a man who controls his temper than one who takes a city."* (Proverbs 16:32)

35. Good News and Bad News

Which do you want first, the good news or the bad? Both? Well I'll tell you the story first. I was on my way to Holeshot MX in Loranger for a race one Sunday morning. I had a few problems getting up, getting the bike loaded, forgot this and that; well you know how it goes. The next thing I knew I was running about twenty minutes late. That wouldn't be so bad, but I was to lead the worship service for the racers at 7:00am. Did I tell you I'm not a morning person?

I stretched the back roads speed limits in a few places. I love to twist the throttle in the curves. Kids don't try that at home. Anyway, I pulled in about 7:25, thinking they would be sitting in the bleachers, wondering where I was, and I would apologize and start the Bible study/prayer time.

I pulled up just in time to see them walking away. Some of the regulars like Heavy D, Carl Langley, Shay Racca and Alan Hobgood were easing back to their pits with peaceful smiles on their faces. "We missed you this morning." "Yeah, good thing Hoot was here, he did a good job."

"Well, how dare they start a worship service without the chaplain!" Just kidding. That was not what I was thinking. I was thinking, praise God! You know why? He took care of His important business with just the right person. I didn't screw things up, in fact I may have advanced God's work in their lives and Hoot's life by my tardiness.

Hoot Parker is a former pro MX racer who can still challenge for a podium spot in the money class at the age of 35. He has a family and a motorcycle shop in Denham Springs (H & S Motorsports) and sponsors several riders. But more than that he is a godly Christian man who is not afraid to take a stand for what he believes. He is one of the few team managers I can hand the microphone to, and he will talk calmly and positively about what's going on.

Even though he had a lot on his mind that morning, with his race, his racing team, getting the bikes prepped, etc.; he took a Bible and led the worship service.

So what's the good news/bad news? It's NOT ALL ABOUT ME! We can get to thinking that the whole world revolves around us, but it doesn't. That's bad news for our egos, but good news for our peace of mind, because it takes the pressure off of us. I work in partnership with God and His Holy Spirit. If I can't make it, He'll raise up someone who will. I can't save anyone anyway, only God can. I'm not a salesman, just a witness. There are others who love God more than me, work harder than me and are smarter than me. It's not just about me.

At that rider's meeting I made that point that God loves each one of the riders and their families, and He'll go to great lengths to let them know, and then publicly thanked Hoot for stepping in for me.

Scripture for the Day: *"What, after all, is Apollos? And what is Paul? Only servants, through whom you came to believe – as the Lord has assigned each his task. I planted the seed, Apollos watered it, but God made it grow. So neither he who plants nor he who waters is anything, but only God, who makes all things grow."* (1 Cor. 3:5-7)

Hoot Parker doing what most people fear, addressing the crowd with the microphone at a race at Wildwood MX.

Wally Diaczenko in our pirogue after a successful hunt. My retriever (Brassy) on his right, his retriever and Brassy's sire, Stryker on his left. (Don't laugh at his hat, he's a former Navy Seal and an expert with explosives.)

36. A Few Steps Ahead

Being from Louisiana, I've had the opportunity to go duck hunting. When I had my best hunting buddy, Wally Diaczenko and our best retrievers, Striker and Brassy, we had some memorable hunts. One of the hard parts about hunting is you have to get up and be out in position about 30 minutes before daylight. I am not a morning person, so getting out of bed at 4:30am and getting all those hunting clothes on is not easy. I would finally begin to wake up while struggling with a bundle of decoys, a shotgun and an excited retriever in a pirogue. You ever try to paddle a pirogue? It does not have the stability of a canoe or kayak, to say the least.

After we would get near the blinds, we would have to walk through the marsh in our hip waders. You duck hunters can almost smell the rotting grass odor and hear the slurp of the boots stepping through the black mud, can't you? Most times I would leave the gear in the pirogue and pull it behind me. Brassy would get out and run (or marsh-hop), and I would have a flashlight pointing ahead of me. I did not want to shine the light up into the air or out to the horizon. I would keep it pointed down in front of me so I could see where I was stepping.

Walking through the marsh or the woods in the dark is different than walking during daylight. Everything looks so different. All you can really see are the next few steps.

Life is like that. Many times we can't see what's coming. Though we are going in a certain direction with a vision in our minds, we can't see around the bends. But God can. He's been there. He wants to guide you around the obstacles. He wants to protect you from the gators, water-moccasins, sink-holes, traps and other dangers. So turn on His light. (Psalm 119:105) The light is His Word, the Bible. It is a lamp to our feet. It's not a searchlight that lights all the way to the horizon. We would probably feint with fear if we saw all of our future obstacles and the dangers ahead. We'd also have a new struggle with pride if we could see that far ahead in our lives. His Word lights up our path right before us. All we have to do is step ahead in obedience and trust His Word.

I will lead the blind by ways they have not known, along unfamiliar paths I will guide them; I will turn the darkness into light before them and make the rough places smooth. These are the things I will do; I will not forsake them. (Isaiah 42:16)

"In his heart a man plans his course, but the LORD determines his steps." (Proverbs 16:9)

37. Abandon Ship!

It was about 11:30 at night. The scene was my kitchen. I heard the tinkling of a bell. I got up to see and it was my son's friend. "Come see this," he said excitedly. He carried a piece of paper and a jar of change over to the corner of the kitchen. There on the floor was the bell. He slipped the paper under the bell and proceeded to lift the whole thing up and position it right over the jar. Then he carefully slid the paper out while shaking it. "What is it?" I asked. "You'll see," he answered without looking up.

All of a sudden a black spider the size of a quarter dropped over the edge of the jar and took off across the floor under the table. Josh groaned in agony, as he hates spiders. I thought I would scare him and reached down to pick up the spider. As soon as I touched it, little black dots exploded from the spider in all directions. Baby spiders! No, not in my kitchen! I think I heard them yell, "Every man for himself. Abandon ship!"

I reached for the paper towels and told Josh where the insect spray was in the pantry. I reached down with the paper towel and grabbed the Momma and the babies that stayed with her. I squished her in the towel and tossed her out the back door. Josh sprayed the scattered babies. He said, "I hope that was just a ranger spider or something." I said, "Oh no, that was a navy poisonous shark tarantula." You should have seen his face. Being the entertainer he is, he recognized the joke and smiled.

You know where the baby spiders that survived were? They were still attached to Mom. Mom died, but I'm sure many tiny spiders survived and crawled out of that paper towel in the yard. The ones that scattered in the kitchen were drowned in poison.

Many people hear the truth of God. But when a threat comes, they abandon it. They fall back on old habits or impulse. They take the easiest way out. They don't trust God when the bullets start flying. So they become a victim of the enemy; spiritual road-kill on the highway of life. Hopefully it's not permanent, but the damage is done. And God has to start all over with them, building their trust and faith.

Jesus told a parable about seeds. The seeds represented the Word of God. The soil was the minds and hearts of the listeners. Some seeds were choked out when trouble came. The seeds that grew and produced a great harvest were the ones that put down roots. Don't abandon what you know is right in your time of testing. Trust God and His Word today. Put it into practice. Hold onto Him when the trial comes your way. Then you will see God at work in you life, and your faith will grow stronger to face another day.

Read Matthew 13:18-23

38. Surviving a Wreck

Mario Andretti did the unthinkable at a race in 2004. He hit the wall going over 100 mph during practice testing. The car flipped several times before coming to rest on the track. He walked away.

Have you ever been in a wreck? In 1980 I was in a truck wreck. I was riding in the back of a Toyota truck with a camper top with two golden retrievers. My friend, who was in the front driving, got a little reckless and went off the road near my home in Thibodaux. I remember flipping over a few times then coming to a stop, right side up. Now I know what it feels like to be inside of a clothes dryer! We all walked away with only a few cuts and bruises. His truck was totaled. I still have the picture of the wrecked truck and the dejected look on our faces when we got home.

In life, we get in wrecks. Not just car wrecks, but life wrecks. Whether it is a divorce, a loss of job, the arrest of our teenager, the failure of a course at school, the loss of a house to a disaster, the loss of a friend, a personal failure, an investment gone sour, a death or a loss of health, we all have to face them from time to time. Disappointments and trials are a part of life for all of us.

For those of us who are in relationship with God, we have a certain protection. We do experience the material or physical loss, but not the spiritual. NOTHING can separate us from the love of God and His protecting, providing hand. Listen to Romans 8:31:

• *"If God is for us, who can be against us?"* You and God are a MAJORITY!

• *"Who shall separate us from the love of Christ?"* Go ahead and write their names here. Are they more powerful than God? His love for you is so powerful he sent His only son, Jesus to die on the cross to pay for your sins. If you were the only person in the world, he would have done it for YOU!

• *"Shall trouble..."* Write down the problem that is troubling you here. Is it bigger than God?

• *"or hardship..."* Write down what is so hard that God can't handle for you. You say, "It's not God I'm worried about. It's me that can't handle it." You're right. You hit the nail on the head. You can't handle it. That's why God allowed it into your life to begin with, so you would turn it over to Him and let Him handle it. He wants you to learn to TRUST him more.

- "...or persecution or famine or nakedness or danger or sword? No, in all these things we are more than conquerors through him who loved us."

Is God's Word true? Then you need to trust Him today, not your own abilities or manipulations or education or contacts or money or looks or charm. Trust Him. If you have Jesus Christ in your heart, you have the crown of a prince upon your head. Who's gonna mess with the kings' kid?

Scripture for the Day: *"He will call upon me, and I will answer him; I will be with him in trouble, I will deliver him and honor him."* (Psalm 91:15)

39. Winter of the Soul

This last month I have noticed that Coy "Boogeyshoes" Hobgood, a local motocross racer who has been winning everything he's entered in the local races. He competes in the money class, which is for the local pros. He's a quiet and unassuming 20 year-old from Slaughter, La. who does his bragging on the track. He will be competing in a couple of National AMA races with the pros this summer. He is achieving what all racers dream of: breaking into the top level of racing. He is in the "spring" of his professional career. He and his Dad are just reaching the beginning of the harvest; the years of practice, the thousands of dollars in parts and bikes, the miles of travel are about to pay off.

We go through seasons in our lives. Have you ever noticed that? You go through a period of plenty. You go through another time of fun and enjoyment. Then there's the time of barrenness, emptiness or discouragement. That's the winter of the soul.

I've just come through that season in my life. It's when the things you attempt don't seem to work. The fruit isn't growing yet. You break the hard ground, you sow the seeds, you work in hope that it will pay off later. You toil and labor in hope. You look heavenward for confirmation that you are doing the right thing, that you are working the right place, using the right tools, digging the right depth, sowing the right seeds. You look over the fence at your neighbor's yard and his is growing very well. He's sitting in the shade taking a break. But that is between him and God. You look back to your own plot of ground God has assigned you and wrestle with the doubts.

That's what I'm doing with this book. I'm sowing seeds into your life. Even though doubts come to me about, "Is it worth it? Will anyone buy it or read it? Am I doing the right thing?" Still I make the sacrifices to spend the time of writing and getting it published. If you have read this far, you are going to reap the benefits of taking in God's principles (if you act on them). One day, God will reward me, either in this life or the next. But I press on, like the bare tree in winter, keeping the roots down, soaking up the rain, waiting for the new buds of spring. I'll just trust God that He'll bring in HIS harvest.

If you are in a season of winter like me, here is some advice.

1. <u>Rest</u>. You've come through a harvest, you are being prepared for the spring, and you need rest of spirit.

2. <u>Learn</u>. Read everything you can about whatever struggles you are dealing with. But make sure it is biblically sound, godly advice. God is preparing you for something.

3. <u>Be patient</u>. In God's economy, He has to prepare you before He will promote you. When the time is right, He'll put you where He wants you to serve.

4. <u>Qualify</u> the opportunities that come your way. You may have offers that are not for you, but they look very tempting. Approach them with much wisdom, prayer and godly advice from a trusted friend.

Like the barren tree of winter covered by cold snow, there is life, but it's not showing on the outside yet. Soon, when the time is right, the winds will change, the temperature will rise and new growth will spring forth! God hasn't forgotten you. Just wait.

There is a time for everything, and a season for every activity under heaven:
a time to be born and a time to die,
a time to plant and a time to uproot,
a time to kill and a time to heal,
a time to tear down and a time to build,
a time to weep and a time to laugh,
a time to mourn and a time to dance,
a time to scatter stones and a time to gather them,
a time to embrace and a time to refrain,
a time to search and a time to give up,
a time to keep and a time to throw away,
a time to tear and a time to mend,
a time to be silent and a time to speak,
a time to love and a time to hate,
a time for war and a time for peace. (Ecclesiastes 3:1-8)

Coy "Boogeyshoes" Hobgood winning at the Arenacross in Jackson, Ms in 2004.

#2 Gage Hutchinson's Dad gives last minute instructions at the line at New Iberia.

40. "I Don't Know What to Pray!"

I was interviewing a 6 year old boy in the tower during the intermission of a race. His name was Noah Nicoh. His father's name was Earl. I wish you could have seen his little freckled face with the broad smile. I was asking him about a gnarly crash he had the weekend before at an Arenacross race. He was answering the easy questions ok, but kind of got stuck when we got into the details of his crash. His Dad was standing right behind him. Like is often the case, I could almost feel the love the father had for his son. It was like an invisible force field.

When the son couldn't think of what to say, I looked up at his father. His father told him what to say, according to the truth of what happened. The little boy had the biggest smile, but it dimmed a little when he got stuck. But when his father reinforced his words, the fullness of his smile continued when he had the answers. I'm sure Earl was happy to help his son speak the right words into the microphone that transmitted the conversation all over the track.

Sometimes we struggle when we are transmitting our words into heaven to the God we cannot see. We get stuck with what to say or how to say it. But we have the Holy Spirit of our loving heavenly Father standing beside us, translating, encouraging, giving us words, transmitting, empowering our prayer. Never be afraid to pray. As long as you have the desire, just humble yourself and be honest, tune out the world, imagine a loving, understanding Father standing there listening with open arms and ears. He'll do the rest.

Scripture for the Day: *"...the Spirit helps us in our weakness. We do not know what we ought to pray for, but the Spirit himself intercedes for us with groans that words cannot express."* (Romans 8:26)

Quote for the Day: "When the road of life is steep and slippery, prayer in action gives us traction." (unknown)

41. It's Raining

Have you ever seen people scatter when it starts to rain? You know what I'm talking about. You are at some outdoor event (like a race) and the warning comes as a clap of thunder or the approach of clouds or even a few drops on your face. At first you just hope it will pass with just a few sprinkles. When it gets harder you calculate how you can continue the activity. But if the downpour comes, everybody runs for cover.

I was just at a race where people went to the track owner and got their money back and left. But the skies cleared and the front came through, lowering the humidity (which is a big deal in south Louisiana). The track dried out and we had a great race. The track needed it, the grass and trees needed it, our lawns needed it. It was a blessing.

Many times God sends rain into our lives to bless us. But we see it as an interruption. If we entrust our life into God's hands, He WILL send the interruptions for our good. We may not see them as good, we may even curse them. But that's a lack of maturity on our part. If we run from them, we may miss God's best. If we want growth in our spiritual lives, vitality in our bodies, peace in our emotions, cleanness in our minds, we must let God bring the rain. It doesn't last any longer than is good for us.

In fact, you might want to build a cistern to catch some of the water for another day. What I mean is, keep a diary. Write down what you were thinking, feeling, what happened, etc. Then write down your prayer. Then come back and write down how God answered. When I do that I am always amazed at how God answered my prayers.

So whatever happens today, don't get "knocked off your horse." Be ready for the interruptions. Don't curse them or run from them. It may be a blessing in disguise.

Scripture for the Day: *"For our light and momentary troubles are achieving for us an eternal glory that far outweighs them all. So we fix our eyes not on what is seen, but on what is unseen. For what is seen is temporary, but what is unseen is eternal."* (2 Corinthians 4:17-18)

Quote for the day: "Make sure that you let God's grace work in your souls by accepting whatever He gives you, and giving Him whatever He takes from you. True holiness consists of doing God's work with a smile." (Mother Theresa of Calcutta. Quoted in Malcolm Muggeridge, *Something Beautiful for God*)

42. When God allows Bad Things to Happen

In this book I've built a bridge from the Bible to common issues of life. Most of what I've presented are situations that I've been through at least once (or someone close to me). Today let's consider a question that we all ask and that I can't really answer. But I will take you to the Bible and let you wrestle with the problem for yourself. Why does God allow some bad things to happen?

We've all heard people use this question against God. "If God is good, why does he allow babies to die, the innocent to suffer, good people to struggle or bad people to prosper?" One quick answer is that we are looking at the temporary here on earth. God's judgment and mercy doesn't end in this life. He's got all eternity to set things right. Also, we live in a fallen, sin-sick world that is diseased ever since the fall of man in the garden of Eden. (Romans 8:22)

Another truth to consider is that God has all the facts and we don't. While it may seem that the wicked are happy, we don't know how tortured their souls are from shame, guilt or fear. While it may seem that it wasn't fair for that good person to lose an arm in an accident, we don't see how it develops their relationship with God. While it may seem that a baby shouldn't have died, we don't see what God was rescuing it from, or how He used his short life span to change others' lives forever. While it may seem that injustice is going unpunished, God may be calling us to do something about it as partners with His kingdom. But sometimes we may be just a little too lazy/indifferent/afraid/preoccupied to pray or act.

I've got a couple friends in wheelchairs from racing accidents. I thought I could pray them back into health. I was wrong. Not because God isn't good, because God loves them and knows much more than I do. It's not about me. It's about them and God's eternal plan for them which only He knows.

So I don't understand why they are not healed. I don't understand why God hasn't answered my prayers the way I want. I'm just going to have to trust Him. Take a look at another interesting Bible verse that addresses this issue. The greatest missionary under Jesus was the Apostle Paul. God used him to pen over half the New Testament. He was God's most important man in the last part of the 1st Century. Yet look what Paul was NOT delivered from:

Five times I received from the Jews the forty lashes minus one. Three times I was beaten with rods, once I was stoned, three times I was shipwrecked, I spent a night and a day in the open sea, I have been constantly on the move. I have been in danger from rivers, in danger from bandits, in danger from my own countrymen, in danger from Gentiles; in danger in the city, in danger in the country, in danger at sea; and in danger from false brothers. I have labored and toiled and have often gone without sleep; I have known hunger and thirst and have often gone without food; I have been cold and naked. Besides everything else, I face daily the pressure of my concern for all the churches. Who is weak, and I do not feel weak? Who is led into sin, and I do not inwardly burn? If I must boast, I will boast of the things that show my weakness. (2 Corinthians 11:24-30)

Does this sound like someone you want to trade lives with? Maybe your problem isn't so bad after all. Yes there is suffering in this world, but even Jesus had to suffer unimaginable horrors as He endured temptation, provoked evil attacks, was persecuted for righteousness and speaking against powerful religious leaders. He was publicly humiliated, tortured, beaten and crucified – for us.

God hasn't deserted you. He's working His long-term plan for you that is infinitely better than a quick-fix band-aid.

Quote for the Day: "Don't pray that God will remove the trial, but that He will give you the strength to make it through and you will remember the lesson so you won't have to go to that class again." (R.J.)

43. The Cross Room

An old story is told about a man who was struggling with a great difficulty as he dreamed. In this dream he walked toward a light. As he got closer to the light he recognized the source. It was his Lord Jesus Christ. Jesus asked him why he was so sad. He replied that his cross was too heavy to bear. So Jesus led him to a door. The sign on the door read, "Cross Room." Jesus said, "you can put your cross down in this room. But you must pick up another one."

The man was so relieved. How he had prayed for this moment. He thanked Jesus three times and they entered the room. He put his cross down and breathed a sigh of relief. Then he began to look for another. As he walked through the room he saw crosses of many shapes and sizes. There were crooked crosses, worn out crosses, old crosses and modern crosses. There were signs on the crosses in every language he could think of and some he'd never seen before. He was sickened to see some bloody crosses, some with pieces of flesh still in the nails. Some crosses were bigger than he was. Many had sharp edges and course grains. He even tried to pick up a couple but they were too heavy. He looked questioningly at Jesus and He just waved His hand across the room indicating the others.

Just as the man was about to give up, he spied a small cross leaning against the wall by the door. He went and picked it up. He couldn't believe his good fortune. "Can I have this one?" he asked. Jesus replied, "My son, that's the one you came in with." (Author unknown)

Just like the man in the cross room, we are looking for an easy way out. Our struggles can sometimes seem too much. But God knows just how much we can take and will not give us more than we are able to bear.

No temptation has seized you except what is common to man. And God is faithful; he will not let you be tempted beyond what you can bear. But when you are tempted, he will also provide a way out so that you can stand up under it. (1 Corinthians 10:13)

Not only does He not overload us, but He will help us carry it, too.

Come to me, all you who are weary and burdened, and I will give you rest. Take my yoke upon you and learn from me, for I am gentle and humble in heart, and you will find rest for your souls. For my yoke is easy and my burden is light. (Jesus in Matthew 11:28)

Kevin Mancuso tries to finish his race despite the mud at High Rollers MX in 2004.

The author doing maintenance to his BMW F650 after his trip to Canada.

44. Tune Up

My 1989 Ford pick-up truck was waiting outside for her tune-up. In the last couple years I'd installed: a new motor, radiator, clutch, starter, plugs, points, wires, fuel pump, fuel line, power steering unit, tires, brakes, oil filter, battery, alternator, heater core, hoses, belts, exhaust system, sensors, filters, fan clutch, trailer hitch, electric trailer brakes, water pump, universal joints... well, you get the picture. The only thing I didn't do is have it painted. My wife says I've replaced everything on it. When I'd say "I haven't replaced the ...," then that part seemed to break. Hey, I can't afford 20,000 dollars for a new truck. I'll just keep fixing mine.

But now she was running rough, especially when cold. That's my truck … not my wife. So for the second time in three years, the plugs, distributor cap and rotor were sitting there waiting for me on the front seat. I needed to restore the fire of the system.

Sometimes we need a tune-up. We have taken care of everything else, but something on the inside of us is just not running right. We lack spark, our ignition system is misfiring; when we try to go there is a hesitation. Maybe a little moisture is blocking the flow of electricity. This moisture I will call "sin." It's all the little mistakes, wrong-doings, wrong-thoughts, wrong-motives, wrong-words that have accumulated in our minds. We might not even remember what they were, but deep in our heart, where we connect with God, they have gummed up the works. Shame or guilt consciously or subconsciously steals our joy and confidence in God.

The only way to get the spark back is to get in there and clean them up. Otherwise, your life will have poor gas mileage, hesitation, be hard to start, often back-fire, knock and ping and may even leave you stranded along the highway.

If this is you, here's a suggested remedy. Set aside a time alone with God; no distractions, noises, or any outside influences; just you, your Bible and an open, humble heart.

1. Open your Bible to Psalm 103. Read it out loud, slowly. Let the Bible paint a portrait of who God really is on your mind. Now turn to John 14:6. Read it and believe it. Next John 7:38. Luke 7:48. 1 John 1:8-9. Let God's Word wash your spirit.

2. Pray. Praise God for who He is. Not some little god that is a figment of your imagination, but ask Him to reveal Himself to you. Say, "God, I am a sinner in need of forgiveness. In the name of Jesus, I come to you. Jesus take control of my heart, my life; be my Lord and master. Please send the Holy Spirit to cleanse my heart and mind. Purge me from anything that is offensive to you. Give me the mind of Christ." Read Isaiah 1:18-20.

3. Confess your known sins. Anything you can remember. He already knows and won't be shocked. Tell Him you've put those sins away, never to touch them again. Read 1 John 1:9.

4. Ask Him to reveal sins you have forgotten. There are some in your sub-conscious. The Holy Spirit will bring them out. As each one comes to your mind, picture yourself handing it to Jesus. He'll remove them "as far as the east is from the west." (Psalm 103:12)

5. Ask Him to heal your inner wounds. Give Him any pain you may be feeling. Allow it to be an ongoing process for the rest of your life. Read 2 Chronicles 7:14

6. Ask Him to fill you with His presence. If you have confessed your sins, you have made room for His Holy presence. That's why the Old Testament priests had to go through ritual cleansing before they could enter the Holy Place of the temple. That's why the people had to bring animals to sacrifice before they could enjoy God's presence. Here are some scriptures for related study if you want to pursue this issue: Leviticus 10:8-10; Lev. 20:26; Deuteronomy 13:17; Joshua 7:12-13; Acts 24:16.

7. Thank Him for every good thing He has given you.

Now go live like someone who just got their heart replaced with a new heart – the heart of a champion.

45. The Greatest Opportunity

Once upon a time there was a teenager who loved motocross racing. He asked his father to help him get started. His Dad bought a motocross bike for the son. Every day after school he would ride it around the yard. Each day he would ask his Dad to come out and watch, but his Dad was too busy with other things. His son soon outgrew the large yard behind their house and asked his Dad to take him to a nearby track. But his Dad didn't have time, so the son got his Uncle Stoney to take him to practice and to the races.

After several months of practice the boy started being noticed for his skill by other riders. He started racing. He asked his Dad to come and watch, but his Dad replied, "I've got a golf tournament this weekend," or "the Saints are playing on TV." As the boy got better he moved up in class. He began to compete at other tracks. He asked his Dad, "Can you come to the next race? It's really important and I have a good chance to win. You can spend the night in the camper with us." The Dad replied, "Not this weekend. I've got a fishing trip with the boss. Maybe next time." So he went with Uncle Stoney as usual.

The son began winning some races in the novice class at tracks in other states. He would always ask his Dad to come but the story was always the same, just the excuses were different.

Eventually he won enough races that he got a sponsorship. After winning several more races he decided it was time to compete in the National Amateur Championship. He traveled to the different qualifying events and won those races. His picture appeared in the paper. He cut the articles out of the paper and presented it to his Dad with pride. "Look Dad, I'm going to the AMA National Championship at Loretta Lynn's next month. Could you please go? You haven't seen me race a single time." "I know son and I've been meaning to. It's just that something always comes up. I'll be there."

But August rolled around and the Father begged out at the last minute. The disappointed son came to say good-bye as he was leaving for the biggest day of his life. "Dad, I really wish you could be there to watch me race." "I'm sorry son, something came up that is out of my control. I'll watch it on TV." So the boy left with his racing team.

The championship race was televised and the father was watching from home with a group of family and friends. The living room was filled with excitement and expectation. He told everyone how proud he was of his son and all that he had accomplished. The race was difficult, but the boy prevailed and won all his races. When he stepped up on the podium to receive his national championship trophy and number plate he was clearly excited. During the post-race interview the announcer asked him who he'd like to thank. Back home the father told everyone to shut up and he turned up the volume on his TV. After naming his sponsors he said, "... and there is someone very special that has really made all this possible. Without him, I would not be standing here today. He has supported and encouraged me all the way."

Back home the Father sat forward in his chair with a big expectant smile. The son continued, "I'd like to introduce my Uncle Stoney." The camera focused on Stoney. "He's taken me to the races, fixed my bike, and given me encouragement and inspiration. Without him I wouldn't be here today." Back home the stunned Father sat back in silence. The party died out around him as the people graciously left him alone.

As soon as the son returned home, the clearly disappointed Father asked him, "Son, I can appreciate Stoney's help with your racing, but you never mentioned me. Have you forgotten your own Father, you know, the one who gave you the bike?"

The son spoke slowly, with hurt in his voice, "Father, I wanted you to be there. I wanted you to be there when I first learned to ride, but you never came. I wanted you to take me to the track, help me with the bike, watch me learn, give me advice. I wanted to show off my riding skills for you, but you always had an excuse. I invited you many times to travel with us, to hang out with us, to celebrate with us, to work on my bike, but when you didn't come, Uncle Stoney filled in. He was always there, encouraging me and helping me. I finally figured out that it wasn't racing that you didn't want to be around. You just didn't want me."

Some people feel that way about God. He is trying to reach for relationship. He sends preachers, neighbors, chaplains, family members, TV and radio ministers and certain situations to them. But they always have an excuse. They can't make it to church, they see a hypocrite, they don't believe the Bible is literally true, they have their own philosophy, they don't like the preacher, they think the church just wants their money, they'll do it later, etc., etc., etc. But the truth is they just don't want God, only what He can do for them.

This is nothing new. Even Jesus Christ had to deal with this when he walked the earth. John the Baptist, who was preparing the way for him with his preaching and baptizing was quite a character. He lived in the wilderness, ate locusts and wild honey and dressed in animal skins as he preached about the kingdom of God and called people to repent.

When Jesus came He lived differently than His cousin John the Baptist. Jesus traveled through the villages and towns with people, went to parties, ate and drank and celebrated with them. He had the same message, that the kingdom of God had come and called people to repent as He healed and taught. But many people rejected John because he was too extreme in one direction and rejected Jesus because He was too extreme in the other. They just didn't want God. Read the words of Jesus yourself:

To what can I compare this generation? They are like children sitting in the marketplaces and calling out to others: "We played the flute for you, and you did not dance; we sang a dirge, and you did not mourn" For John came neither eating nor drinking, and they say, "He has a demon" The Son of Man came eating and drinking, and they say, "Here is a glutton and a drunkard, a friend of tax collectors and 'sinners.'" But wisdom is proved right by her actions. (Matthew 11:16-19)

If you feel God knocking at your door, don't keep putting Him off. The more you reject Him, the harder your heart becomes. So His messengers aren't perfect, that doesn't change the message. If you keep rejecting God, He will eventually leave you alone. He doesn't force Himself on anyone.

Seek the LORD while he may be found; call on him while he is near. Let the wicked forsake his way and the evil man his thoughts. Let him turn to the LORD, and he will have mercy on him, and to our God, for he will freely pardon. (Isaiah 55:6-7)

Daniel Vining and Clint Plauche enjoy a podium moment as top finishers in the 250 Novice at the 2004 Winter Series. (Not shown, is 2nd place finisher -Jay Ledet)

125 Novice in the heat of battle at Wildwood MX in 2004.

One of La.'s race chaplains, Mac Edmonston racing his Vintage '73 Yamaha DT1 at Holeshot MX in 2004.

46. Nooooo! I Wish I Hadn't Done That!

This is an old story that illustrates something we all struggle with – giving in to temptation.

A preacher goes to a nursing home to meet an elderly parishioner. As he is sitting there he notices this bowl of peanuts beside her bed and takes one. As they talk, he can't help himself and eats one after another. By the time they are through talking, the bowl is empty. He says, "Ma'am, I'm so sorry, but I seem to have eaten all of your peanuts."

"That's okay," she says. "They would have just sat there. Without my teeth, all I can do is suck the chocolate off and put em back in the bowl." (Author unknown)

Like this impulsive preacher we have all done things that we shouldn't have. "I just couldn't help myself," is an attitude of giving into temptation (Matthew 6:13). We can save ourselves a lot of grief if we will just make the right choices; we know this! (Galatians 5:16) But how can we do it?

The answer is simple - LET GOD DO IT. But how? By ASKING. And what does He do when we ask? He sends His Holy Spirit to live inside us and give us the power, grace, desire, to do the right thing (John 14:16-17; Romans 8:4). The Holy Spirit guides our consciences and guides us into all truth. He fills our hearts with godly desires.

Prayer for today: "Dear God, please forgive me for my sins. I believe Jesus died for me and rose again. I release my selfish desires and receive your Holy Spirit. Now guide me into truth and work your power through me. Make me your instrument of goodness today."

Scripture for the Day: *"You will receive power when the Holy Spirit comes on you."* (Jesus in Acts 1:8)

47. Explaining our Difficulties

When you watch pro motocross racers on a track they look so smooth. They make it look like anyone can do what they are doing. It almost looks as though they are on a smoother track. But if you walk the track you will see the same holes, ruts, rocks, roots, kickers (dangerous bumps at the tops of jump faces) and braking bumps that amateur riders ride on. In fact, most pro riders feel, "the rougher, the better." It's not that these top level, experienced riders get easier tracks, it's that they have developed the skills to handle the difficulties before them.

Some people mistakenly believe that the longer you walk with God by faith, the easier life gets. No, the mature believers, like the pro racers, have developed a level of skill and trust that allows them to take on the race with the smoothness and success of an experienced competitor.

If you have entered into a relationship with God through Jesus Christ, you are aware that God doesn't keep all difficulties away from you. The difference is, He goes through them with you (Deuteronomy 31:6; Matthew 11:28-30). He also monitors what comes your way so as not to overload you (1 Corinthians 10:13). A third benefit of being a Christian is God works all things in your life for good (Romans 8:28). But the pain of the struggles and trials are still part of life in this world.

Listen to a part of another devotion book by Oswald Chambers entitled, *My Utmost for His Highest.*

God is not concerned about our plans; He doesn't ask, "Do you want to go through this loss of a loved one, this difficulty, or this defeat?" No, He allows these things for His own purpose. The things we are going through are either making us sweeter, better, and nobler men and women, or they are making us more critical and fault-finding, and more insistent on our own way. The things that happen either make us evil, or they make us more saintly, depending entirely on our relationship with God and its level of intimacy. If we will pray, regarding our own lives, *"Your will be done"* (Matthew 26:42), then we will be encouraged and comforted by John 17, knowing that our Father is working according to His own wisdom, accomplishing what is best. When we understand God's purpose, we will not become small-minded and cynical. (May 22 devotion)

Read Jesus' prayer to the Father before his crucifixion in John 17.

Houston Gammons does the "Faith Walk" with blacked out goggles while Ross Dimm (left) and Brandon Brignac help on the obstacle course at G2G camp.

The author about to jump into a training tank to work on a project with taped helmet in Dive School in Houston. This was preparation for working in muddy water.

48. "I Can't See"

One of the rising stars of MX racing in Louisiana is Jamie Ellis. You can find him contesting the money class at tracks in La. and Tx. He also gives lessons during the week. Recently I was announcing a big qualifying race for the National Championships at Gravity Alley in Breaux Bridge.

When he competed on Sunday in the 250cc expert race he began having some trouble. We noticed he was getting out of the ruts, hitting tires, getting caught up in the soft stuff and unable to move up into the top three positions. He stalled his bike in a turn one time and had to restart it. He made a gallant push at the end, catching the 3rd place rider and winning by 6 inches at the finish line (but that is a story for another devotion).

After the race I asked him what happened. His reply brought back memories to me, "I got some chunks of dirt in my goggles and they kept popping up in my eyes. My eyes were so full of dirt I couldn't even close them." He couldn't see on the track. He was literally riding on instincts, glimpses and memory! Good thing he was on his home track.

Sometimes in life we just can't see. We are distracted by some problem that pops up again and again, keeping us distracted and without real vision. It can wear us down, discourage us and even tempt us to give up. That's when our faith becomes even more important. Whether this "dirt in our goggles" is another person, a situation, a health problem, a wrong attitude or finances, we have to fight our way through it until it is gone.

If this is happening to you, you should refocus on two areas:

1. Who God is *"He did what was right in the eyes of the LORD, just as his father Amaziah had done. He sought God during the days of Zechariah, who instructed him in the fear of God. As long as he sought the LORD, God gave him success."* (2 Chronicles 26:4-5)

2. Who you are *"I praise you because I am fearfully and wonderfully made; your works are wonderful, I know that full well. My frame was not hidden from you when I was made in the secret place. When I was woven together in the depths of the earth, your eyes saw my unformed body. All the days ordained for me were written in your book before one of them came to be."* (Psalm 139:14-16)

"'I am the Lord's servant,' Mary answered." (Luke 1:38)

49. Keep Trying

Part II

I mentioned Jamie Ellis's race one day at Breaux Bridge. He had dirt in his goggles and could not see very well. The dirt kept popping into his eyes until they were so dirty he couldn't even close them. He ran into several obstacles during that race, including stalling his bike in a turn, hitting a tire, going off the course and getting bogged down in the soft sand. But he never gave up. Late in the race he was able to make a final push to win 3rd place by only 6 inches at the checkered flag. After the race he said, "I guess I learned again, that no matter what happens in the race, you should never give up."

You can see where I'm going with this one If you know you are supposed to be doing what you are doing, then you must keep trying. In every goal we try to reach, there will be obstacles and setbacks. The difference in success and failure is simple. The winners are the ones who learn from their loss, make the adjustments and keep trying all the way to the finish line.

Hey, If success were easy, everybody would have it.

Scripture for the Day: *"Therefore, my dear brothers, stand firm. Let nothing move you. Always give yourselves fully to the work of the Lord, because you know that your labor in the Lord is not in vain."* (1 Corinthians 15:58)

Quote for the Day: "A professional writer is an amateur who didn't quit." (Richard Bach, A Gift of Wings)

50. Riding with the Brakes On

Mac Edmonston's motorcycle seized up during practice at a race. So he borrowed another racer's bike. The brakes were not adjusted correctly, so Mac changed the adjustment according to how the adjustment was set on his bike. He took it to the line and raced it in the money class without practicing on it first. The result was a couple of trips over the handlebars and a sore neck and back for Monday.

He later told me that the adjustment was wrong, causing the front brake to be on during the race. He said, "I wondered why I just sat there spinning my wheels while everyone else took off from the start. Then, when I was in the air, the front end came down. When I landed, the wheel locked up sending me over the bars."

What he needed was a little adjustment. Since he had one little bolt on the brake lever set wrong, he was riding with the brake on. He could get away with it for a little while, but it finally caught up with him. What started out as a sluggish bike turned into a nasty crash.

Does your life ever feel like that? Does it ever seem as if you are "riding with your brakes on?" Maybe something in your life is out of adjustment. It could be something that you don't know about, or it may be something you know about, but refuse to change. If you line up your thoughts with the thoughts of God, the little inconsistencies, false ideas or wrong attitudes will eventually be straightened out. This sets you free to run unhindered the way you were designed. It also avoids a lot of those self-inflicted wounds we have to suffer sometimes.

Why don't you pray this prayer today, "Father, I come to you in Jesus' name, asking you to search me and see if there is anything wrong in me. I want you to line up my mind with the mind of Christ. Forgive me for what I have thought wrong. I yield to your terms of right-ness right now."

Scripture for the Day: *"For our offenses are many in your sight, and our sins testify against us. Our offenses are ever with us, and we acknowledge our iniquities: rebellion and treachery against the LORD, turning our backs on our God, fomenting oppression and revolt, uttering lies our hearts have conceived.*

So justice is driven back, and righteousness stands at a distance; truth has stumbled in the streets, honesty cannot enter." (Isaiah 59:12-14)

Related Scriptures: Isaiah 59:1-2; Romans 12:2; 1:28; 7:23; 8:6-7; 1 Cor.2:16; Col. 2:18; 1 John 1:9-10.

51. Who is He?

One of the embarrassing moments of being a race announcer is when you've been talking about a rider during a race while he is on the far side of the track. Then, when he gets near the tower, a closer look at the number reveals you've been talking about the wrong rider. A few times (more often than I care to admit), I've talked about a certain rider that I thought was out front, giving details about him, where he's from, sponsors, age, previous races won, only to have that person come up behind me, tap me on the shoulder and say, "I'm not in that race." Then I have to ask, "Then who is that on the track?" Again, apologies are necessary over the intercom and I have to identify the real rider.

If you've ever watched a race, you know that sometimes it's hard to identify the riders until they are close enough to see their numbers clearly. Then, even though you've seen the riders on the track, you don't really know the rider, until you actually meet him face to face. If you really want to know him, you have to spend time with him between races.

It's the same thing with God. You might think you know Him and what He is like. But you may have the wrong idea. The more you read His Word, the more you understand Him, the more you can get an accurate picture of Him. But if you really want to know Him, you must meet Him. Not just talk about Him, not just hear someone else talk about Him, not just pray to Him, but encounter Him personally.

Jesus told His disciples that He must go away so He could send the Holy Spirit to live with them. The Holy Spirit is the person through whom we encounter God personally. He reveals the Son, Jesus Christ. He also communicates our prayers to the throne of the Father.

On the last and greatest day of the Feast, Jesus stood and said in a loud voice, "If anyone is thirsty, let him come to me and drink. Whoever believes in me, as the Scripture has said, streams of living water will flow from within him." By this he meant the Spirit, whom those who believed in him were later to receive. Up to that time the Spirit had not been given, since Jesus had not yet been glorified. (John 7:37-39)

"Those who obey his commands live in him, and he in them. And this is how we know that he lives in us: We know it by the Spirit he gave us." (1 John 3:24)

Ask the Holy Spirit to reveal Himself in your life today.

Related Scriptures: 1 Cor. 2:10-14; Acts 1:2-5; 8:15-19; 9:17.

52. Which Voice is God?

I called a tire company today and a man answered the phone. I asked him to check and see if a part came in for me. When he put me on hold a pre-recorded voice came on the phone that sounded exactly like his! This voice even seemed to pick up the conversation where his left off: "Ok, let me check..." (recorded message in similar voice) "We have some specials here at..." I almost answered before I realized I was on hold and listening to a recording.

When you are listening for God's direction, you may hear voices in you mind. Which one is God? Which one is your own wishful thinking? Which one is temptation from the evil one? How do you know? We must be very careful about the voices in our mind that we listen to. Just last week I heard about a mother in Texas that murdered her child and said that God told her to do it.

Here are some guidelines to help discern the voice of God.

1. The voice/instruction must line up with scripture. God never breaks His Holy Word. Jesus said, *"Scripture cannot be broken."* (John 10:35)
2. God's voice/instruction will always be for good, never evil. There is not even a shadow of evil in Him. (1 John 1:5)
3. Which voice/instruction glorifies Jesus? Even the Holy Spirit gives glory to Jesus, not Himself or us. (John 15:26)
4. Can the voice/instruction be confirmed by godly counsel? Pass it by a couple other Christians you can trust who know you and know God's word. (Proverbs 15:22)
5. Does the voice/instruction lead to temptation? God never temps us to evil. (James 1:13)

Be very careful in listening for God's direction from your mind. Feelings are deceptive and unreliable. We are experts at rationalizing what we really want. Most of all, the consequences for sin may be more than we want to pay.

Scripture for the Day: *"My friends, do not believe every spirit, but test the spirits to see whether they are from God, because many false prophets have gone out into the world. This is how you can recognize the Spirit of God: every spirit that recognizes that Jesus Christ has come in the flesh is from God."* (1 John 4:1-2)

53. Track Racer or Bench Racer?

Do you know what bench racing is? It is the sport of talking about racing. Get a couple racers together and they will start. Tales of races, starts, crashes, passes, wash-outs, missed gears, block passes and other heroics are swapped like trading cards. After the race, standing around the back of a pick-up truck, sitting at the counter of the motorcycle shop during the week, even on an internet message board, you can hear the good, the bad and the ugly from the weekend before.

Sometimes a "wannabe" sneaks into the conversation. You know who he is. He's not bad, it's just that, well, he's never "hung the skins on the wall," you know, his trophy case is bare. He may be able to talk with race cliché's, but has won few, if any races in actual competition. He may have been around a track at practice, have decals on his truck, wear the hats or shirts, but has never won the respect that only winning races will bring. He's a "bench racer" only. The racers tolerate him, but he's not really one of the "fast guys." You see them in the chat rooms and message boards criticizing what they don't really understand. Maybe one day they will make it to the podium, but until then, they're "wannebies or newbies" as successful racers.

There are Christians like that, too. Maybe they have made a decision to trust Jesus Christ as their savior, prayed the prayer, but their heart is full of worldly pride. Maybe they go to church, but hang out in the wrong places and with the wrong people during the week. They might read the Bible but don't really put it into practice. The Spirit of God is not upon them. Even though they can speak with the godly clichés, they live frustrated lives. They can "talk the talk" but can't "walk the walk." The church has many hypocrites (bench racing Christians). They dabble in Christianity, but their lives are no different than unbelievers.

Jesus called people to follow him. Some dropped what they were doing and followed without reservation and enjoyed true forgiveness, a changed and purposeful life, and the power and presence of God. They were called disciples (learners or followers). Others rejected Jesus' offer. Then there were those in-between souls who said they would follow, but just watched from a distance. They were too timid to participate. "Yes Lord, I will follow You, but..." (Luke 9:61)

These bench racers or "newbies" of the 1st century were called hypocrites. (All real believers still sin from time to time, but I'm referring to those who play the game of Christianity but are not true believers). These bench racers or hypocrites will not enjoy power from God, but confusion and disappointment. When difficulties come their lives will come crashing down around them. (Matthew 7:24-27)

Are you enjoying the power of God in your life? Do you look forward to reading His Word, hanging out with other believers, singing songs of praise to Him? It could be that you have slipped into "bench racing." Or you never really became a follower of Jesus Christ to begin with.

Take some time now to pray and ask God to reveal the truth to you. Then admit your sin, recognize your need for Him and ask His forgiveness. Then give your heart to Him today. Now here comes the hard part. Whatever you know He wants you to do – DO IT! It's your first pop-quiz. Don't fail. Make your creator proud of you today.

Scripture for the Day:

"There was a man who had two sons. He went to the first and said, 'Son, go and work today in the vineyard.'

'I will not,' he answered, but later he changed his mind and went.

Then the father went to the other son and said the same thing. He answered, 'I will, sir.' But he did not go.

Which of the two did what his father wanted?'" (Jesus in Matthew 21:28-31)

Prayer for the Day: Dear Father, I know I have failed you. I'm sorry. Please forgive me for my sins. I ask Jesus to come and live in my heart, be my new Lord and Master. I yield my life to you. Teach me your ways, help me come to know you personally. Reveal to me what is offensive to you and give me the power to remove it from my life. Help me live life well today. Amen.

54. The Bible teaching Serial Killer

The other night, the network news reported the capture of a prime suspect for a serial killing. DNA evidence and a history of crime was enough to arrest Derrick Todd Lee on charges of kidnapping and murder. As many as five young women fell victim to this evil menace. Yet Lee reportedly was nice, charismatic and led Bible studies. This is evil at its' worse, working in the human heart, using God as a disguise.

I've seen this first hand when I was involved in prison ministry. One night as we were making our rounds in December at the St. Tammany parish jail, we distributed Christmas cards to the inmates. Most were thankful, but the leader of an inmate Bible study group (who looked like Lee now that I think about it) came back to me and demanded I give him another Christmas card because he didn't like the one he had. I didn't like his attitude but swapped cards.

Later, as I was talking to another inmate, I heard a commotion. A fight had broken out at the table where this "Bible teacher" was sitting. Apparently, he didn't like what one of his students had said and punched him out of his chair, opening a bloody cut under his eye. Then he taunted the confused man into a fight. Some Bible teacher! I think he just used the Bible to get power over people.

How would you recognize a false teacher? They have been around since day one. Jesus gave instructions on what to look for:

Watch out for false prophets. They come to you in sheep's clothing, but inwardly they are ferocious wolves. By their fruit you will recognize them. Do people pick grapes from thorn bushes, or figs from thistles? Likewise every good tree bears good fruit, but a bad tree bears bad fruit. A good tree cannot bear bad fruit, and a bad tree cannot bear good fruit. Every tree that does not bear good fruit is cut down and thrown into the fire. Thus, by their fruit you will recognize them. Not everyone who says to me, 'Lord, Lord,' will enter the kingdom of heaven, but only he who does the will of my Father who is in heaven. Many will say to me on that day, 'Lord, Lord, did we not prophesy in your name, and in your name drive out demons and perform many miracles?' Then I will tell them plainly, 'I never knew you. Away from me, you evildoers!' (Matthew 7:15-23)

Another way to protect yourself from false teachings is check with your Bible to make sure that what is being taught lines up; and that includes THIS DEVOTION BOOK! (Acts 17:11)

Three papas in MX (from left) Craig Moran, JR Manuel and Heavy D.

Kaitlyn Hayes and Regina Hebert at Breaux Bridge

Glenn Guidry steps forward to receive his prize at the Mid-South Shoot-Out while track owner Becky Andre holds the box of names.

55. Don't Worry, Be Happy

Remember that little song? It has a reggae beat to it. I have it in my guitar book. You want me to play it for you? Ok. Maybe next time.

We all know God doesn't want us to worry. One of the most common questions I got asked in Bible class by the teenagers was, "Is it a sin to worry?" What they wanted was to worry in peace - without guilt. Worry in peace is an oxymoron. They don't go together. They are mutually exclusive. Faith pushes worry away, and worry (or apathy) fills in where there is no faith.

Whatever it is that you are worrying about today, write it down on a piece of paper. . . . Come on, get a piece of paper. Now right it down. Put it on the table. You must pull ALL of the problem out BY THE ROOTS and place it ALL on the table. Come on. You can pick it back up later if you want. Trust me. Put that issue out on the table. Now - the issue you are worrying about is NOT inside of you right now, it is on the table, right? Right? Come on, let it go, for now. You can worry about it later if you want. Did you get that problem out of you? Did you put it on the table? Don't go any further until you do.

Ok, now let me ask you a question, "Does God want you to worry about that problem?" No, of course not. "Does Jesus live in your heart? Are you His child? Will He take care of you?" You have to come to terms with these questions. Go back and meditate on those questions if you are not sure. Read these scriptures and meditate on each word of their truth. I hope you are reading them from your Bible.

> *Don't be anxious about anything (don't worry), but in everything, by prayer and petition, with thanksgiving, present your requests to God. And the peace of God, which transcends all understanding, will guard your hearts and your minds in Christ Jesus.* (Philippians 4:6-7)

> *So do not worry, saying, 'What shall we eat?' or 'What shall we drink?' or 'What shall we wear?' For the pagans run after all these things, and your heavenly Father knows that you need them. But seek first his kingdom and his righteousness, and all these things will be given to you as well. Therefore do not worry about tomorrow, for tomorrow will worry about itself. Each day has enough trouble of its own.*
> (Jesus in Matthew 6:31-34)

"He himself (you) will dwell in prosperity." (Psalm 25:13)

"(your) life is hidden with Christ in God." (Colossians 3:3)

"God is our REFUGE..." (Psalm 46:1)

Now, may I ask you another question? "Is God's Word true?" If it is, then not just "CAN He", but "WILL He" take care of you? Then if His Word is true, and He PROMISED to take care of you and nothing can touch you that He doesn't approve of first, and He is on duty and loves you, then, HE WILL HANDLE THE PROBLEM!

Now there might be a part that you have to play, but ultimate responsibility for your safety is in His hands, since He promised to be your protector, refuge, and God.

Now use your faith and pray this prayer, "God, I don't know exactly how you will handle this problem, but I trust you with it. I put it in your hands. Help me not to worry about it anymore. Show me what part I must play, but the ultimate responsibility is yours. I give it to you."

Now take that piece of paper with the problem and either put it in your Bible (showing that God will handle it); or throw it away (showing you have so much confidence in God that you don't even want to look at it anymore); or put it in your pocket (showing you think He might do something to help, but you're not sure); or tape it to your forehead (showing everyone that you don't trust God and the problem has control over you).

Quote for the Day: "Every tomorrow has two handles. We can take hold of it by the handle of anxiety or the handle of faith." (copied)

Nicholas and Robbie Burgess at their track in Gonzales in 2003

Shannon Silva in a happy moment as he is leading a National Vintage race at Mid-Ohio in July, 2004 on Orazio's '77 MT125.

56. There is a Cure

What is wrong with our world? In every society, on every continent, people from every religion since the beginning of time do it. They treat each other badly: lying, stealing, cheating, abusing, murdering, lusting, rebelling, breaking laws, injuring, perjuring, insulting, obsessing, destroying, etc., etc., etc.

Money doesn't solve the problem. It just gives more options for wrongdoing. Education doesn't solve the problem, it just makes the person more equipped. Religion doesn't help much, it just helps people cover their desires for some things and justify their actions on others. Philosophy and Psychiatry have their place but hasn't stopped this plague of wrongdoing. (America is one of the richest, best educated, best counseled, productive societies that ever lived, yet we have more crime than ever.)

The problem exists in the human heart. The Bible calls it sin. It is the desire to get what I want, when I want it, no matter what someone else says or does. You can see it in children at the grocery store as early as age two. A child is being dragged by the embarrassed Mom down the aisle because he/she can't have the candy/drink/toy or whatever.

If you don't think you have this problem called sin, you are already full of pride and in rebellion against your creator. We could probably find some of your schoolmates, teachers, co-workers or family members who could make some accusation of wrongdoing against you, right? Don't worry, though. We are ALL sinners. I am, you are, the preachers, Sunday School teachers, priests, nuns, etc.

The Bible says there is none righteous, no NOT ONE. (Romans 3:10; 23) Our attempts to cover them from God will not work (Isaiah 29:15; Psalm 44:21) and will bring poor health (Psalm 32:3-4). In the words of Dr. Charles Stanley, "We can't get better, we only get craftier, slicker, better able to hide it; learn from those times we got caught. We might find new ways to express our sinful nature," but it's still a sinful nature that causes us and the people around us problems.

That's enough bad news. Now here comes the good news: God made a way out. He sent His only Son, Jesus Christ to die on the cross 2,000 years ago as payment for our sins. *"God made him who had no sin to be sin for us, so that in Him we might become the righteousness of God."* (2 Corinthians 5:21)

The one who admits he is in need of forgiveness, asks God to forgive him (Acts 3:19), receives this free gift of salvation (Ephesians 1:8-9; John 1:12). He will get a new heart (Ezekiel 36:26-27) and new kind of life in relationship with God forever (John 3:15-16; Romans 5:21; Titus 3:6-7; 1 John 1:2; 5:11; Jude 21)

Isn't that Great News? Ask for yours today!

Scriptures for the Day: *"'Come now, let us reason together,' says the LORD. 'Though your sins are like scarlet, they shall be as white as snow; though they are red as crimson, they shall be like wool.*

If you are willing and obedient, you will eat the best from the land; but if you resist and rebel, you will be devoured by the sword.' For the mouth of the LORD has spoken." (Isaiah 1:18-20)

"This righteousness from God comes through faith in Jesus Christ to all who believe. There is no difference, for all have sinned and fall short of the glory of God, and are justified freely by His grace through the redemption that came by Christ Jesus. God presented Him as a sacrifice of atonement, through faith in His blood. He did this to demonstrate His justice, because in his forbearance He had left the sins committed beforehand unpunished – He did it to demonstrate His justice at the present time, so as to be just and the One who justifies those who have faith in Jesus." (Romans 3:22-26)

Quote of the Day: "Human nature's way of salvation is 'do, do, do.' But God's way of salvation is 'done, done, it's all done.' You have but to rely by faith on the atonement which Christ accomplished on the cross." (Charles Haddon Spurgeon)

57. What you DO have

Sometimes I fall into a trap. This trap makes me unhappy and discontented. It makes me more impatient with others and the "stuff" that is lying around the house. One Monday morning after a big race weekend, I dreaded going out to the camper and unloading it. Not only that, but I had crushed in part of the camper at a drive-through restaurant on my way home. I started the day aggravated and the trap was about to close on me.

But I did something right that helped me out of the trap. I sat down for my morning devotion. A prayer, a scripture reading, more prayer, meditation on the verses, then God showed me a truth. This truth changed my day, revealed the trap, and re-set my attitude. The trap was being discontent with what I had, and wanting things I did not have. Have you ever fallen into that trap? Read this section of scripture from John 6 and see if you can find the truth that keeps you out of that trap.

Jesus was about to perform one of His great miracles, feeding the 5,000 men (plus the women and children). If you look closely, you'll see the truth in the difference in the attitude of Philip and Andrew. Jesus tests them with a question, "Where shall we buy bread for these people to eat?" I saw my attitude that morning in Philip's answer, "Eight months wages would not buy enough bread for each one to have a bite." Compare that attitude with the one of Andrew, "Here's some food!" See the difference?

> *When Jesus looked up and saw a great crowd coming toward him, he said to Philip, "Where shall we buy bread for these people to eat?" He asked this only to test him, for he already had in mind what he was going to do. Philip answered him, "Eight months' wages would not buy enough bread for each one to have a bite!"*
>
> *Another of his disciples, Andrew, Simon Peter's brother, spoke up, "Here is a boy with five small barley loaves and two small fish, but how far will they go among so many?"*
>
> *Jesus said, "Have the people sit down." There was plenty of grass in that place, and the men sat down, about five thousand of them. Jesus then took the loaves, gave thanks, and distributed to those who were seated as much as they wanted. He did the same with the fish.* (John 6:5-11)

Did you find it? Here is the truth: Philip had his focus on what they didn't have. Andrew focused on what they did. In other words, Andrew was thankful for what he did have, and gave that to Jesus. Then he trusted Jesus to meet the need.

That Monday morning I was so like Philip, "I need a newer camper." "I need more money." "I need someone to do all these jobs." "I need... I need... I need..." Wah, wah wah. What a crybaby! When I started looking at the fact that I did have a camper and truck, on loan from God; I did have a home to live in; I did have food in the fridge; I did have some cash in my pocket; I did have a family who loves me; I did have opportunity and resources to fulfill my calling; I started getting a thankful heart. I started seeing the "stuff" as gifts given to me to use, not just things in the way. I was set free from being in bondage to these material things. Now I became the master of them. God loaned them to me to be used for Him. My attitude adjustment allowed me to go out and attend to the repair and maintenance of these things with a thankful attitude. My mind was no longer on what I didn't have, but on what I did!

Quote for the day: "You can't have everything, where would you put it?" (Unknown)

"Oh, and I need a garage." ☺

58. Growing

I'm wiping the sweat off my forearms as I type. I just came in from working my vegetable garden. It's June 2nd and the summer heat of Louisiana is here already. I pulled some weeds from around the peppers and tomatoes. I chopped the soil around the cucumbers, peppers and tomatoes. Then I dug a trench and added a garden soil mix with earthworms that my wife had in her first grade class (it was a science lesson). After re-covering the bed with leaves and pine needles I set the sprinkler and watered.

Life is a lot like a garden. Some people mistakenly believe that God will just bring them everything they need if they just pray hard enough. No, there is work that we must do. He provides for the birds of the air, but he doesn't take the food to the nest. They have to gather.

In the same way, we must sow seeds. The Bible says we will reap what we sow (Galatians 6:7) and we will reap the amount we sow (Luke 6:38). The worries of life and the deceitfulness of wealth may choke our faith, destroying our peace and joy (Matthew 13:22). God expects us to produce a harvest of good fruit for Him with the abilities, faith, resources and gifts He has given us (Matthew 3:8-10; 12:33). Sometimes, our lives need pruning and some things must go (John 15:2) to make us more productive. Other times God adds fertilizer to our lives to bring new life (Luke 13:6-9).

Are there seeds you need to sow in someone's life today? Do you need to be more generous? Do you need to pull some weeds of worry or material desires? Are we using the abilities and gifts God gave us for His good? Is God trying to remove something or someone from our lives? Are we getting a second chance at something that we need to do right this time?

Let's work with God today. Then we'll be in awe as He produces so much good that we know it could have only come from Him.

Quote for the Day: "A wise farmer puts as much thought into sowing as he does to reaping." (Unknown)

59. Just Believe

What does God want you to do? This is a question many people ask themselves, especially when they need help. Have you ever gotten an answer to that prayer? Would you like one today? What is our job with God? What work does God want us to do? I'll show it to you in black in white, just as plain as day from the Bible. Are you ready? Will you do it?

Here's the setting of the scripture. Jesus had just fed the multitudes from five loaves of bread and two fish. After he left, the crowds went after Him and found Him on the other side of the lake. Jesus told them a harsh truth. *"You are looking for me because you want more food."* Then He directed them to a better motive, a more worthy way, a higher road. He told them not to pursue food that spoils, but food that lasts forever.

Listen now to the major question on the minds of the people from John 6:28. Jesus' reply to all of us is in verse 29.

Then they asked him, "What must we do to do the works God requires?"

Jesus answered, "The work of God is this: to believe in the one he has sent."

So here is a word to think about today, BELIEVE. The word in the original greek language is "pistuo", which literally translated means, "to faith." It is not just mental agreement. It is an action word. You take action, then you open the door for God's power.

So when God says, "meditate on these scriptures day and night" (Joshua 1); and "trust me and see how much good I'll pour into your life" (Malachi 4); and "to all who received Him He gives eternal life" (John 1); and "your sins are forgiven" (1 John 1:9); "live my way" (10 commandments) and "life will be better" (Deuteronomy 28).

You must BELIEVE/TRUST "pistuo" Him. So let's "faith" God today.

Scripture for the Day: *"If you believe, you will receive whatever you ask for in prayer."* (Jesus in Matthew 21:22)

Quote for the day: "Now you just believe. That is all you have to do; just believe." (Advice from an old Ohio farmer)

60. "If I Have to Explain, You Wouldn't Understand"

One fall night I was leaving a skating rink after having chaperoned an event for our school. I had my helmet in one hand, and my leather jacket in the other. The father of one of my students was escorting his family to his truck. I wished them a good night as I strode over to my Honda Shadow for the drive home. "Probably dealing with a mid-life crisis," I heard him say to his wife just loud enough for me to hear. I smiled and shot back, "I already went through that." I donned my helmet and jacket, started her up and enjoyed the ride home.

You've experienced this critical attitude before. Some guys just don't understand why we ride. Maybe their egos are threatened by the rebel image. There are those who assume we are all gang members. Others think motorcycles are dangerous. Then there are those who are harboring a little envy. Perhaps they never had the guts to swing a leg over and discover what we know. Motorcycling is FUN.

One of my relatives once asked, "why do you have to have that 'Harley' sound?" as he blipped my throttle while I was preparing to leave. "If I have to explain that sound, you wouldn't understand," I said as I buckled my helmet. Most bikers know there is a difference between the rumble of a Harley and the thumping of a Honda, even if the Honda IS an 1100, V twin. But whether you are riding a bike powered by V-twin, an in-line 4, a single cylinder, or a two-stroke, you know there is magic on a motorcycle. It doesn't matter if it's built in America, Italy, Great Britain or Japan, something about it moves you (pun intended). Tourers, sport-bikes, cruisers, dual-sports or dirt bikes, the thrill is there. Motorcycling is just plain, fun. Call it the "poor man's airplane," "crotch rocket," "scoot," "machine," it doesn't matter, fun is still its middle name. From mopeds to race bikes, they are selling in record numbers. Why? F - U - N.

But we knew that. That's why we buy them against the warnings of fearful, but well-meaning family members, brave the wind-chill, expose our bodies to traffic, make room in the garage, sit near the window in restaurants, read the mags, wear the brand names and buy the gear. So, what's the point? Don't worry about what others think - go out and enjoy. I've finally figured out I can't please everybody, so I'll please God, be true to myself and family, and let others' opinions fall where they may. Just ride and be safe.

Before you go, take this prayer with you:

"Dear heavenly Father, protect me from danger, my bike from mechanical problems, and my family while I'm gone. Guide my wheels, my thinking, my words and my actions. Assign my angels and my purpose. Thank you for the wind in my face, the horsepower in my hand and the freedom to ride. Help me not to be anxious for the destination, but to enjoy the journey; and when my time is done, bring me back home safely - in Jesus name."

Scripture for the Day: *"We are not trying to please men, but God."* (1 Thessalonians 2:4)

Quote for the Day: "If a man does not keep pace with his companions, perhaps it is because he hears a different drummer. Let him step to the music which he hears, however measured or far away." (Henry David Thoreau, Walden)

The author(left) interviews Kyle Chaney as Frank Fletcher steadies him.
Kyle is recovering from a racing accident.

Carl Langley prays and asks God's blessing with son Michael
before a race at Wildwood MX in 2005.

61. Getting Blessed

When we ask God to bless us, or ask for God's blessing, what do we mean? Or more importantly, what do we need to do to obtain God's blessing? The answer is put in simple terms in Deuteronomy 28. God had just set the Israelite nation free from 400 years of slavery in Egypt. They were on the verge of entering the promised land. God spoke through Moses, their leader as He prepared this rag-tag group of former slaves to become a civilized, prosperous society.

As you read further into the Bible you will find that God now works through His people, the church of Jesus Christ. If you have trusted Jesus as your savior, you are the "new Israel" and "descendants of Abraham by faith" because we believe in God. (Galatians 3:7)

Listen to the requirement for blessing from Deuteronomy 28 in verse two, "You will experience these blessings if you obey the LORD your God."

Now read further in that chapter of your Bible and see some of the great promises of blessing He has waiting for you.
1. Location (whether you live in town or in the country)
2. Family (many children)
3. Work (productive fields)
4. Food
5. Travel
6. Protection from enemies (even though they attack, they won't succeed)
7. You will be God's special people (above those of the world)

But you still say, "I believe in God, what can I do to be blessed?" Jesus answered that in practical terms in Matthew 5:3-10:

Blessed are the poor in spirit, for theirs is the kingdom of heaven.
Blessed are those who mourn, for they will see God.
Blessed are the meek, for they will inherit the earth.
Blessed are those who hunger and thirst for righteousness, for they will be filled.
Blessed are the merciful, for they will be shown mercy.
Blessed are the pure in heart, for they will see God.
Blessed are the peacemakers, for they will be called sons of God.
Blessed are those who are persecuted because of righteousness, for theirs is the kingdom of heaven."

Open your heart and mind to receive God's blessing today.

62. Learning from Paul's Troubles

You say you've got troubles? If you are a believer, you want to be reminded what you can learn from them? Take a careful look at what the Apostle Paul said about his troubles (and he had many).

"To keep me from becoming conceited..." the trouble is to keep our attitude right (humble)

"because of these surpassingly great revelations, there was given me a thorn in my flesh..." The word for thorn literally means "a sharp stick that pierces the body." The trouble causes pain, pain gets our attention, requires a response and re-arranges priorities. It also helps us appreciate the blessings we have.

"a messenger of Satan to torment me..." God only allows Satan to attack us when it fits His goal for our long-term good
(check Job 1). Satan wants to torment and destroy, God wants to use this in our lives for personal growth.

"Three times I pleaded with the Lord to take it away from me." Paul asked God to remove it. The first two times he got no answer. On the third time God answered, "No." It's ok to ask God to take away the problem. Paul did. But be ready to accept His terms. He may say yes, no or wait.

"But he said to me, "My grace is sufficient for you, for my power is made perfect in weakness." Here we come to the crux of the matter. God allowed this painful problem into our lives for a reason. We can hang on a long time if we know it's for a purpose. God will give His grace, His love, His power, His presence in enough measure to pull us through and take us to victory. His promise is, "I'm enough."

"Therefore I will boast all the more gladly about my weaknesses, so that Christ's power may rest on me. That is why, for Christ's sake, I delight in weaknesses, in insults, in hardships, in persecutions, in difficulties. For when I am weak, then I am strong. (2 Corinthians 12:7-10)

If we are trying to handle a painful problem in our own strength, God may step back and let us struggle until we run out of strength. There can be only one leader in the battle, so there is no room for God's power if we are running the show. He'll wait for us to hand it over to him.

It's like the person who is drowning. With all that fighting and flailing around, no one can come near to rescue them. Once they get tired and cease from struggling, there is opportunity for the rescuer to save them.

Whatever you are fighting against today, STOP! Just give it to God. Tell Him you surrender the whole problem to Him. Ask Him to show you what you should do. Then trust Him. Just REST in Him!

Scripture for the Day: *"Since ancient times no one has heard, no ear has perceived, no eye has seen any God besides you, who acts on behalf of those who wait for him. You come to the help of those who gladly do right, who remember your ways."* (Isaiah 64:4-5)

63. Harvest

I love to put out a summer vegetable garden. I invested in a roto-tiller a couple years ago and use it to till up a plot of ground in the back yard. I put pine needles and leaves from the yard in twice a year. Periodically I replenish it with worms and fish scraps from fishing trips. The hardest work is pulling up the rows with a hoe.

Both of my kids (and exchange students) provided some free labor and heard my little sermons touting the benefits of sweating in the sun to bring fresh food to the table. They've heard me take in a deep breath, sigh and then say, "I love the smell of fresh-turned dirt." I guess I am just an incurable "dirt-a-holic". I love digging in the dirt and racing in the dirt.

Today I went out to my garden and opened the fence. To my delight I found lots of snap beans waiting to be picked underneath the huge green leaves of the bushes. I thanked God for the food that came from His generous hand. I filled my t-shirt up with about 30 beans. Then I worked my way over to the corn. The stalks were maturing and sending forth seed. A couple small ears were starting to protrude. I looked behind me on the ground and gazed at the big leafs on the cucumbers. I could only find one half-ready cuke to take.

Next I scouted the peppers. A few baby yellows were showing, with the promise of flowers on the jalapeno and bell. But my tomatoes didn't let me down. Over a dozen healthy tomato plants each carrying five or six green specimens. In a few days I'll be eating fresh BLT's!

Then I shuffled down the row to my one and only cherry tomato plant. I had already picked over twenty from this plant in the last two weeks. I like to put them in a candy dish on the kitchen counter and snack on them as I walk by. Today there were at least twenty ripe cherry tomatoes that came right off in my hand. I picked some orange ones to ripen in the window. Now my t-shirt was bulging with bounty. How many of you know I ate a few on the way into the house?

I was so proud of that bush. I had lovingly planted it in the prepared soil. I had fertilized it, provided water and support (cage and stake). I pulled weeds from around its roots. I plucked bugs from off its leaves. Now it was doing what it was created to do and I was sooooo gratified.

Maybe God thinks of us this way. He has a purpose and plan for our lives (Jeremiah 29:11) before he even plants us (Jeremiah 1:5). He provides for our needs (Matthew 6:33) so we can grow. He protects us from things that would weaken or destroy us (sin). He builds a fence around us to keep out destructive pests (moral law). He gives us the sun (Son) to provide life and direction. Then He expects a harvest from us (bearing fruit).

Are there any pests sucking the life out of you today (wrong company or influences)? Is there a hole in the fence (law breaking) allowing varmints in to eat away at your leaves? Have you been getting your waterings (scripture)? Are you allowing the Son to shine in your life? Have you fertilized your soil lately (godly teachings)? If not, then you may not be producing fruit.

Give God a healthy person with which He can bring forth His fruit. You are His highly favored tomato bush!

Scripture for the Day: *"Blessed is the man who does not walk in the counsel of the wicked or stand in the way of sinners or sit in the seat of mockers. But his delight is in the law of the Lord, and on His law he meditates day and night. He is like a tree planted by streams of water, which yields its fruit in season and whose leaf does not wither. Whatever he does prospers."* (Psalm 1:1-3)

64. The Old Tree

If you take a drive through Tickfaw State Park in Springfield, La., you can see one of the oldest trees in the area. A roadside sign tells the story. Years ago when the loggers (my grandfather was one) were harvesting the cypress trees from the swamp, one tree was spared. They left it intact, probably because the top was broken off and it was hollow inside. It was of little commercial value to them.

This tree now stands as a testimony to two great truths. The first truth, as reported on the memorial is that this tree is between 700 to 800 years old. That means that it was alive when Christopher Columbus discovered America. It has seen many other trees, Indians, settlers, hunters, trappers, explorers and wildlife come and go. It has survived hurricanes, floods and droughts. Many birds, squirrels and insects found food and shelter in this tree.

The second truth is for us. The very injury that scarred the tree made it valuable to those around it. What seemed like a defect to the loggers was the very thing that insured its survival and nourished the inhabitants around it.

We have all been injured in one way or another. Parents cannot raise their children without injuring them in some way. Whenever you pick up a glass, you leave fingerprints on it. Sometimes we mishandle it and damage it. I carry deep scars from my parents, school, friends, mistakes and circumstances. So do you.

So we have defects, but DON'T MAKE THE MISTAKE of buying into the lie that our injury, or "so-called" weakness is a defect and makes us less valuable. According to God's higher purpose, it might be the very thing that makes us valuable to those around us. If we submit our whole selves to our creator, He who created us that way or possibly allowed that injury to happen, will use it as a great blessing to others. Our scar/injury/loss might just be someone else's inspiration/provision/gain.

I'm not saying that it was God's will for the abuse or injury, quite the contrary: God has commanded us to love others as we love ourselves. But in this sin-sick, fallen world, we get mistreated and have to suffer pain – especially from someone who has suffered pain themselves. That's why God commands us to live a certain way, so we won't harm ourselves and others. But when the injustice, sin, accident, call it what you will, happens, God can "redeem" the pain or injury and bring good from it, while healing us deep down in our souls where no band-aids can reach.

Like that old tree with the broken off top and hollowed out center, we can become a living testimony to others for our creator who *"causes all things to work together for good"* (Romans 8:28).

For a related story read John 9:1-7.

But we have this treasure in jars of clay to show that this all-surpassing power is from God and not from us. We are hard pressed on every side, but not crushed; perplexed, but not in despair; persecuted, but not abandoned; struck down, but not destroyed. We always carry around in our body the death of Jesus, so that the life of Jesus may also be revealed in our body. (2 Corinthians 4:7-10)

Quote for the day: "God designed the human machine to run on Himself." (C. S. Lewis, Mere Christianity)

Fernwood MX's King of MX winners from left, Larry Hayes, Coy Hobgood, Samantha Mouton, Dustin Manuel, Nick Phillips, Skylar Phillips, Mark Lunstra, #21 Chad Pattison and #973 Jon-murry Barr

Two Hall of Fame motorcycle racers enjoy a meal together at the AHRMA supper at Mid-Ohio in 2004: Gary Nixon and Jay Springsteen have earned 6 National Championships between them. They know about success.

65. The Path that Determines Success

One of the wisest men I've ever listened to is Rev. Mike Murdock. One of the truths I've learned from him is, "your habits determine your success." Think about it. What are you in the habit of doing each day? I'm not talking about the big inspirational events, but the day to day drudgery of life that fills the in-between. It's what you do there that determines the quality of your relationships with family, your work ethic and the rewards it brings, the environment you make to live in, how others perceive you and perhaps most important, your character.

In 1 Peter 1:4-5, God says that we have become "partakers of the divine nature" and we should "make every effort" to form godly habits. We are not born with habits, we form them. Step by step, decision by decision, book by book, action by action, thought by thought, word by word. We can't always choose our circumstances but can choose how we interpret and respond to them (our thinking). We can't choose our family but can choose how we relate to them. The battlefield is our mind. Jesus said, "if the eye is good, then the whole body will be good." In other words, we determine to think according to the divine nature God has placed within us, even if it goes against our human reasoning. If we think according to God's way, and do it daily then we are allowing God to unleash His power, provision and grace in our lives. His promises can then flood our lives, unhindered by our circumstances.

We can change, we can receive healing, and we can receive forgiveness and peace and love; if we would just live according to God's plan for our lives. How do we get there? First we need to KNOW God and His way. This comes by reading God's word daily, and receiving His son, Jesus into our lives. When He becomes our LORD, we then give up all rights to ourselves, allowing room for God's grace, protection, and ownership.

Step by step, decision by decision, thought by thought, word by word, action by action each day in the small things. Jesus said, "take up your cross and follow me DAILY." He also said, "if you try to save your life you will lose it, but if you give your life away, you will find it." (my loose paraphrase)

The new habits lead to a new lifestyle which leads to a new character which leads to a new life.

Scripture for the Day: *"Do not conform any longer to the pattern of this world, but be transformed by the renewing of your mind. Then you will be able to test and approve what God's will is - His good, pleasing and perfect will."* (Romans 12:2)

Zachary Riggins takes a spill and is helped back up at Gravity Alley MX.

Eddie Ketchum #87 crosses paths with Casey Paulk at Wildwood MX.

66. Facing Reality

Any successful racer has already come to terms with the realities of the sport. In motocross racing, there will be falls (with injuries). It's not a question of "if" but "when." There will be mechanical breakdowns. It's not a question of "if" but "when." There will be bad weather that ruins the track. There will be someone who gets mad at you. There will be people who are jealous when you win.

The big challenge is not "if" it happens, but "when" it happens, how will we respond? Will we get mad and quit? Will we, lose our temper and retaliate? Will we shun the offending track or person forever? Will we "payback" that person or company for "getting in our way" of victory?

I'm not talking about learning from our mistakes and making adjustments, I'm talking about having unrealistic expectations that will surely not be met, then giving up on something or someone. It's the same way with our human relationships. The Bible says that *"all have sinned and fallen short of the glory of God."* (Romans 3:23) The human heart is *"deceitfully wicked, who can know it."* (Jeremiah 17:9) This is the reality of our world.

So rather than seeing everyone as "innocent," which they are not, recognize that people are "sinners" and don't be surprised when they let you down. We have a sinful human nature. But don't let that make you cynical or distrustful. Jesus didn't trust human nature, but He trusted what He could do for humans and who they could become if they cooperated with the Kingdom of God.

> *Now while he was in Jerusalem at the Passover Feast, many people saw the miraculous signs he was doing and believed in his name. But Jesus would not entrust himself to them, for he knew all men. He did not need man's testimony about man, for he knew what was in a man.* (John 2:23-25)

Get forgiveness from Jesus. Offer forgiveness to others when they sin against you. Know that it is not a question of "if" they will sin against you, but "when." When you recognize this principle at work in the world, you will be fore-warned and fore-armed to deal with others.

Scripture for the Day: *"Forgive us our sins, as we also have forgiven those who have sinned against us. And lead us not into temptation, but deliver us from the evil one."* (Matt. 6:12-13)

Quote for the Day:

"People are unreasonable, illogical, and self-centered; love them anyway. If you do good, people will accuse you of selfish, ulterior motives; do good anyway. If you're successful you win false friends and make true enemies; try to succeed anyway. The good you do today will be forgotten tomorrow; be good anyway. Honesty and frankness will get you nowhere; they make you vulnerable. Be honest and frank anyway. People favor underdogs, but they follow the top dogs; fight for some underdogs anyway. What you spend years building may be destroyed overnight; do it anyway. People really need help but they attack you if you try to help them; try anyway. Give the world the best you have and you get kicked in the mouth; give the world the best you have anyway." (Karl Menninger on his 87th birthday)

67. Racing on Today's Fuel

One of the habits that racers should get into early is re-fueling their bikes before the race. They MUST have fuel for their engine or they will get that sickening feeling of a bogging engine with no throttle response; and it seems it happens at the most inopportune times. For instance, their bike runs out of gas when they are in front, or way on the back side of the track, or trying to clear a double, or making a pass. So racers check their fuel tanks and usually top it off before going to the starting gate. They simply can't run on yesterday's fuel. They already burnt it.

It's like that in life, too. We can't run on yesterday's grace. It is just not sufficient for today. God's mercies are *"new every morning."* (Lamentations 3:23). His grace is *"sufficient for the trials of today."* (2 Corinthians 12:9) What is grace? It is God's supernatural power for living. It is the Holy Spirit at work inside us giving us strength, wisdom, encouragement, direction, hope and love. He reveals it as the fruits of the Spirit: love, joy, peace, patience, kindness, goodness and self-control. These are things that there are no laws against.

Jesus said *"streams of LIVING water will flow from inside the believer."* (John 7:38) This is not dead water, like a pond. It is living water, like a river, constantly flowing new and fresh. More power than we can use overflowing in our spirits.

So instead of saying, "I'll just grit my teeth and bear this difficulty then pray about it later." You can pray right away and receive God's new and fresh grace for today. The key word is NOW. God is with you NOW. He has power available to you NOW. His Holy Spirit lives in you right NOW, interpreting these words NOW. He is filling your heart with hope NOW. Because you have trusted Jesus as your savior, He has come to live in your heart and is "closer than a brother." (Proverbs 18:24)

So don't try to live on yesterday's experience with God. He's got some fresh grace for you right now; and it will be available the rest of the day and the rest of the week and the rest of the month and the rest of the year and the rest of this life on earth. But there's more. He will be your faithful provider of grace into eternity. You just have to be faithful to trust Him - NOW.

Quote for the Day: "Remember, grace is pouring in on you all the time and it is not conditioned by the fact that your eyes are shut." (Evelyn Underhill, The Letters of Evelyn Underhill)

68. Food and Faith

At most motocross races the pits are filled with the aromas of food cooking and the cooks who have perfected their favorite dishes. From the venison sausage breakfast biscuits of Potts Thomas to the jambalaya crew of Glenn and Dana Guidry, or Dirk Cortez's big breakfasts and gumbo, or even Doyle Westbrook's chicken fricassee, racers in this area know how to eat. If you've been to a race in south Louisiana, you know what I mean. You have been invited over to a pit for some Cajun hospitality and spicy food.

If we drop back in history to the time of the Old Testament, God provided a tasty food to the Israelites called "manna." It was a kind of bread that had the taste of honey and coriander seed. Just after the exodus from slavery in Egypt, God's chosen nation was traveling through the desert under the leadership of Moses. Since they were on a journey to the promised land and had no food, God supernaturally gave them food from heaven. Exodus 16 and Numbers 11 give the story. God provided exactly what they needed for each day. If they would just trust Him for their daily provision they would have all they needed whether their food requirements were great or small.

When the dew was gone, thin flakes like frost on the ground appeared on the desert floor. When the Israelites saw it, they said to each other, "What is it?" For they did not know what it was. Moses said to them, "It is the bread the LORD has given you to eat. This is what the LORD has commanded: 'Each one is to gather as much as he needs. Take an omer for each person you have in your tent.'" The Israelites did as they were told; some gathered much, some little. And when they measured it by the omer, he who gathered much did not have too much, and he who gathered little did not have too little. Each one gathered as much as he needed. (Exodus 16:14-18)

But some got greedy, and that human "hoarding mechanism" kicked in, and they tried to gather more than they needed for the day, and the manna went bad.

Then Moses said to them, "No one is to keep any of it until morning." However, some of them paid no attention to Moses;

they kept part of it until morning, but it was full of maggots and began to smell. So Moses was angry with them. (Exodus 16:19-20)

The point is some people RESTED in God's provision. Others anxiously hoarded the manna in disobedience to God's instructions. The first group had provision and peace. The second group had worry and disappointment. How many of us are like the second group? Have we shifted our focus from God's provision to our own ability to hoard possessions? If we want to live in peace and avoid needless worry, we should not become so attached to the accumulation of possessions. Not that there is anything wrong with possessions, but we should hold them loosely, setting our heart's affections on things above (Matt. 6:19-20). Otherwise our lives will be filled with distress, worry and fear.

Prayer for the Day: "Dear Lord, I surrender my life to you. All I have is yours. If there is anything I shouldn't have, take it away. I trust you to give me my daily bread. Help me to think and act according to your way. Give me strength and guidance in my daily work. Help me to make the right decisions according to what you have blessed me with."

69. Humor

One of God's richest gifts to us is humor. He knew we would need it to endure some of the things we have to put up with in life. He also wants to give us joy. Joy is a happy feeling of well-being that comes from the Holy Spirit and is a by-product of faith in God (Galatians 5:22). It is not based on situations or happenings around us. That would be happiness. You can have joy even during times of tribulation. (James 1:2-4; 2 Corinthians 8:2)

But He gives all humans a hint of this joy whether or not they are in relationship with Him or not. This gift called humor is part of being human. Some have more than others. Jerry Seinfeld and Tim Allen perfected theirs and turned them into hit TV shows. We should all develop our sense of humor and use it as often as possible. Laughter is medicine for the soul.

Look at this humor displayed by Qantas airlines between the pilots and the engineers. This is taken from actual "gripe sheets" that pilots fill out after a flight to let the mechanics know about problems with the aircraft. On the lower half of the form the ground crew records what action was taken so the pilots can review it before the next flight.

P = the problem logged by the pilot.
S = the solution and action taken by the engineers.

P: Left inside main tire almost needs replacement.
S: Almost replaced left inside main tire.
P: Test flight OK, except auto-land very rough.
S: Auto-land not installed on this aircraft.
P: Something loose inside cockpit.
S: Something tightened in cockpit.
P: Dead bugs on windshield.
S: Live bugs on back-order.
P: Autopilot in altitude-hold mode produces a 200 feet per minute descent.
S: Cannot reproduce problem on ground.
P: Evidence of leak on right main landing gear.
S: Evidence removed.
P: DME volume unbelievably loud.
S: DME volume set to more believable level.
P: Friction locks cause throttle levers to stick.

S: That's what they're there for.
P: IFF inoperative.
S: IFF always inoperative in OFF mode.
P: Suspected crack in windshield.
S: Suspect you're right.
P: Number 3 engine missing.
S: Engine found on right wing after brief search.
P: Aircraft handles funny.
S: Aircraft warned to straighten up, fly right, and be serious.
P: Target radar hums.
S: Reprogrammed target radar with lyrics.
P: Mouse in cockpit.
S: Cat installed.

Scriptures about Joy:

"The Kingdom of heaven is like treasure hidden in a field. When a man found it, he hid it again and then in his joy went and sold all he had and bought that field." (Jesus in Matthew 13:44)

"I have told you these things so that my joy may be in you and that your joy may be complete." (Jesus in John 15:11)

"Yet he has not left Himself without testimony: He has shown kindness by giving you rain from heaven and crops in their seasons; He provides you with plenty of food and fills your hearts with joy." (Acts 14:17)

"The jailer brought them into his house and set a meal before them; he was filled with joy because he had come to believe in God - he and his whole family." (Acts 16:34)

"For the kingdom of God is not a matter of eating and drinking, but of righteousness, peace and joy in the Holy Spirit." (Romans 14:17)

70. Baking a Maturing Life

Sometimes we wonder, "What did I do to deserve this?" or "Why did God have to do this to me?"

A daughter is telling her Mother how everything is going wrong; she didn't make the cheerleading squad, her boyfriend broke up with her and her best friend is moving away.

Meanwhile, her Mother is baking a cake and asks her daughter if she would like a snack, and the daughter says, "Absolutely Mom, I love your cake."

"Here, have some cooking oil," her Mother offers.

"Yuck" says her daughter.

"How about a couple raw eggs?"

"Gross, Mom!"

"Would you like some flour then? Or maybe baking soda!"

"Mom, those are all nasty!"

To which the mother replies: "Yes, all those things seem bad all by themselves. But when they are put together in the right way, they make a wonderfully delicious cake!" (Author unknown)

God works the same way. Many times we wonder why He would let us go through such difficulties. But we see only a small portion. God sees the whole mix. God will take that mix of circumstances and heat it up in the oven of adversity. When EXACTLY the right amount of time has passed, He will pull out a masterpiece life that will be a blessing to all and a splendid example of His power and goodness.

Scripture for the Day: *"In this you greatly rejoice, though now for a little while you may have had to suffer grief in all kinds of trials. These have come so that your faith - of greater worth than gold, which perishes even though refined by fire - may be proved genuine and may result in praise, glory and honor when Jesus Christ is revealed."* (1 Peter 1:6)

71. The Price of Freedom

Have you ever wondered what happened to the 56 men who signed the Declaration of Independence? Five signers were captured by the British as traitors, and tortured before they died. Twelve had their homes ransacked and burned. Two lost their sons serving in the Revolutionary Army; another had two sons captured. Nine of the 56 fought and died from wounds or hardships of the Revolutionary War. They signed and they pledged their lives, their fortunes, and their sacred honor.

What kind of men were they? Twenty-four were lawyers and jurists. Eleven were merchants, nine were farmers and large plantation owners: men of means, well educated. But they signed the Declaration of Independence knowing full well that the penalty would be death if they were captured. Carter Braxton of Virginia, a wealthy planter and trader saw his ships swept from the seas by the British Navy. He sold his home and properties to pay his debts and died in rags. Thomas McKeam was so hounded by the British that he was forced to move his family almost constantly. He served in the Congress without pay, and his family was kept in hiding. His possessions were taken from him, and poverty was his reward.

Vandals or soldiers looted the properties of Dillery Hall, Clymer, Walton, Gwinett, Heyward, Ruttledge, and Middleton. At the battle of Yorktown, Thomas Nelson, Jr. noted that the British General Cornwallis had taken over the Nelson home for his headquarters. He quietly urged General George Washington to open fire. The home was destroyed, and Nelson died bankrupt. Francis Lewis had his home and properties destroyed. The enemy jailed his wife, and she died within a few months. John Hart was driven from his wife's bedside as she was dying. Their 13 children fled for their lives. His fields and his gristmill were laid to waste. For more than a year he lived in forests and caves, returning to find his wife dead and his children vanished. A few weeks later he died from exhaustion and a broken heart.

Norris and Livingston suffered similar fates. Such were the stories and sacrifices of the American Revolution. These were not wild-eyed, rabble-rousing ruffians. They were soft-spoken men of means and education. They had security, but they valued liberty more. Standing tall, straight and unwavering, they pledged: "For the support of the declaration, with firm reliance on the protection of the divine providence, we mutually pledge to each other, our lives, our fortunes and our sacred honor." (Copied from internet, author unknown)

Freedom is not free. In the same way if you want personal freedom from bad habits, the pain of the past, irrational anger, uncontrollable desires, or any other human affliction, you must pay the price. The price is setting it free, letting it go. Uhhh, excuse me, before you even try I must warn you: YOU CAN'T DO IT UNDER YOUR OWN POWER! You must rely on the supernatural power of God. How? By admitting your need and desire for His help; getting real with Him - that's what He responds to.

Pray this prayer: "O God, I realize I am a sinner in a sinful, fallen world. I ask your forgiveness for all my sins. I believe Jesus died on the cross for me. I accept His payment for my sin and ask Him to come into my heart. I give you my life. I set free my right to myself and let you be God of my life. I yield all my problems, shortcomings, weaknesses, and sinful desires to you. Whatever it takes, no matter how long, set me free from each area and give me the mind of Christ. Fill me with your Holy Spirit. Amen"

Now tell a friend. Join a Bible-believing church. Set aside regular times to pray and read scripture, and obey what you know God wants you to do. You are now in for the ride of your life!

Scripture for the Day: *"I am the Way, the Truth and the Life. No one comes to the Father except through me."* (Jesus in John 14:6)

Quote for the Day: "I know not what course others may take; but as for me, give me liberty or give me death." (Patrick Henry, Speech, Virginia Convention, March 23, 1775)

72. Return to Sender

There was a story going around the internet. I don't know if it's true, but it has the ring of truth in it. It also illustrates how dumb we can be.

Two Michigan duck hunters went out onto a frozen lake for a hunt. They were well-equipped with everything they would need for an easy hunt. They drove their brand new $42,500.00 Lincoln Navigator out onto the ice filled with shotguns, shells, a Labrador retriever and some dynamite to create a honey hole. They lit a 40 second fuse on a stick of dynamite and threw it as far as they could. The lab dutifully went after the fizzling stick. When he returned with the still-lit explosive in his mouth, the horrified hunters shot him. But you know how hard-headed labs can be, and though stunned, he continued to do what he was trained to do. He brought the stick back to his master. His master, fearing for his life, fired again. The panicked dog dove for cover under the new SUV. Moments later the lab went to heaven and the SUV went to the bottom of the lake.

Justice was served as the owner was told by his insurance company that they don't cover accidents caused by illegal use of explosives. The $560.00 monthly payments would remain in effect until the full purchase price was met.

Justice, judgment, a final reckoning for us all. It's coming (Revelation 20:11-12). Like the retriever bringing back the lit dynamite to the man who threw it, our sins have consequences (Romans 5:12; Hebrews 10:28-31). We might not have thrown an explosive, but we have rebelled against God through thoughts and deeds. Lies told, things taken that don't belong to us, gossip passed damaging a reputation, lust conceived, greed acted upon, idols served, pain inflicted - you don't have to be reminded. We have a sinful human nature. We stand under the judgment of a holy and righteous God (Ezekiel 16:59).

Who is perfect? Only one. Jesus Christ, God's son. He walked the earth, taught us the truth about God, fulfilled the holy scriptures, then was punished for our sin (Mark 15:24). It's as if He ran out onto the ice, took the stick of dynamite away from the dog, walked a safe distance away and blew up in the process. He took what we had coming to us. Yet, He reappears some distance away alive again, beckoning the stunned hunters to follow Him to a new city on the ice. The hunter that is willing to walk away from his possessions and leave the old life, will discover a new kind of life that his creator has lovingly prepared for him. An eternal city with a new life.

We can't take the story out too far, but the point is clear. Make peace with God before your dynamite returns! What good is material wealth at the bottom of a lake? If the price for your sins has been paid, why not receive the offer of forgiveness from God?

Scriptures of the day:
"How will we escape if we ignore such a great salvation?" (Hebrews 2:1)

"What does it profit a man if he gains the whole world, but loses his own soul?" (Jesus in Matthew 16:26)

Quote for the Day: *"And if your eye causes you to sin, gouge it out and throw it away. It is better for you to enter life with one eye than to have two eyes and be thrown into the fire of hell."* (Jesus in Matthew 18:9)

73. Johnny Medlin

Johnny Medlin is a 42-year old motocross racer from Marrero, La. He used to be a threat in the money class. Last year he settled into the Senior class. Nowadays you can find him helping younger racers in the mini class, especially his son, Brandt. This past weekend his son turned 11 years old and won his class. But Johnny wasn't doing so good. He was wearing a clavicle brace on his shoulders. Most MX racers have had to endure a clavicle as broken collarbones are a common injury. Patrick Meche, who won the Senior B class two weeks earlier in Breaux Bridge went over the bars that same race day and broke his collarbone, sprained his ankle and put a big contusion on his hip.

I asked Johnny how he broke his collarbone. He said,

I was practicing up at Kentwood, trying to get back in racing shape. I was on a brand new Kawasaki. I had just pre-loaded my weight on the suspension to clear a step-down double jump and the carburetor sucked a piece of metal into the main jet, causing it to lose power on the jump face. I crashed, and it wasn't even my fault.

Isn't that just like life? One little thing goes wrong in our day and it can set off a chain of events that causes us pain - and it wasn't even our fault! I learned Murphy's law in dive school, "If anything can go wrong, it will." One little piece of metal shaving was in Johnny's brand new carburetor. If it had sucked into the main jet ANY OTHER TIME, he would have felt a cough and sputter and resumed his practice. But losing power on the face of a jump when he's trying to clear the second jump can be disastrous - and was.

How can we protect ourselves from every little thing in this world that threatens us? We give ourselves to our creator, and let that be His problem. Once we stop battling wills with God and submit to His plan, we become His special property, His unique children, different from the other people of the world. Listen to what God said to His people in Exodus 19:5-6: *"Now if you obey me fully and keep my covenant, then out of all nations you will be my treasured possession. Although the whole earth is mine, you will be for me a kingdom of priests and a holy nation."*

Scripture for the Day: *"'Because he loves me,' says the LORD, 'I will rescue him; I will protect him, for he acknowledges my name. He will* *call upon me, and I will answer him; I will be with him in trouble, I will deliver him and honor him. With long life will I satisfy him and show him my salvation.'"* (Psalm 91:14-16)

Chris Brian breaks free from the bonds of gravity on his way to victory in the Expert Quad class at Holeshot MX.

Kaitlyn Hayes chats trackside with Lindsey Escoyne during practice at Wildwood MX.

74. Why Are We Still Here?

Why doesn't God just take us to be with Him once we become a Christian? Since life is full of trials and struggles and tribulations, once we make peace with God and get His forgiveness and Jesus comes to live inside us, why not just go on home to heaven?

I was thinking this thought today as I prayed in my quiet time. I asked, "Lord, I just want to be with you. I get tired down here. When can I come home?" The answer came in my daily Bible reading. I had been reading through Philippians. Here was my daily reading. Can you see the answer God gave me? Look at chapter one, verses 21-24:

For to me, to live is Christ and to die is gain. If I am to go on living in the body, this will mean fruitful labor for me. Yet what shall I choose? I do not know! I am torn between the two: I desire to depart and be with Christ, which is better by far; but it is more necessary for <u>you</u> that I remain in the body.

The key word is in the last sentence is "you." It is necessary for "you" that I remain in the body. Paul was asking himself the same question. He wanted to leave this world and be with Christ. I can see why, he was in prison. He said it was better for him to go home to be with Christ. But it was better for "you" (them, his readers) that he remain in his physical body here on earth.

This makes perfect sense. If our focus is on ourselves, if we are self-absorbed, self-centered, selfish, we cannot be of much help to God or others, or even ourselves. It's when we become servant-minded that we are most gratified with life. The good seeds that we sow into the lives of others grow to produce a harvest that comes back to bless us. Life becomes not only tolerable, but meaningful and joyous. I'm not talking about trying to please others and living for them, because you can't. But please God then do what you think is right. Let their opinions fall where they may.

Another reason God leaves us here on earth is to train us for eternity. This life is just the first few seconds of eternity. Once we graduate to our permanent home in heaven, we will be placed into a position of service for God based on what we did and learned down here.

Be a blessing to others today, your family, friends, co-workers and even strangers. God will help. Then you will be a blessing to yourself and realize God's purpose of why He leaves you here.

When he had finished washing their feet, he put on his clothes and returned to his place. "Do you understand what I have done for you?" he asked them. "You call me 'Teacher' and 'Lord,' and rightly so, for that is what I am. Now that I, your Lord and Teacher, have washed your feet, you also should wash one another's feet. I have set you an example that you should do as I have done for you. I tell you the truth, no servant is greater than his master, nor is a messenger greater than the one who sent him. Now that you know these things, you will be blessed if you do them. (Jesus in John 13:12-17)

Quote for the Day: "Do all the good you can, by all the means you can, in all the ways you can, in all the places you can, at all the times you can, to all the people you can, as long as ever you can." (John Wesley)

75. Leaves

Have you ever wondered how God can hear prayers from so many people at one time? His switchboards must be all lit up all the time with so many people praying at the same time, huh? How about watching over us? How can He protect a missionary in Zimbabwe and a housewife in China and a racer in Louisiana at the same time? Well, I can't explain it, but I trust Him to do it.

In one of my frequent moments of weakness I was crying out to God in prayer. I had my head down on the table and eyes closed. I felt Him say (in my mind), "Look up. What do you see?" I lifted my head and looked out the window. In my neighborhood in Covington, La. there are many trees. My wife and I have planted a lot of shrubs and trees in our yard over the last 14 years. What I saw when I looked out the window were LEAVES. Thousands and thousands of leaves as far as I could see, tuned into the morning sun. Oaks, pines, wild persimmons, maples, sweet gums, ash, sweet bays and magnolias were all stretching their leaves to the sky for nourishment. Elder, crepe myrtle, azalea, and ligustrum bushes were doing the same. Even the grass was lifting it's blades to the sky. The sun was shining brightly on all of them. How many leaves were getting life from the sun in that moment just on my street? How about the street over? How about in our parish, state, country or hemisphere? Countless!

God is like that. He provides His nourishing life to all who tune in to Him. He is able to reach out to all people at the same time. We just need to open our hearts and minds to Him through His Holy Spirit. If there is something blocking His warmth to you today, ask Him to remove it. Whether it is a sin, wrong attitude, self condemnation, lack of confidence, distractions, stress, people or problems, He can break through and give light and warmth.

Don't grope around in the spiritual darkness today. Don't despair. The SON is out, Jesus Christ. He broke through the clouds of darkness when He died for you at the cross. Now He's alive and shining brightly just on the other side of your self-made clouds. Ask God to blow away the doubt and fear that have hidden you. Ask God to open your eyes and turn your leaf to His source of life today.

Scripture for the Day: *"For the eyes of the Lord range throughout the earth to strengthen those whose hearts are fully committed to Him."* (2 Chronicles 16:9)

Quote for the Day: "The Christian should work as if all depended on him, and pray as if it all depended on God." (Charles Haddon Spurgeon)

Friends converge to fix a broken clutch at High Rollers MX. Joseph Pizzuto and Michael Santangelo perform the surgery on Nick Curole's Yamaha.

An old "Whizzer" with an early Harley coffin rivet tank on display at the Swap Meet in Ohio.

76. The Most Common Mistake

Can you imagine a racer with just the frame and wheels of his motorcycle at the starting gate of a race? His bike has no engine, no fuel, no self-propulsion - just handlebars, body, suspension and tires. Oh, it looks good. It's shiny; the decals and numbers are well-placed. But with no power, he must push it around the track.

On a straightaway with no obstacles, especially at the beginning of the race when he is still fresh and excited, he has no problem. He just runs alongside, pushing his bike down the track. He's not that far behind the others yet. But then he encounters his first jump. With enough momentum he can just barely make it up. He may take a break at the top to catch his breath and re-group mentally and physically. The downhill side is a piece of cake. He may even get to jump on and ride for a change! He thinks to himself, "I really like this racing! I'm doing well." But he sees others so far out in front of him that he wonders if something is wrong.

As he pushes his bike slowly around the track, he grows tired and discouraged. Finally he encounters an obstacle that he can't make it over or through. Disgusted, he finally gives up and pulls off the track and out of the race. He decides this really isn't working and looks for alternatives.

Have you ever felt this way about life? Have you ever tried a little bit of God or Christianity and grew discouraged and quit? You could be among a majority of people who have missed the most important part of a true life of faith. They treated Christianity as a religion. They see Jesus and the Bible as a teacher - ONLY. It is true that Jesus was a great teacher, and the Bible a great teaching book. But Satan, our enemy would love us to believe that's all He was.

Jesus was more than a great teacher. He was a SAVIOR. He came to rescue us, to send His Spirit to live INSIDE us, to EMPOWER us with his GRACE. Trying to keep all the rules and live up to His teaching is like trying to race without fuel and no motor. It just cannot be done. Jesus' teachings are too hard on PURPOSE. Listen to Jesus in Matthew chapter 5:21-22:

> *You have heard that it was said to the people long ago, "Do not murder, and anyone who murders will be subject to judgment." But I tell you that anyone who is angry with his brother will be subject to judgment. Again, anyone who says to his brother, "Raca," is answerable to the Sanhedrin. But anyone who says, "You fool!" will be in danger of the fire of hell.*

Is that teachings easy for you? It is impossible for me, at least under my own power as a mere man. Should I list the 10 commandments, too? I've broken them all, at least in my mind, at least once. God set the standard of righteousness high so we would see our need for Him and His forgiveness. He wants to rescue us. We can't live the Christian life without Him.

If you are just trying to keep the religion and reach this level of teaching, you might be happier if you didn't know it. The first step to discovering the power of the kingdom of God is emptying ourselves (poor in spirit) and being submissive to God's authority (meek). When we recognize our spiritual poverty and receive the forgiveness and new life of God (born again) we will have a motor that propels us and fuel that sustains us through the ups and downs of life.

Want more good news? We are justified (declared not guilty before God) by FAITH, not by keeping the law. The law reveals our need for God and His forgiveness, and leads us to the cross where we die to ourselves and get new life in Christ.

Scripture for the Day: *"So the law was put in charge to lead us to Christ that we might be justified by faith."* (Galatians 3:24)

Prayer for the Day: "Dear Lord, I have sinned against you in many areas (name specific ones). I ask you to forgive me and rescue me from the power of sin and evil. Fill me with your Holy Spirit. Give me the mind of Christ. Live your life through me today. In Jesus name, Amen."

Chad Kennedy hits turn 2 at Wildwood MX so hard that his foot comes off the peg while leading the money class.

Trent "Cannonball" Cannon at Holeshot MX the night of his crash.

Dylan McClendon racing at High Rollers MX on a cloudy day.

77. The Let Down

Trent "Cannonball" Cannon, a 21-year old motocross racer from Gonzales has had his share of disappointing crashes and injuries that have hampered his shot at a racing career.

One night he was practicing for an upcoming national championship race at High Rollers Motocross track. He committed to a big double jump when his bike's motor stalled in the air. This caused the front end to dive sending him over the bars.

Trent was depending on the bike to do its job and launch him up the ramp of the first jump thirty feet to the next jump where he would land on the downhill side. But it didn't happen. The bike let him down. He crashed and injured his shoulder rendering his whole left side useless for a few weeks. This caused him to miss the big race.

Another night at Holeshot in Hammond he was accelerating down the back straight and tangled with another rider sending him off the track and into the woods. He dodged the trees the best he could but finally crashed into a downed tree and went over the bars. He got up to race later, but was out of contention for the money. Presently he is back racing again and took third in the Open Money class at River's Edge Grand Opening race on January 2, 2005. He is not giving up although he has limited funding and resources.

Does this sound like your life at times? You depend on someone or something and they let you down. There are consequences that you must pay and it wasn't even your fault. Whether it was a boss that forgot to tell you, a spouse that didn't do what they promised, a child that made a bad decision or a friend that didn't come through, life has its let-downs. Many of these events are out of our control, but we can control our attitude toward them and how we respond.

The Apostle Paul stated that he was not perfect, and so he was, *"forgetting what is behind and straining toward what is ahead..."* (Philippians 3:13)

Jesus said that we should not hold grudges *"blessed are the merciful, for they will be shown mercy."* (Matthew 5:7). He also warned about condemning others in Matthew 7:2:

"For in the same way you judge others, you will be judged, and with the measure you use, it will be measured to you."

The sooner you let it go, the sooner it will let go of you.

Quote for the Day: "The fastest way to get round-shouldered is to carry a grudge." (unknown)

78. Clouds

Clouds obscure the sun. They darken the land. The darkest clouds may bring storms. Yet we need them. We need a break from the heat of the blazing sun. We need the refreshing rains. We need the moisture that cycles through the earth's atmosphere.

In the Bible clouds represent the trials, sorrows, struggles and pain of life. But that's when God comes to us. He comes on the clouds of life's crises and let-downs because that's when we are most open and teachable. Do you cry out to God for help when things are going fine? No. It usually comes at a time of distress or sorrow. When your heart breaks it creates a crack of opportunity as you strongly desire for God to come in and help. He comes to help you unlearn bad habits and ideas. He is teaching us how to walk by faith. He is teaching us how to reach out in the storm and hold his hand for guidance, comfort and hope. He comes to help us trust Him the way a child trusts a loving parent.

The next time a cloud of pain, disappointment, doubt, confusion, despair or grief comes into your life, look for Jesus. He is coming in the cloud and He has healing, comfort and hope in His hands. Open your heart and your mind for His work in your life. Reach out and take His hand.

Scripture of the Day: *"Behold, He is coming in the clouds..."* (Revelation 1:7)

Quote for the Day: "Trouble causes some people to go to pieces; others to come to their senses." (Unknown)

79. Cutting the Bight

My first job as a commercial diver was with Dave Barker in Thibodeaux, La. At first I drove his truck with the dive gear down to little docks in south Louisiana for "wheel jobs." Wheel jobs were propeller clearing jobs. Boats that got cables, traps and ropes caught in their propellers would call a diver to get it free. I would usually get the call at about 2:00 A.M. I would call a helper (dive tender), load my helmet and gear and go pick up the dive truck. On the truck were dive compressor, volume tanks, tools, dive radio, welding machine, underwater cables, and umbilical hoses.

We would pull up next to the boat and I would don wet-suit, boots, overalls, gloves and harness. The tender would start the compressor, hook up my dive helmet, hang the ladder into the water and uncoil the hoses. I would go in and inspect the propeller. If it was cable, I would use the underwater cutting torch. If it was rope, I would use a hatchet, butcher knife, cutting pliers and hacksaw.

It didn't take me long to discover that there was always one "bight" that was holding the whole mess together. One part of the rope or cable had tied it all together. Since the water was always dark I had to work by feel. I would pass my hand along the tangled mess until I felt the one tight strand on the outside. That's where I started working. When I got that piece cut, the rest usually unwound without much difficulty.

What is the "bight" that has you today? Is there one main thing that is worrying you? Ask God to feel around in your soul and point it out. Usually it is the sore spot. This one problem could be creating a tangled mess in your heart. Instead of trying to medicate it, or unleashing pain on others, why not just cut it loose? Give it to God. It may be something you did or didn't do. It may be something someone else said or did. Whatever it is, God wants to set you free.

Scripture of the Day: *"To the Jews who had believed him, Jesus said, 'If you hold to my teaching, you are really my disciples. Then you will know the truth, and the truth will set you free'."* (John 8:31-32)

Quote for the Day: "When I look back on all these worries I remember the story of the old man who said on his deathbed that he had had a lot of trouble in his life, most of which had never happened." (Winston Churchill, *Their Finest Hour*)

The author preparing to hit the water in 1978.

80. Striking the Arc

As I stated earlier, I used to be a diver for Dave Barker's Diving Service in Thibodeaux, Louisiana. For a while we did small jobs until he won the contract to clean out the sunken vessels in Bayou Lafourche. If you've ever taken the beautiful ride down Highway 1 to Grand Isle you have driven along that bayou. For years it was not navigable very far. There were over 200 sunken vessels all the way to Larose.

Since I had salvage experience (and was his only diver) I did the big vessels. He hired a small crane and barge to pick up the smaller ones. My largest job was a sunken barge near Larose. I had to go down into the murky water and cut it in half before the crane could pick it up, a half at a time.

I enjoyed cutting with underwater torches, so it was my favorite job. However, the barge had several layers and compartments to cut through so it took me almost a week. But eventually I heard the loud "clummmmmp," when one side let the other side go.

I know you guys are wondering so I'll give you the technical details. An underwater cutting torch is connected to a topside welding machine with reverse polarity. The voltage goes through a "knife switch" that a tender on the surface engages when the diver is ready. A ground clamp is placed on one part of the metal underwater. A gouging handle is used with hollow rods of different thicknesses. Two strands feed the head: the electrical insulated wire and the oxygen hose. When the rod is "struck" to the metal with the ground clamp, it creates intense heat. Then the handle is pressed which blows the oxygen through, gouging a hole. The diver must strike the ark and keep it from sticking (like topside welding). Then he pulls the trigger on the handle, blowing oxygen through the molten metal. He carefully pulls the arc along, blowing the oxygen through until the rod is consumed, which usually cuts about six inches.

It takes a steady hand. If you hold the rod too far away, then no fire, too close and the rod sticks, allowing current to flow through and again, no fire.

Life is like that cutting technique. Your kids require just the right amount of monitoring and freedom. Your job requires just the right amount of obeying your boss (or customers) and thinking for yourself. Your relationship with your spouse requires just the right balance of closeness and space. Your relationship with God requires the balance of meditation, intimacy and action upon His principles.

Is there any area of your life out of balance? If there is there will be pain in that area. Ask God to re-balance your life today. Like the underwater cutting torch, not too close, not too far, strike the arc for the fire, then squeeze the trigger for action.

Scripture for the Day: *"Let us hear the conclusion of the matter, fear God and keep His commandments."* (Ecclesiastes 12:13)

Quote for the Day: "The heaven themselves, the planets, and this centre, observe degree, priority, and place, insistence, course, proportion, season, form, office, and custom, in all line of order." (William Shakespeare, Troilus and Cressuda)

81. Friendship with God

We all need at least one friend. Friends are people who will tell us the truth when we need to hear it, listen to us when we need to be heard, spend time with us when we need companionship and share the experiences of life. How many times have you had a great experience and thought, "I wish so and so were here to enjoy this!" Shared fun is multiplied fun. Shared grief is divided grief. A shared work load is a lessened work load.

Did you know God wants to be your friend? (Proverbs 18:24) One of the differences between human friends and a divine friend is that in human friendship you must provide something the other person needs. But God requires that you provide nothing but yourself. You need no ability, no money, no personality, no power, no virtues (1 Corinthians 1:26-30). It's not your strength of character or knowledge, talent or abilities that will impress God and earn His acceptance. You must only bring yourself, empty, needy, without agendas, without pretenses. You must be REAL. He loves us without condition and wants relationship with us.

It's like the young man who wants to win the love of a lady who owns the flower store. She doesn't need for him to bring flowers. She has all the flowers she wants or needs. She just wants him, his heart, his love.

That's how God feels about us. We don't have to conquer the world for Him to love us. He has done that already. We don't have to get others to like us. Some never will. But God loves us already. We don't have to clean ourselves up enough for God to love us. He loves us just like we are; but He loves us too much to let us keep wallowing in the sins that drag us down. He'll clean us up as we trust Him and yield areas of our lives to Him.

But you say, "I'm already friends with God." How can you tell if you are friends with Him? In John 15:14 Jesus said, *"You are my friends if you do what I say."* You might say, "How do I know God wants to be my friend?" In John 15:13 Jesus said, *"Greater love has no man than this, that he lay down his life for his friends."* That's exactly what Jesus did. He stood between us and judgment by taking the payment of death at the cross on our behalf. He proved He loved us. What more could He do? You might say, "He did that in a general way for everybody. If He really loves me, He would tell ME." Congratulations, He just did.

Quote for the Day: *"Two are better than one, because they have a good return for their work: If one falls down, his friend can help him up. But pity the man who falls and has no one to help him up!"* (Ecclesiastes 4:9-10)

82. Raymond Hendry

Raymond Hendry is a 38 Year-old MX racer who came on to the scene in 1997. You can always spot Raymond's bike because it is always a Honda with #916 on the plates. This past race we were having a little trouble with some hot-shot riders not getting off the track when it wasn't their turn to practice. I called down to the flagman to get them off. They still continued to practice a portion of the track while the little 50cc riders were on. Twice a little mini rider almost got jumped on. I yelled over the P.A. system for them to get off, and for parents to help wave them off. Finally Raymond came walking up and said, "You want me to get them off?" He walked out onto the track and waved them off.

But one thing Raymond couldn't wave off was the devastation of a fire. He got home one evening and found fire trucks at his house. His home had caught fire and he lost almost everything except for what he had in a fireproof safe. I asked him how he coped with it. He answered, "The Lord said He'd handle it, so I don't worry about it."

As you can tell Raymond is a Christian. Some things God allows to happen to His children, but only what will be for their long-term good. God didn't put us here to be comfortable, but to show people His power and truth so they can be saved (Matthew 5:13-14). Another reason He leaves us on earth is to grow us up into the men and women who are mature (Ephesians 4:13, Colossians 4:12) and complete.

Scripture for the Day: *"Consider it pure joy, my brothers, whenever you face trials of many kinds, because you know that the testing of your faith develops perseverance. Perseverance must finish its work so that you may be mature and complete, not lacking anything."* (James 1:2-4)

Quote for the Day: "It isn't what you have, but who you are, that makes life worthwhile." (unknown)

83. The "P" Word

You know what the number one obstacle to relationships is? I'll give you a hint. It's the same obstacle that keeps people from a relationship with God. Need more hints? It causes fights and quarrels in your own home. It causes marriages to break up. It keeps people from saying they are sorry and making up. By now you've guessed because you have recognized it in yourself - Pride.

Just when I think I have arrived at a place of humility I discover another obstacle to relationships. God usually reveals it to me. Last night He used the book, *Getting Anger Under Control,* by Neil Anderson and Rich Miller. Yes, I struggle with anger periodically. Under the chapter of "Steps to Freedom" I found a list of specific ways people live in a proud manner. Here is the list. I submit it to you so you can run a check of your own life and see how prideful you are. Ready? Here we go with the "Areas of Pride."

- Being too busy doing "important" things to take time to do little things for others
- Finding it hard to admit when I am wrong
- Having a tendency to think that I have no needs
- Being more concerned with pleasing people than pleasing God
- Being concerned about getting the credit I feel I deserve
- Being driven to obtain recognition by attaining degrees, titles, or positions
- Often feeling that my needs are more important than another person's needs
- Having a stronger desire to do my will than God's will
- Leaning too much on my own understanding and experience rather than seeking God's guidance through prayer and His Word
- Considering myself better than others because of my academic, artistic, or athletic abilities and accomplishments
- Being more concerned with controlling others than about developing self-control
- Thinking I am more humble, spiritual, religious, or devoted than others
- Relying on my own strength and abilities instead of depending on the power of the Holy Spirit

If you are like me and failed this test, here is the prayer that goes with it.

Dear Father, I agree that I have been proud in (<u>name the area</u>). Thank you for forgiving me for my pride. I choose to humble myself before you and others. I choose to place all my confidence in you and none in my flesh. In Jesus' name. Amen.

Related Scriptures: James 4:6-10; 1 Peter 5:1-10; Proverbs 3:5-7; 16:18; Matthew 6:33; 16:24; Romans 12:10; Philippians 2:3

84. Why Believers Have Suffering

Now that's a hard question. Theologians, philosophers and teachers have been struggling with this one for a long time. I can't answer this for every case, but I can give you something to think about. Why would God allow you to face suffering when you were doing His will, believing Him, praying and reading His word?

As a young man and new parent I faced a similar situation. I had just re-committed my life to Christ. A short time later my wife Linda gave her life to Him and was baptized in our church. Our family was now dedicated to Him. Shortly thereafter I lost my job and our new-born baby daughter, Lacey was close to death. Our cars were broke down and the house needed repair. We couldn't pay the bills and things looked bleak. Why would God allow this to happen after having rescued us from similar problems a few months earlier? We looked around at others who were not serving God, even living a sinful lifestyle and they seemed to be untouched by trouble or lack of money. Why did God allow His children to suffer? Maybe you are going through it now.

Looking back over the years I can see an answer. God was developing our faith and strengthening our relationship with Him and each other. The faith we have today was born in struggles. He meets all our needs and protects us, but every once in a while trouble comes our way. But now it doesn't scare us like before. Now we take it to God and KNOW He has a plan and a purpose for the trial. We KNOW He will be with us all the way through and provide a way out. We KNOW He has something new to teach us, a new place to bring us, and the trial is the only way for us to learn it. Through the uncertainty, the doubt, the fear, the discomfort, and the suffering, He is in control. He is orchestrating it for our own good. When it is over and the skies clear we KNOW we will be at a new place of faith, peace and love.

How do we KNOW? Because He brought us through all the others, and in His Word He promised to take us through them.

Scripture of the Day: *"Consider it pure joy, my brothers, whenever you face trials of many kinds, because you know that the testing of your faith develops perseverance. Perseverance must finish its work so that you may be mature and complete, not lacking anything."* (James 1:2-4)

Quote of the Day: "Apparently, most believers are permitted to go through emotional and spiritual valleys that are designed to test their faith in the crucible of fire. Why? Because faith ranks at the top of God's system of priorities." (Dr. James Dobson, When God Doesn't Make Sense)

Someone ran into the back of me on the Mississippi River Bridge in Baton Rouge one foggy morning while on my way to a race and wrecked my Dad's camper.

Chase Guedry takes the checkered flag from Mike Burgess at Gonzales. At far right is his son Robbie, the track owner.

85. Mentoring

I've had some good mentors in my life. Mentors are teachers who take a special interest in you, take you aside and share their experience and knowledge. They are not just cheerleaders, but they do encourage. They are not just authority figures, but they're not afraid to correct you.

Mike Burgess, Sr. was my first mentor in motorcycle racing. He was the first to bring competition-ready off-road motorcycles to the New Orleans area. He picked up where my Dad left off in being a mechanic on my own bikes. He took me, and his sons, Robbie and Mikie to motocross, Enduro and flat track races in the early 70's. I won my first motocross race on a Penton 100 when I was on his race team.

Last week I saw this pattern in action again. Chase Guedry, also known as the "Cajun Cowboy" is a 19-year-old racer from Gonzalez. He spent a day with one of the fastest motocrossers in the world, Kevin Windham, at his track in Centreville, Ms. Kevin took a day from his schedule to work with Chase. He gave him some pointers, then cut him loose on his track. At first Chase was a little self-conscious riding under the watchful eye of one our sport's dominant racers. After a while, the old Cajun Cowboy came back as he loosened up and knocked off the rust, increasing his lap times. I'm sure Chase will never forget the time Kevin invested into his life.

If you have a teachable attitude and a desire to learn your trade, you will attract a mentor. But one day the mentor will be gone and you will be on your own to put your knowledge into use. Maybe, if you continue to grow and develop your skill and knowledge, God may lead a young student into your path so you can continue the circle of mentoring. If you are wise, you will be a mentor and have a mentor at the same time. Watch for students God sends your way. Ask yourself the question, "What does God want me to teach this person?" Then model it.

Read in 2 Kings, chapter 2 about a prophet who mentored another prophet before he died. Notice that Elisha (the student) had to go through the pain of departure with Elijah (his mentor), before he had the strength and authority to become a successful prophet. Notice also that Elisha took what he learned from Elijah and added it to his life to do even more than his mentor. Therefore Elijah played a key role in his student's ministry, sharing in his successes even after he was gone. Don't you want to leave something good behind after you are gone?

Quote for the Day: *"For lack of guidance a nation falls, but many advisers make victory sure."* (Proverbs 11:14)

86. I Wonder

I was always a dog lover. I raised and trained golden retrievers. They don't judge you, criticize you, second-guess you or say no. They just want to please. A simple pat on the head will make their day.

My wife was always a cat lover. She knows cats and how to deal with them. She has always had cats and probably always will. When our children were small, a stray cat showed up at our door. "Can we keep him, Mom?" Her reply? "Ask your Daddy." My answer? "No." Of course you can guess what happened. They bugged me until I gave in. That was our first cat, but not our last. The first one is long gone, but we have two more. They came to us the same way - stray kittens looking for a home.

Have you noticed that you can't train cats? They come to you when THEY want. If you call them, they'll sit down and yawn. If you are busy and they want attention, they'll jump up into your lap and interrupt whatever you are doing, because it's ALL ABOUT THEM. They'll learn to train you. (Guys who does that sound like?)

Anyway, our oldest cat Minnie is lying next to me right now as I write. Minnie is the most loving cat in the world. He just wants some lovin'. He curls up in my lap when I watch TV. He lays his head on me when I am reading. He even lays on the floor next to me stretching and rolling when I'm doing my push-ups and sit-ups. He sleeps on the bed next to our feet. He is never mean, sometimes playful and always wants to snuggle up for love.

I know not all cats are this way. How did he turn into such a lover? I wonder if my daughter's gentle affection did it? I wonder if my wife's tender petting and kind words did it? I wonder if the absence of meanness and abuse had anything to do with it? I wonder if consistent care for his physical needs had anything to do with it? This cat has always known the security of love and kindness, even from an old dog-lover like me. I wonder, does this environment of trust have anything at all to do with the making of a sweet-natured, loving cat? Now Kyle has been mean to Minnie a few times and Minnie doesn't trust him.

I wonder if there might be a principle here that can translate into our relationships with other people? I wonder?

Scripture for the Day: *"With the measure you use, it will be measured back to you..."* (Jesus in Luke 6:38)

Quote for the Day: "There is no beautifier of complexion, or form, or behavior, like the wish to scatter joy and not pain around us." (Ralph Waldo Emerson, The Conduct of Life)

Who do I need to treat better?

87. Cleaning Fish

Before we start, how about a riddle? What has four legs, four arms, three eyes, and is called "Ronnie?" I'll give you the answer in a minute.

I like catching fish. I just don't enjoy cleaning them. Yesterday I was fishing with my cousin and step-dad in a 17 foot bay boat along the marshes outside of Delacroix Island in south Louisiana. You guys want to know, "how did you do?" Well, we caught eleven trout of average size and one big nine pound redfish (my step-dad caught it). We got rained on most of the day (no cover) and fought a choppy bay back to the marina. When we got back to my step-dad's house we had to clean the boat and the gear. Then I drove for another hour and a half home.

The good news is, I was given all the trout. The bad news? You guessed it. How did you know? Oh yeah, I forgot about the title. I put up a couple saw-horses in the yard and a laid a board across them. I sharpened a couple knives and went to work. At first it was tedious, but as I went along I got better at it. Make the cut behind the head, slice along the backbone, slap a bug, cut the fillet off the fish, slice the skin, slap a bug, toss the tiny piece of meat into the water-filled pan, drop the carcass into the scrap bucket, slap a bug. I never could understand why I had fish scales on my face.

After the last fish was done I cleaned up, put the fillets in the kitchen (Linda did that), and went out and buried the fish carcasses next to plants that needed nourishment. Later I rinsed the fillets and separated them into freezer bags, leaving one batch in a marinade of water and Tabasco sauce for frying. Do you think the people who eat this fish will appreciate the work that was involved?

Parenting is like that. When we were young, we couldn't appreciate all the sacrifice our parents did for us. We just wanted what we wanted, when we wanted it, and pouted when we didn't get our way. Most parents (to varying degrees) work hard for money and sacrifice their own needs to provide for children who have no real appreciation for their parents or their efforts.

For you parents who are too tired to go on I have some good news. It will not always be this way. One day your children will grow up ... yes they will ... yes they will!... Ok, let's stop arguing. You know they will, it just doesn't feel like it right now. They will grow up and leave. Then one day they will be dealing with their own budgets, diapers, schoolteachers, doctor bills, sibling rivalries, discipline, etc., etc., etc.

So keep cleaning the fish, slapping bugs and picking up. One day you'll sit down to eat. The answer to the riddle? The two "Ronnie's" I went fishing with - Ronnie and Ronnie. My step-dad has a glass eye, so between them they have three eyes.

Scripture for the Day: *"At the proper time we will reap a harvest if we do not give up."* (Galatians 6:9)

Quote for the Day: "When a child is born into the world, God draws His hand out from near His own heart, and lends something of Himself to the parent, and says, 'Keep it till I come.'" (Henry Ward Beecher, Proverbs from Plymouth Pulpit)

88. "Get Out of the Car and Face Me!"

I was on my way across the Lake Pontchartrain causeway to go on the fishing trip I told you about earlier. My cousin Ronnie was in the passenger seat and it was 4:00 A.M. I was half asleep with the cruise control set on 57. I was almost to the south shore when a causeway cop came flying by in the left lane. She slowed down, rode alongside, then backed way off. I asked Ronnie, "why is that cop slowing down? She must be looking at something."

When I hit the 35 mph sign I turned off my cruise control, then something caught my eye in the mirror. The cop's light's came on. Then she came right up on my bumper. "Oh no, not me?" I said in disgust. (I'm sure this has never happened to you, right?)

"Pull over!" a young voice said over the cruiser's PA system as we got to the end of the bridge. I pulled over to the right. "Pull over to the left," was the command. I pulled over. Then I hear, "Get out your driver's license, proof of insurance and registration." I got it out and handed it to the cop. She checked my brake tag. She couldn't have been over 21 years old. She took my paperwork back to her cruiser and ran the checks. We waited 15-20 minutes.

"Sir, get out of the truck!" I walked to the back of the truck, half asleep and half in disgust. I put my foot up on my bumper and waited, head down. She walked up with her ticket book. I stood up.

"Face me." I looked at her. "No stand here and face me!" So I turned and faced her trying to hide my growing anger. "I need to let you know that you are being recorded by video and audio. I clocked you going 57 in a 35."

"I turned off my cruise control at the 35 sign," I offered. "I clocked you going 57 in a 35," she repeated. I felt like arguing. I let her write for a while as I thought of a way to get my point across without challenging her authority, "You know what's funny? I wasn't speeding on this bridge. People flew by me left and right, then I'm the one that got pulled over," I complained.

"Well, if it makes you feel any better, everyone's getting pulled over," she replied.

She offered the ticket to me and I hesitated. "By signing the ticket you don't admit guilt, you just agree to pay the fine or appear in court." I liked the "don't admit guilt" part, so I signed.

I went on to my step-father's house, now 45 minutes late. I didn't let it ruin my day, but I thought about it from time to time. I had been pushing the edges of the speed lately, but now I was ticketed for a crime I didn't feel I committed. The worst part (besides paying the fine and getting it on my record) was the way she said, "turn and face me...no, face me." I hadn't had anyone talk to me like that since I was a kid. But wait, it sounded familiar. I had recently put my finger in my son's face with the same tone, the same controlling authority. Maybe God was trying to tell me something. Maybe I was being disciplined by God.

Not every bad thing that happens to us is from the devil. Not every painful experience is bad. Even when we submit ourselves to God and do the right thing, we get corrected and disciplined. For the people who have truly allowed God to be God of their life and allowed Jesus to come into their heart, they must expect God to do His work and some of it is uncomfortable. The work of sanctification (cleaning up) is God's work and we must cooperate or we will never mature. We need to allow Him to do it, whatever the cost. If we fight against God's work of sanctification, we will remain shallow and weak, unable to be used of God to do any great thing.

We can be blind to areas in our life that need work. If we are to grow in faith and spiritual maturity, we must remain flexible in God's hands. We must not think we have God or ourselves all figured out. We never "arrive" in this life. We are a work in progress. Maybe that's why God says, *"a prideful spirit comes before a fall."* (Proverbs 16:18)

The next time some painful experience comes into your life, instead of asking "why me Lord?" We should ask "what are you trying to teach me, Lord?" Then pay attention, remain flexible and humble and don't get discouraged.

Scriptures of the Day: *"My son, do not make light of the Lord's discipline, and do not lose heart when he rebukes you, because the Lord disciplines those he loves, and he punishes everyone he accepts as a son"* (Hebrews 12:6, 11)

"May God Himself, the God of peace, sanctify you through and through. May your whole spirit, soul and body be kept blameless at the coming of our Lord Jesus Christ. The one who calls you is faithful and he will do it." (1 Thessalonians 5:23-24)

Quote for the Day: "Correction is better than Corruption." (R.J.)

89. Breaking Point

You want to know where God is easiest to find? You're not gonna like this. You sure? It's the same place I have always found Him - ALWAYS. I find Him at my breaking point. When I can't take it any more and I cry out for help. There He is.

Jesus told the parable of a man who found treasure buried in a field. He went and sold ALL he had to buy the field. (Matthew 13:44) There is a price to pay. Do you think you can afford it? You must give up something that is very precious, something that breaks up marriages, sends kids out of the family, divides churches, corporations, communities, nations; it even caused every war. Have you guessed the word yet? It is Control.

To meet with God in a very real way you must give up control. One of my closest friends, a strong Bible-believing Christian has been struggling and failing for a couple months until he spoke those key words, "God I give you control." I have another friend who's not a Christian (at least doesn't live like one), and his wife is not a Christian and he started a work of God in his life by issuing these words in sincerity, "Lord, what do you want me to do?"

Do you know what brings new life in nature? Death. The plant bearing seed must let the seed go (let go of control), then the seed must die, before new life springs forth. Some of you are struggling with your faith; have been your whole lives because you just won't "let go and let God..."

God is like a gentleman, He won't force Himself on us. He invites, sends signs, waits with open arms until you let go. God won't be your co-pilot. The "God position" is the pilot's seat. If He is to unleash His power in your life, make the necessary changes, bring forth new life, you must yield to Him. He's not God in your life if He's not God of your life. If you want Him, you must come on His terms. The first of the 10 commandments is, *"Thou shalt have no other gods before me."* Other gods may include, money, fame, position, popularity, another person, even you.

This is so simple, yet so hard; and it's not just a one-time thing. I did it once long ago, yet I tend to take back control from God. Then I mess things up. When I've had enough I repent, that is turn back from the direction I was going and give Him back control. As He takes the helm of my ship, He gradually eases me back on course while I finish suffering the consequences of whatever wrong I have done.

Real Christianity is not learning what to do. It's doing what you already know (with God's help). Then God will reveal more. As you obey that, He will reveal more. But we must learn to let God be God in our lives. Then we will open the door for His love, power, knowledge, wisdom, peace and life to pour in. But first things first, die to your self-centeredness, and ask Him to take control. When you do, super-natural changes will begin to occur that can only be explained supernaturally.

Scripture for the Day: *"I tell you the truth, unless a kernel of wheat falls to the ground and dies, it remains only a single seed. But if it dies, it produces many seeds. The man who loves his life will lose it, while the man who hates his life in this world will keep it for eternal life."* (Jesus in John 12:24-25)

Quote for the Day: *"You, O Lord, are our Father. We are the clay, you are the potter."* (Isaiah 64:8)

90. A Columbine Parent Speaks to Congress

The Columbine High School shooting at Littleton, Colorado needs no introduction. I'll not re-visit the events but show you something good that came from it. Darrell Scott, father of Rachel Scott, one of the teenage victims addressed the House Judiciary Committee's sub-committee. What he said to our national leaders is something that everyone should hear. I believe God used him to speak to our nation. Following is an excerpt from his speech.

Since the dawn of creation there has been both good and evil in the hearts of men and women. We all contain the seeds of kindness or the seeds of violence. The death of my wonderful daughter, Rachel Joy Scott, and the deaths of that heroic teacher, and the other eleven children who died must not be in vain. Their blood cries out for answers. The first recorded act of violence was when Cain slew his brother Abel out in the field. The villain was not the club he used. Neither was it the NCA, the National Club Association. The true killer was Cain, and the reason for the murder could only be found in Cain's heart.

In the days that followed the Columbine tragedy, I was amazed at how quickly fingers began to be pointed at groups such as the NRA. I am not a member of the NRA. I am not a hunter. I do not even own a gun. I am not here to represent or defend the NRA - because I don't believe that they are responsible for my daughter's death. Therefore I do not believe that they need to be defended. If I believed they had anything to do with Rachel's murder I would be their strongest opponent.

I am here today to declare that Columbine was not just a tragedy-it was a spiritual event that should be forcing us to look at where the real blame lies! Much of the blame lies here in this room. Much of the blame lies behind the pointing fingers of the accusers themselves.

I wrote a poem just four nights ago that expresses my feelings best. This was written way before I knew I would be speaking here today:

Your laws ignore our deepest needs, Your words are empty air. You've stripped away our heritage, You've outlawed simple prayer.

Now gunshots fill our classrooms, And precious children die.

You seek for answers everywhere, And ask the question "Why?"

You regulate restrictive laws, Through legislative creed.

And yet you fail to understand, That God is what we need!

Men and women are three-part beings. We all consist of body, soul, and spirit. When we refuse to acknowledge a third part of our make-up, we create a void that allows evil, prejudice, and hatred to rush in and wreak havoc. Spiritual presences were present within our educational systems for most of our nation's history. Many of our major colleges began as theological seminaries. This is a historical fact.

What has happened to us as a nation? We have refused to honor God, and in so doing, we open the doors to hatred and violence. And when something as terrible as Columbine's tragedy occurs – politicians immediately look for a scapegoat such as the NRA. They immediately seek to pass more restrictive laws that contribute to erode away our personal and private liberties. We do not need more restrictive laws. Eric and Dylan would not have been stopped by metal detectors. No amount of gun laws can stop someone who spends months planning this type of massacre. The real villain lies within our own hearts. Political posturing and restrictive legislation are not the answers. The young people of our nation hold the key.

There is a spiritual awakening taking place that will not be squelched! We do not need more religion. We do not need more gaudy television evangelists spewing out verbal religious garbage. We do not need more million dollar church buildings built while people with basic needs are being ignored. We do need a change of heart and humble acknowledgment that this nation was founded on the principle of simple trust in God!

As my son Craig lay under that table in the school library and saw his two friends murdered before his very eyes - he did not hesitate to pray in school. I defy any law or politician to deny him that right! I challenge every young person in America, and around the world, to realize that on April 20, 1999, at Columbine High School prayer was brought back to our schools. Do not let the many prayers offered by those students be in vain. Dare to move into the new millennium with a sacred disregard for legislation that violates your God-given right to communicate with Him. To those of you who would point your finger at the NRA - I give to you a sincere challenge. Dare to examine your own heart before casting the first stone!

My daughter's death will not be in vain! The young people of this country will not allow that to happen!"

Jeremy Domingue uses an extreme outside line and takes advantage of the side of a nearby jump to hold his momentum through a turn at Gravity Alley MX on his way to victory in December, 2004.

New Orleans racer and motorcycle dealer owner Sebastien Ramuscello waits at the starting grid of the 2004 AHRMA road race at No Problem Raceway. He used the horsepower advantage on his 999 Ducati to win his race.

91. Seize the Opportunity

Many times races have been cut short because of something out of the track owner's control: An impending storm, lightning or other dangerous conditions. We cut the laps of the second moto to beat the darkness at tracks that don't have lights. We tried to seize the opportunity of daylight before it got too dark to see.

You've had this happen to you; whether it was fishing, playing a sport, getting the pictures, watching a TV program, making an appointment, closing the sale, getting into shore, keeping a promise or just not being late. Maybe you'll get another chance, maybe you won't. Sometimes we think we'll get another chance, but the window of opportunity slams shut on our fingers forever. We need to take advantage of good opportunities when they present themselves.

Some of you have heard the gospel about Jesus Christ many times. Some will hear it again. But there is someone who is reading this that will never get another opportunity to respond to God's invitation for forgiveness and new life. This might be the closest to a Bible you'll ever get for the rest of your life. The rest of your life may be shorter than expected. Maybe God put these words before you one last time.

Don't delay. Recognize your need for God. Ask God to forgive you for all your sins. Tell him you are turning your life over to Him. Ask Jesus Christ, who died to take your punishment for sin at the cross, to come into your heart. Receive Him as your Lord and Savior. Tell somebody who'll encourage you. Join a Bible-believing church. See ya in heaven!

Scriptures of the Day: *"Then Jesus told them, "You are going to have the light just a little while longer. Walk while you have the light, before darkness overtakes you. The man who walks in the dark does not know where he is going. Put your trust in the light while you have it, so that you may become sons of light."* (John 12:35-36)

"Yet to all who received him, to those who believed in his name, he gave the right to become children of God—children born not of natural descent, nor of human decision or a husband's will, but born of God." (John 1:12-13)

"I tell you, now is the time of God's favor, now is the day of salvation." (2 Cor. 6:2)

Quote for the Day: "Raise the sail while the wind is fair." (proverb)

92. Hotpatch from God

Another Internet worm attacked computers all over the world last week. Since I send race reports each week to media outlets, my computer is on the net, exposed for a couple hours. I had allowed my Antivirus software to expire so I was in a position of vulnerability. So I got a "hotpatch" from Microsoft. I clicked on the link, and they verified my license, then they asked if I wanted the "Service Package." I clicked, yes. Next I sat back for a while as our computers interfaced.

I couldn't see what was going on deep within my hard drive, but assumed that Microsoft was downloading and uploading files, patching holes, fixing weak areas, and fine-tuning the software. Their new information was based on the latest developments and circumstances of the computer world since I bought my computer several months ago. I wouldn't let just any company have access to my computer files, but I trust Microsoft because they are the manufacturer. It's in their best interest if my software succeeds. When that hotpatch was done, my computer ran faster, was updated and now protected from the newest viruses and worms.

That same day I got a "hotpatch" from God. I had some financial set–backs (car and air conditioner problems). I was facing some parenting challenges (2 kids trying to face the challenges of college). I was just overwhelmed with circumstances. So I found a quiet place on the bedroom floor and tapped into God.

I recognized who He was, my Lord, Savior, and Judge. I worshipped Him as the King of Kings of the whole universe, submitting again to His authority over me. I loved Him as my intimate and merciful Heavenly Father. I came to Him in the name of Jesus Christ, the name above every name in heaven and earth, the only one who died for my sins, making me right with the Father. I thanked Him for the Holy Spirit who lives in me, comforting and empowering me for daily living. Then I just rested before Him, as the Spirit interceded for me with silent groanings that I could not understand (Romans 8:26).

As I lay there on the floor, my manufacturer downloaded new files into my spirit. He uploaded those files that needed to go. He patched holes, fixed weak areas, and fine-tuned my spirit. He ran a heavenly "service package" on me. He prepared me to face the future that He holds the keys to. He knows what is coming; I don't. He knows which road I should take; I'm not so sure. He knows where the danger is; I'm vulnerable. He knows what I've done wrong and has the power to forgive and forget. I need that. I need His hotpatches. I need Him.

As I lay on the floor I could feel the sunshine breaking through the clouds and lighting the room. It was if the Lord Jesus Christ was standing beside me, waking me to get back into the race of life. I got up with a renewed sense of well-being, new faith and new confidence in my God.

I'm not alone. The God of the universe walks with me. Bring on the viruses and the worms, because *"no weapon formed against me shall prosper.!"* (Isaiah 54:17)

Scripture for the Day:

"Even youths grow tired and weary, and young men stumble and fall; but those who hope in the Lord will renew their strength.

They will soar on wings like eagles; they will run and not grow weary, they will walk and not faint." (Isaiah 40:30-31)

Quote for the Day: "Prayer may not change things for you, but it for sure changes you for things." (Samuel M. Shoemaker)

Chase Romero taking a tear-off in the air at Down South MX in 2005.
(photo by Kyle Jenkins)

Bobby Handy at Wildwood MX in 2004.

93. The Battle of Old and New

Bobby Handy is a former professional motocross racer who still competes from time to time even at the age of 44. On some Thursdays you can catch Bobby and his son Chris practicing at Glory to God MX track near Gonzales. Money class racers hate it when he gets the holeshot because he is so difficult to pass. He knows every trick in the book having learned on the same track with national legends Mark Barnett, Bob Hannah, Broc Glover and David Bailey. Handy, from Baton Rouge, is used to winning.

Chase Romero is an up and coming talent in the money class. This talented teenager has grown up racing with his brothers Shaun and Corey at tracks in western Louisiana and Texas. Chase is on the cover of my first book, "Devotions for Racers." Chase only knows one speed - wide open. But he has the balance and skill to keep it on the track. He, too is used to winning. This New Iberia native hadn't raced in several months, then decided to join his brother Corey for a shot at a $2000.00 purse at a race in Baton Rouge.

In August of 2003 these two forces came together on the same Arenacross track on LSU's campus. As the announcer for that race I got a ringside seat for this spectacular melee. Young verses old. Experience verses impulsive youth. The cunning old buck against the young lion, both known for their fiery tempers.

My announcing partner was Mike Burgess, Jr., Handy's former mechanic and driver when he ran the pro circuit back in the 80's. "If Bobby gets the holeshot you better watch out," Burgess's crusty voice crackled over my headset. Sure enough, when the gate dropped, that big Honda 450f with number 227 on the plate dashed into the lead through the first turn. Handy had the lead and Burgess was whooping like an Indian. Before the first lap was over Chase Romero was on his tail.

The two racers, one from the past and one for the future engaged in their deadly dance. Grabbing handfuls of throttle they unleashed all the ponies from their big four-stroke engines, sling-shotting those light-framed Hondas down the straights. Inches from the wall, bumping each other in the air on the jumps, they delighted the crowd. But the crowd was not their focus. They were playing a fast paced game of chess.

Romero would fake outside and take the inside. Handy anticipated the move and went outside. It got rougher. Romero backed off temporarily then dashed into Handy's outside line with a block-pass. Handy pivoted his bike on a dime, clipping Romero's back wheel for the inside. They drag-raced down the straightaway over the double-jump, then the triple. As they set up for the sweeper Handy pushed Romero to the other side of the track as they wrestled for the next turn. Back and forth they went. Eventually Blake Kennedy moved up to the front and battled with Handy for second. The two bumped tires at speed in the sweeping turn and both went down, allowing Romero to post the win.

Just like these two riders, Christians have two natures at war. The new nature, implanted by the Holy Spirit of God is directing us to go one way. The old nature, our old habits, selfishly wants its way. Something has to give. This mental and spiritual battle can get tough. Although we may want to follow God and do what is right, it is easy to be impulsive with a wrong word or action. An intense struggle ensues as one nature tries to bully the other. Sometimes the battle is instantaneous, other times it can be prolonged as in a decision that has to be considered.

How can we overcome that old nature? How can we let God win in our lives? There is an old Chinese proverb that goes like this: "A black and white dog are always fighting. Feed the white dog and it will grow stronger and win."

What you feed is what will grow strong. Feed your spirit by reading the Bible, praying throughout the day, obeying God and spending time with other believers.

Scripture of the Day: *"Watch and pray so that you will not fall into temptation. The spirit is willing, but the body is weak."* (Jesus to his disciples when they fell asleep during guard duty. Matthew 26:41)

94. Missed Opportunities

One thing I am not good at is picking lines. Whether it's the bank, post office, building supply or especially the grocery I seem to pick the wrong lines. You've been there. You're in a hurry, you come to the check out lines, you scan for a short line, you check their baskets, you're watching for competitors and you make your decision. When you get near the cash register something goes wrong. The lady forgot something and leaves her stuff. "Excuse me, I'll be right back," she says as she goes by. Or maybe there's a price-check on an item. How about the time the lady pulls out fifty seven coupons? (Oh, that was you? Don't take it personally, I understand -you were saving money. Just NOT IN FRONT OF ME! Sorry, sometimes I can be selfish.)

What really gets me is the opportunities I missed. You know, when another register opens up down the way and I hesitate, then five people jump in line? Or how about when you forget about the 15 item express line? It's true. I'll be standing in a line behind someone with two-baskets full with my handful of stuff, when suddenly I remember the express lane. Now it's too late and I feel like a fool.

Missed opportunities. I've seen them from the other side, too. I've planned some good reward for one of my teenage children, then they make a foolish decision and miss the blessing. Want an example? Several times I've invited them to go out with me on jobs. I didn't tell them I would pay them more than it was worth. They declined and missed the reward. A couple times I was given older furniture. I asked them to help re-finish it. They declined. Now it's mine. In their defense they have responded well and received rewards. But they did miss opportunities that would bless them.

God works like that. He offers opportunities. We hesitate. We miss the reward in our own life. God lays out a blessing on one of our "life roads." We choose another way and miss out. It might have been something we were praying for. We don't even know we missed it.

When I asked my kids to help me refinish furniture, my purpose was to help them learn to take care of their stuff. When they refused, they were showing me they weren't ready for it. When God reveals Himself to you in a new way, you must act upon it. When He reveals a new truth, you must put it into practice, or you'll miss the opportunity for growth or blessing. Maybe you didn't have enough faith to receive what you were praying for.

Many people's prayer lives have ground to a halt because they were not acting upon what He has already revealed to them. We must go through first and second base to get to third. We must finish eleventh grade before we can graduate to twelfth. We must obey what we already know before God will bring us to a higher level.

Is there anything holding you back today? Is there an opportunity you're afraid to reach for? Has God given you a new inheritance in something, but you hesitate to move forward? Has He asked you to do something or stop doing something and you haven't responded yet?

Don't be like the Israelites who were given the promised land, but didn't have the faith to go in and possess it. They lacked FAITH. God didn't force it on them. He just sent them back out into the wilderness until that generation died. He preserved the lives of the two who had faith, Joshua and Caleb. (Numbers 13-14)

Whatever opportunity God has put before you, take it. Whatever He has revealed to you on the mountaintop, take it down into the valley of everyday life. There is no telling what great blessing God has just around the corner for you today. Walk forward in obedience and faith. Expect the miraculous and don't be surprised when He answers your prayer!

Scriptures for the Day: *"Walk while you have the light, before darkness overtakes you. The man who walks in the dark does not know where he is going. Put your trust in the light while you have it, so that you may become sons of light."* (Jesus in John 12:35-36)

"Everything is possible for him who believes." (Jesus in Mark 9:23)

Prayer for the Day: Dear Lord, forgive me for missing opportunities and not acting upon your revealed word. Help me see what you are trying to show me. Give me the strength to act upon it and the faith to believe, in Jesus name, Amen.

95. First Name Basis

I don't like to shop, but I do like going to buy things at certain stores. One example is the local auto parts store. I like what they sell (except when a component doesn't work and I have to pull it off and exchange it). I also enjoy not having to wait in lines to check out. They see me so much they recognize me when it's my turn. We're on a first name basis. Hey, I have to keep three vehicles running that have over 100,000 miles (not to mention the lawn mower, rotor-tiller, motorcycle, outboard motor, etc). They see me pretty often.

I enjoy being at the races also. I am on a first name basis with most of the racers and their families. We're like a big family. We watch out for each others' kids. We loan our stuff freely. We work on each others' bikes. We hang out and talk.

It takes time to develop that kind of trust and relationship. It's the same way with God. He knows everything about you. He created you. He loves you and wants relationship with you. But are you on a first name basis with Him? Do you look forward to going into His presence? Are you there every day? Or do you feel uncomfortable going before Him in prayer?

There is a key to unlocking this door. In order to feel comfortable in God's presence we must obey Him. Do what He wants us to do. Say the things that He would want us to say. Recognize who He is and His authority over us. When we sin, we need to come into His presence in an attitude of humility and sincere repentance. Then we ask for forgiveness.

If we claim to have fellowship with him yet walk in the darkness, we lie and do not live by the truth. But if we walk in the light, as he is in the light, we have fellowship with one another, and the blood of Jesus, his Son, purifies us from all sin. (1 John 1:6-7)

Next we need to BELIEVE that He has forgiven us. It is only then that we can come confidently before Him and enjoy His presence.

Dear friends, if our hearts do not condemn us, we have confidence before God and receive from him anything we ask, because we obey his commands and do what pleases him. And this is his command: to believe in the name of his Son, Jesus Christ, and to love one another as he commanded us. (1 John 3:21-23)

If you are out of sorts with God, why not take some time to get it right? Find a quiet place where you can be alone with Him. He has been waiting for you. You can present your needs to Him and He won't rebuke you for it.

If any of you lacks wisdom, he should ask God, who gives generously to all without finding fault, and it will be given to him. But when he asks, he must believe and not doubt, because he who doubts is like a wave of the sea, blown and tossed by the wind. (James 1:5-6)

96. Painful Healing

One of the problems with getting older is declining health. At 49 I'm too young to be in that category. But I do have some chronic back pain caused by old racing injuries in my right ankle. I've been getting some physical therapy from my chiropractor, Dr. Mike Petrosky. He has the gift of healing. He can push his thumbs into my back and TELL ME where my pain is. Then he puts a little lotion on his hands and begins to massage the injured area. He uses some force with his thumbs deep into my lower back in the bad spots.

One day I asked him about this and this is what he said, "I'm working out the lactic acid... getting the injured area's attention... stimulating the muscles for healing." The best part of all was when ... he stopped! It was painful while he was pressing and I was trying not to cry out in pain, but I almost didn't make it a couple times. He said I had some muscle tears down there that caused the pain and restricted movement.

I asked him why it hurt so much. He said, "There's no air pockets in your muscle, so the injured area has fluids that build up. That's why there is usually swelling associated with an injury. It's your body's life-force. I massaged out the old fluids. The injury is calling out for fluids with healing cells. Many people ignore it, or take a pill to cover it up. But you must listen to your body. Give it the attention in the area where the injury is."

I don't understand all that stuff, but I think it's kind of like renovating a room on your house. First you have to tear out the old or damaged area. Then you have to clean the walls or floors for the new coating to stick. Next you bring in the new materials. Finally you re-build that section. All the while there is the inconvenience of the mess. Eventually, with time, it will have been worth it and the pain will be forgotten.

So it is with healing. Whether it is emotional, physical or mental pain, in order for healing to occur, the healer must put his hand on the painful area. It must be dealt with. The old waste must be purged. New construction materials must be brought in, then the re-building can begin. It is painful for a while. But it's the only way.

Are you suffering from pain in some area of your life? Rather than covering it up or ignoring it, shouldn't you get a healer? Jesus Christ is the ultimate healer. His words or requirements may be painful at first, but they are necessary to purge the wound. Bring in the right healing and construction material from God's Word. Take it easy on that area for a while. Then give it time.

Scripture for the Day: *"But for you who revere my name, the sun of righteousness will rise with healing in its wings. And you will go out and leap like calves released from the stall."*
(Malachi 4:2)

"...the crowds learned about it and followed him. He welcomed them and spoke to them about the kingdom of God, and healed those who needed healing." (Speaking of Jesus in Luke 9:11)

Quote for the Day: "Many that high-strung patient, 'practice the peace of God which passes all understanding and you will be well.'" (Louis F. Bishop, M.D.)

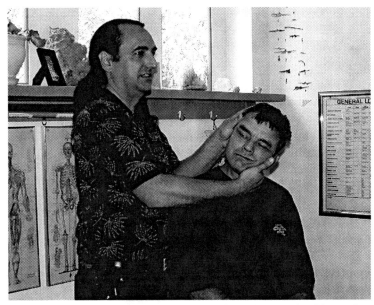

Dr. Mike Petrosky at Abita Chiropractic working his healing magic with an adjustment on an old MX racer's busted up body.

My Son Kyle at 20, working the sound booth at the Jackson Arenacross in 2004.

97. IF

by: Rudyard Kipling

If you can keep your head when all about you,
Are losing theirs and blaming it on you,
If you can trust yourself when all men doubt you,
but make allowances for their doubting too;

If you can wait and not be tired by waiting,
Or being lied about, don't deal in lies,
Or being hated, don't give way to hating,
and yet don't look too good, nor talk too wise;

If you can dream - and not make dreams your master,
If you can think - and not make thoughts your aim;

If you can meet with Triumph and Disaster,
And treat those two imposters just the same;
If you can bear to hear the truth you've spoken,
Twisted by knaves to make a trap for fools,
Or watch the things you gave your life to, broken,
And stoop and build'em up with worn-out tools;

If you can make one heap of all your winnings,
And risk it on one turn of pitch-and-toss,
And lose, and start again at your beginnings,
And never breathe a word about your loss;

If you can force your heart and nerve and sinew,
To serve your turn long after they are gone,
And so hold on when there is nothing in you,
Except the Will which says to them: "Hold on!"

If you can talk with crowds and keep your virtue,
Or walk with Kings - nor lose the common touch,
If neither foes nor loving friends can hurt you,
If all men count with you, but none too much;
If you can fill the unforgiving minute,
With sixty seconds' worth of distance run,
Yours is the Earth and everything that's in it,
And - which is more - you'll be a Man, my son!

98. A Morning Prayer

Dear Lord,

Thank you for waking me in my right mind - that I have my health, family and home.

Thank you for today's sustenance - food in the pantry, running water and clean air.

Thank you for the resources you have bestowed upon me - vehicles, tools and time.

Thank you that I live in a land of opportunity - peace in the community, laws for guidance, authorities for protection.

Thank you for the knowledge from education - wisdom from experience, and the freedom to apply it.

Thank you for those who have sacrificed for me - my parents' love, my friends' trust, my country's resolve.

Thank you for who you are - what you've done, and what you will do.

Help me to cooperate with you - fulfilling my tasks, blessing others, becoming like you.

Protect me from the evil one - the world and my own lusts.

Fill me with your peace - your joy, your grace.

Teach me to love others - myself, you.

Take my sins - I want them no more.

Take my selfishness - it only makes war.

Take my life - Jesus paid the price.

Teach me your ways, until I become a teacher.

Cleanse my soul, until others see Jesus.

Lead me along your path, until I come home.

With Great Expectation and Hope … Your Child.

(R. J.)

99. The First Jane Doe

There are times in our lives when we face difficulties that are more than we can bear - alone. One such case was documented on August 31, 2003. Dateline NBC broadcast a report entitled, "Meet Jane Doe." It was the story of the first victim from the 9/11 bombing of the World Trade Centers. Of the 300 survivors in long-term care, Debbie was the last to leave the hospital. Debbie Martinfeld, a beautiful 30 year-old woman, nearly lost her leg in the tragedy. She and her fiancée, Greg were making plans for marriage when their world was turned upside down.

After several months of bed-ridden pain, Debbie became depressed. She said, "I wish they'd never saved me... I wish I was dead." But Greg hung in there with her. Family and friends continued their prayers and support. Physical therapist Jessica Heine was one of those supporters. She worked with her every day. She said, "my job is to know when to push and when to back off." Greg said, "we're in this together."

Debbie began to respond. By April, 2002, she began to slowly raise herself out of bed. She told her therapist she wanted to walk. Soon, with great difficulty, she stood. On June 25 she took her first step holding on to a walker. But there were set-backs. The sutures on her back began to bleed. Her wedding was postponed. But she didn't give up. On her 31st birthday party well-wishers gave her boxing gloves. From her hospital bed she threw a flurry of punches for the camera with a smile. She fought on.

By July she had taken 50 steps. By September 2002 she was walking with a cane. She was determined to dance at her wedding. When asked what kept her going she mentioned faith, surgeon Melvin and Greg. When Greg was asked the difficult question, "Were there times when you thought, 'we are just not going to get through this.?'" Greg answered honestly, "yes, but we worked them out."

December 19 was her last full day at the hospital. After 15 months and 9 days she finally got to go home. She put it all in perspective when she said, "In many ways, on 9/11 I died. This is a very difficult life. There is triumph, but I still need to figure out how to live this way. I have no doubt I'll yet dance at my wedding." When asked how she would thank all the people who kept her going she answered, "The greatest gift I can give the people who helped me is to dance at my wedding. In some ways this is a Cinderella story. It has a happy ending. I have faith."

1. Like Debbie, we are sometimes faced with trials when we least expect them.

2. God put some people around Debbie to lend support.

3. Like the therapist, our closest supporters need to know when to push and when to back off.

4. Sometimes it gets harder before it gets easier.

5. She had a man who stuck by her during her ordeal, showing her real love.

The most important lesson is she had FAITH. She believed that eventually she would walk - and she did.

Scripture for the Day: *"All things are possible to him who believes."* (Jesus in Mark 9:23)

Quote for the Day: "Just over the hill is a beautiful valley, but you must climb the hill to see it." (Unknown)

100. Facing a Test

When I was a teacher I had to give tests. Except for pop quizzes I always gave the students fair warning. I let them know what the test would be on and gave them a few days to prepare. Inevitably there would be the student that whined "we have a test?" when it was time to start. Most students hated tests. But I had to find out what they knew. I had to motivate them to study. I had to reveal to them how much knowledge they picked up. I had to reveal weakness in the subject matter.

I hate tests in my life, too. But God does have to expose our weaknesses to us so we won't be overcome with pride. He wants us to depend upon Him. He wants to help us, to develop our relationship. He also wants us to grow stronger.

Temptation, on the other hand, doesn't come from God. It comes from one of three areas: Satan, the world or our own desires. The purpose of temptation is to get us to sin. Sometimes a test and a temptation are one in the same situation. Often, we can no more separate them than we can separate our own motives.

When temptation comes, what is the best way to handle it? Jesus was tempted after His baptism and before His earthly ministry. We can learn from Him how to respond to temptation.

Then Jesus was led by the Spirit into the desert to be tempted by the devil. After fasting forty days and forty nights, he was hungry. The tempter came to him and said, "If you are the Son of God, tell these stones to become bread." Jesus answered, "It is written: 'Man does not live on bread alone, but on every word that comes from the mouth of God.'" (Matt. 4:1-4)

I was going through a personal struggle when I came across this verse in my devotion. God showed me three principles from this passage that helped me pass my test. First, God allowed the test. He was overseeing the whole thing. Notice that Jesus was "lead by the Spirit... to be tempted." Sounds pretty close to God tempting, but it's not. The devil did the tempting, God did the testing. The devil wanted Jesus to fall into sin. God wanted Jesus to be strengthened by the test. Jesus was just doing what God wanted Him to do, when the tempter CAME TO HIM. Jesus was not just minding His own business, but minding God's business.

Sometimes the test/temptation comes when you are directly IN God's will, doing what He wants you to do. Then the temptation comes and finds you. Be encouraged in the fact that God knows and is overseeing the big picture.

The second principle is this was an ongoing test/temptation. It wasn't short. It lasted 40 days! I know some of our problems seem to go on forever, but how many of them last almost 6 weeks? Very few. God knows just how much we can take and won't go over the limit. *"... and God is faithful; he will not let you be tempted beyond what you can bear..."* (1 Corinthians 10:13) One of my favorite passages in the Bible is, "this too, will pass."

The third principle that helped me endure was the part I had to do. Notice what Jesus used as a weapon - the Word of God. Scripture is the divine weapon of choice in spiritual warfare. We should not only read it, but learn it and memorize it for times of battle.

Did you notice that Jesus said we can't live without it? He said, we "don't live on food (bread) alone, but on every WORD that comes from the mouth of God." "What words?" you ask. The words you have in the Bible. Every poisonous situation you are faced with has an antidote in the Bible. Every mental, emotional or spiritual bomb has diffusing instructions in the Bible. So in my struggle I realized I needed to go to the Bible every day for ammunition to succeed.

If you are struggling with a problem in your test today, maybe you haven't read the solution. Read the answer key. Look it up. It's not cheating. It's not too late. The teacher wants you to search for the answers. That's why He gave you the test. He wants you to pass, that's why he gave you the answer sheet called the Bible!

Scriptures for the Day:
> *... though now for a little while you may have had to suffer grief in all kinds of trials. These have come so that your faith—of greater worth than gold, which perishes even though refined by fire—may be proved genuine...* (1 Peter 1:6-7)

> *Remember how the LORD your God led you all the way in the desert these forty years, to humble you and to test you in order to know what was in your heart, whether or not you would keep his commands. He humbled you, causing you to hunger and then feeding you with manna, which neither you nor your fathers had known, to teach you that man does not live on bread alone but on every word that comes from the mouth of the LORD.* (Deuteronomy 8:2-3)

101. Don't Be Blown Away

I love to ride my street bike down country roads. I had an 1100cc Honda Shadow that had more power than I needed; but it didn't have to strain at 70 mph when I had my camping gear strapped to it. Another advantage of riding a heavy bike is being able to withstand the wind-shear when passing trucks on the Interstate. When I used to ride my little 250 dual sport on the Interstate at speed, a passing truck would sometimes send me onto the shoulder.

One of the advantages you gain as you get older is perspective. Like a heavier motorcycle on the Interstate, an older, more experienced person is less affected by the wind-shears caused by life's problems. Example: have you ever heard of a teenager being devastated by a small set-back? Maybe it was something as simple as being snubbed by a friend, not being invited to a party, even a bad hair day. They think the whole world is falling in on them. They are like the little 250 being blown off the road.

The same kind of problem can happen to an older person and they just shrug it off. They can endure so much more without being "blown off the road." Why? Because they have been through so much more. They have more perspective. At dinner tables all around the world there are young people expressing a problem to older people. The response is probably pretty close to, "don't worry, it'll be all right." That's easier to say than believe when you are the one being "blown into the weeds, right?" But it is still true.

Still, God has the higher perspective. He's been around billions of times longer than the oldest person. He's got billions of times more wisdom than the wisest person. He loves you billions of times more than anyone else. What's more, He can SEE around the corner, into the future and He's not worried.

Whatever you are dealing with, bring it to God. He is allowing this to happen for your own good. He wants you to depend on Him. He wants your trust. He wants intimacy with you. Why not spend some time alone with Him today? You think it's just a coincidence that you are reading this right now?

Scripture of the Day: *"We were under great pressure, far beyond our ability to endure, so that we despaired even of life. Indeed, in our hearts we felt the sentence of death. But this happened that we might not rely on ourselves but on God, who raises the dead. He has delivered us from such a deadly peril, and he will deliver us. On him we have set our hope that he will continue to deliver us..."* (2 Corinthians 1:8-10)

The author's 1100 Shadow and Steve Kolz's 600 Bandit at Holeshot MX Track in
Loranger during a day trip around the area.

#290 Corey Altazin leads #105 Chase Melancon, #154 Shaun Gunderson and #42 Cody
Smiley through the first turn of the Open Intermediate class at Holeshot MX in 2004.

102. The Key to Surviving the Storms of Life

How do you get to know God better? Possible ideas would be to: read the Bible, go to church, listen to a preacher or teacher, read books or ask somebody who knows Him. No. These things only help you know ABOUT God. It's not the same as KNOWING God. What's the difference?

It's like the difference in knowing about motocross racing and doing it. A man can read all the books on motocross. He can do all the research on the bikes, the tracks, the history. He can begin to talk all about it with others. But he won't KNOW it personally, until he dons the gear, swings a leg over a bike, starts the motor and takes some hot laps. The more he rides, the more he KNOWS motocross. Then the real education comes when he rides in a pressure situation - the race. When the "real bullets are flying" he puts his knowledge to the test; when he has to share the track with other racers who are doing everything they can to pass him. He takes the knowledge he has learned ABOUT motocross and puts it into action in this real life situation. That's when he learns to trust his bike over the jumps, trust his tires around the turns, trust his suspension through the whoops and trust his brakes to slow him down.

How does he KNOW his helmet works? When he crashes and gets knocked in the head and survives. How does he KNOW his boots work? When he gets his foot caught between two bikes and they protect him. How does he KNOW the thrill of winning a race?

Knowing ABOUT God is mentally understanding what He is like. He is good, forgiving, all-knowing, all-powerful, timeless, etc. On the other hand, KNOWING God comes from developing intimate RELATIONSHIP with Him. This comes through TRUSTING him when we enter the storms of life.

Why does it have to be this way? It is our human nature to want to control people, situations and things around us. We can't really trust God, when we're trusting in something else. It's those times when we find ourselves helpless, that we are ready to let Him take over. When we come to the end of our rope, He is just a "drop" away. Those difficult times when we relinquish CONTROL to Him, are the teachable moments when we are open to KNOW Him on a personal level. Those truths we "learned about Him" are then proved true. Our faith is transferred from our own devices to Him.

The more we turn over control to God, the more He reveals Himself to us. The more we experience Him at work in our lives, the more we are willing to trust Him. The more we trust Him, the more we read His Word, spend time in prayer, praise Him for what He has done. The more we experience His goodness, mercy, forgiveness and love, the more we become like Him and pass those on to others. The more we let Him have control, the more we follow the path He has prepared for us, the less we suffer from the self-inflicted consequences of sin.

So if you want to KNOW God and follow His path for your life, what should you do? Ask Him to reveal Himself to you. He will. Seek Him. You might say, "I've already tried that stuff, church, Bible, prayer and it didn't work." Maybe God's not revealing Himself to you anymore because you're not doing anything with the knowledge He's already given you. In other words, what are you already doing with the knowledge of God you already have? Most of us don't need to know more about God, we need to do something with the knowledge we already have. Just concentrate on loving and obeying God. He'll take over from there.

Scripture for the Day: *"If you love me, you will obey what I command. And I will ask the Father, and He will give you another Counselor to be with you forever – the Spirit of truth... Whoever has my commands and obeys them, he is the one who loves me. He who loves me will be loved by my Father, and I too will love him and show myself to him."* (Jesus in John 14:15, 21)

Quote for the Day: "Knowing is one thing. Doin' is a whole 'nother game." (R.J.)

103. Is the Cat All Right?

I have a friend named Michael Brown. He looks just like Santa. He is short and stocky, has red hair and a fluffy red beard. He warms up a room when he enters with his jovial nature and infectious laugh. He's quite a character on the street, too. He rides a custom-painted black Kawasaki Vulcan with leather fringed hand guards and saddlebags. He wears a half-helmet with a Kaiser point on top and leather jacket. He logs thousands of miles a year on his motorcycle when he's not working offshore.

One day he was cruising down the highway when a cat ran out in front of him. He swerved to miss the cat, but made the mistake of looking back to see if he missed it. While his head was turned to the right, the bike wandered off course to the same side. By the time he looked back it was too late. He was crossing the shoulder and headed for the ditch. When he regained consciousness he was on the ground. His bike was lying in the ditch and his spiked helmet was stuck in the ground, upside-down.

Thankfully Mike and his bike survived (motorcyclists always want to know, "how was the bike?"). His body and bike suffered a few scratches and dings. Good thing he didn't turn and look over his left shoulder or he might have ended up in oncoming traffic!

A bike goes where you point it or lean it. You've probably experienced this on a bicycle. When you ride with no hands you have to lean to the side you want to go.

Life is the same way. You will end up where you are looking or leaning. If you are looking at a sin, you'll eventually end up there. If you are leaning toward a goal, you'll eventually arrive. If you keep thinking about failure, you'll be there. If you are concentrating on the things your friends are into, you'll go there. If you put your thoughts and mind on good things, they will come.

What has occupied most of your thoughts this week? Where does your mind drift? In what direction are you leaning? What is your heart set on? Are you looking back too much? Beware of the dangers of leaning toward sin or looking back too long. Don't go there.

Scripture for the Day:
"Finally, brothers, whatever is true, whatever is noble, whatever is right, whatever is pure, whatever is lovely, whatever is admirable—if anything is excellent or praiseworthy—think about such things. Whatever you have learned or received or heard from me, or seen in me—put it into practice. And the God of peace will be with you." (Philippians 4:8-9)

104. The $640,000.00

According to a published report by the Associated Press, a man who had walked off with $640,000.00 returned it two days later. He had been working at a downtown office building when the money fell out of an unlatched door of an armored truck nearby. The truck had just pulled away from the Federal Reserve Bank of Cleveland. He began to grow nervous when authorities published reports of his description and the missing money.

The bank's security director, Ken Kennard said the man called from a nearby pay phone to say he was "worried and wanted to know what to do." He said that he may not have done the right thing and needed some guidance as to what to do next. Kennard said he talked the man into coming into the bank. The man walked into the federal building and returned it that morning. The three, forty-two pound packages of cash were still wrapped in plastic. It was all there to the last penny. Federal prosecutors decided not to file charges.

This man avoided serious prison time by changing his mind. But not only did he change his mind, he returned the money. That's repentance. He changed direction.

This is why so many people don't experience God's forgiveness. They believe God can forgive. They ask for His forgiveness. But they don't show they have really received His forgiveness by doing something different. They don't turn onto the road that leads in the new direction.

Jesus enraged the religious leaders of His day by hanging out with the worst sinners. But instead of becoming like them, He offered them God's forgiveness. Some received it, others didn't. One such case was Zacchaeus. He was a hated tax collector. Tax collectors were known to overcharge and keep the difference. Jewish tax men were seen as traitors by their own people.

When Jesus was dining at Zacchaeus' home he taught about forgiveness. Then Zacchaeus did something that revealed true repentance. Read for yourself:

"Zacchaeus, come down immediately. I must stay at your house today."

So he came down at once and welcomed him gladly. All the people saw this and began to mutter, "He has gone to be the guest of a 'sinner.'"

But Zacchaeus stood up and said to the Lord, "Look, Lord! Here and now I give half of my possessions to the poor, and if I have cheated anybody out of anything, I will pay back four times the amount."

Jesus said to him, "Today salvation has come to this house, because this man, too, is a son of Abraham. For the Son of Man came to seek and to save what was lost." (Luke 19:1-10)

Aaron Sanchez asks his Dad Chip a question at the Fall, 2004 G2G camp

Jeff Posey (left) and Scott Bailey give instructions at the same camp to the young riders.

105. The Rogue Elephants

Elephants are fascinating creatures. A few years ago Pilanesberg National Park in South Africa was having a problem with the increasing violence of its young bull elephants. These juvenile elephants were knocking over white rhinos, kneeling on them, then goring them to death. This is unusual for elephants.

The game wardens finally realized the problem. This new aggressive behavior was caused by a government program that killed older elephants to reduce the population. Almost all of the young rogue elephants were orphaned when they were calves. Normally the older dominant males keep the young bulls in line and serve as role models. Without their guidance and discipline, these "thug elephants" grew up to terrorize the herd.

Our prisons are filled with men who grew up with hardly any contact with a loving father. Zig Ziegler, a motivational speaker quoted his friend Bill Glass who has worked with inmates for over twenty five years. Rev. Glass said, "of the thousands of prisoners he had met, not one of them genuinely loved his dad." "Ninety-five percent of those on death row hated their fathers," according to Dave Simmons, author of, *Dad, the Family Counselor.*

This next generation needs male leadership. One of the things I enjoy at the motocross races is watching all the Dads do their jobs. They not only help lead their own kids, but pitch in to help the other kids as well.

Is there some boy who could use some extra attention from you today? Maybe he lives down the street. Maybe he is a relative. Maybe he lives with a friend. Maybe he lives under your roof. Invest some time and attention into the life of a child this week. You may change his life.

Scripture of the Day: *"those who saw me commended me, because I rescued the poor who cried for help, and the fatherless who had none to assist him."* (Job 29:11-12)

Quote for the Day: "Viewing the child solely as an immature person is a way of escaping confronting him." (Clark Moustakas, Creativity and Conformity)

106. Dropping the Ring

It's a groom's nightmare. The best man hands him the ring during the wedding ceremony and he drops the ring. It's not so bad when they're standing on a solid floor. But what about a wooden deck under a gazebo? What about the spaces between the boards? It happened to us one weekend.

As an ordained and licensed minister of the gospel I get to officiate at weddings. It's a joyful affair for a man and woman to express their love to one another by standing before God and witnesses to make their vows. They are taking their love to the highest level, a life-long commitment. The ceremony inspires me and the people who are in attendance. It reminds us of the eternal love God has for us when He committed His Son to us at the cross.

Jay Burton, an expert class motocross racer from Prairieville was marrying his long-time girl-friend, Tiffany Gravette. Another former expert racer was Nick Burgess, who was given the honor of standing next to Jay as best man. I was standing before them on a wooden deck next to the pool at the Gravette home, leading the vows. When I asked for the ring, Nick reached into his pocket for the ring box. The next thing I heard was a collective gasp from the crowd, with the loudest voice being the bride's. Nick had dropped the ring and it bounced on the deck!

In all fairness to Nick, the ring was not set in the box's grooves. When he opened the box, it fell out. We had joked at the rehearsal that if the ring dropped between the deck boards we would have to pull up the deck during the ceremony. In that moment while the ring was bouncing its way toward a gap in the deck, the groom acted quickly. Jay saved the day by reaching down and catching the ring on the second bounce. I added a sentence to the sermon that went something like this, "Life is like that. Sometimes you drop the ring. But you just have to pick it up and keep on going."

Have you ever done something bone-headed? Has an accident ever happened to you that you weren't prepared for? Have you ever been given an important assignment and something went wrong? Have you ever "dropped the ring?"

I have good news for you. You are not condemned to loser status for the rest of your life. You don't have to go through life with a "dunce's hat." You are not a fool because you did a foolish thing. You don't have to wear the chains of guilt, unless you want to. Don't laugh, some people find it comfortable to keep beating themselves up over something because they won't forgive themselves.

Whether you have taken another man's life in a fit of rage or pocketed a candy bar in a impulse of desire, you can be forgiven. The consequences will be different, but you can be set free from the shame and self-condemnation if you choose. If others won't forgive you, then that's their problem. God will forgive you and remove it "as far as the east is from the west." It may take time others for others to see that you are sincere. You can only "play your side of the net."

If you have "dropped a ring" in the past, just pick it up and go on. We are only human and prone to mistakes. Some things just happen to us through no fault of our own. Ask for forgiveness, then live in peace. God is ready, able and willing to forgive and forget. What are you waiting for?

Scripture of the Day:
Therefore, there is now no condemnation for those who are in Christ Jesus, because through Christ Jesus the law of the Spirit of life set me free from the law of sin and death. For what the law was powerless to do in that it was weakened by the sinful nature, God did by sending his own Son in the likeness of sinful man to be a sin offering. And so he condemned sin in sinful man, in order that the righteous requirements of the law might be fully met in us, who do not live according to the sinful nature but according to the Spirit. (Romans 8:1-4)

107. I Found It

Mac Edmonston and I took a ride on a couple of street bikes along the Mississippi River one Saturday morning. We motored along the curvy River Road from Geismar all the way to the LSU campus. A hint of fall was in the air and we had the road to ourselves.

We pulled up at a red light near the football stadium and Mac asked if we could stop at the Parker Coliseum. Two weeks before we had been to an Arenacross race in that building. The pit area was the livestock stalls adjoining the arena. He had lost a small piece of plastic off his helmet. He wanted to see if he could find it.

We pulled in and got off our bikes. We walked through the stalls, kicking the sawdust and dirt-covered floor with our boots. Would you believe he actually found it? I asked if that was it when he placed it in the hole of his helmet. He answered, "if it's not, it sure will work."

Have you lost something in your relationship with God? Has the joy faded? Has your faith grown weak? Do you lack confidence going before Him? Has it been a while since you've talked to Him - I mean seriously poured out your heart to Him?

Then you must go back where you lost Him. Maybe it was before a certain week-end or a certain encounter with someone. Maybe it was right before the last time you got into trouble. Maybe it was the last time you were in church.

Wherever you lost touch, you need to go back. Ask Him to direct you. Maybe a sin has separated you from Him. Whether it was a person, place or thing, you have allowed something to come between you and God. Look for the path that God is on. Take it. He hasn't turned from you, but you have turned from Him. He looks for you to return with expectant eyes and open arms.

Scripture for the Day: *"... suppose a woman has ten silver coins and loses one. Does she not light a lamp, sweep the house and search carefully until she finds it? And when she finds it, she calls her friends and neighbors together and says, 'Rejoice with me; I have found my lost coin.' In the same way, I tell you, there is rejoicing in the presence of the angels of God over one sinner who repents."* (Jesus in Luke 15:9-10)

Quote for the Day: *"'Return to me,' declares the Lord Almighty, 'and I will return to you'."* (Zechariah 1:3)

108. The Refiner's Fire

One subject I deal with often in this book is trials and testing. The reason is two-fold: One, I want you to make some sense out of your suffering. If you're not dealing with a problem too big for you to handle - you will. Two, I want to encourage you. If you have accepted Jesus Christ as your Lord and Savior, you belong to God. You are under His protection. But trials still come. Why? I don't know the mind of God, but I've found some reasons God has allowed me to suffer pain. See if these make sense to you. First read the scripture from 1 Peter, 3-9:

Praise be to the God and Father of our Lord Jesus Christ! In his great mercy he has given us new birth into a living hope through the resurrection of Jesus Christ from the dead, and into an inheritance that can never perish, spoil or fade—kept in heaven for you, who through faith are shielded by God's power until the coming of the salvation that is ready to be revealed in the last time. In this you greatly rejoice, though now for a little while you may have had to suffer grief in all kinds of trials. These have come so that your faith—of greater worth than gold, which perishes even though refined by fire—may be proved genuine and may result in praise, glory and honor when Jesus Christ is revealed. Though you have not seen him, you love him; and even though you do not see him now, you believe in him and are filled with an inexpressible and glorious joy, for you are receiving the goal of your faith, the salvation of your souls.

Joe Beam, in his book, *Seeing the Unseen*, addressed this question of why God allows suffering. In his chapter entitled, "Why does God let Satan hurt us?" Beam quoted the scripture above. Then he got some insight about the refining of gold from a Christian friend who was a goldsmith and gemologist. Herbert Ledbetter is the Director of Merchandise for the A. A. Friedman Company, the largest privately owned jewelry chain in America. According to Ledbetter the purpose of putting gold through intense fire was to:

- burn away impurities
- bring the gold to such a high gloss that the goldsmith could see his reflection in it
- make the gold malleable enough that the goldsmith could shape it however he chose

- increase the strength of the gold
- increase the value of the gold

Ledbetter went on to reveal that the goldsmith was careful to prevent two things:
- He could never let the gold become too heated, or it would bubble and ruin
- He could not let the gold cool too quickly or it would become brittle

Mr. Ledbetter drew a conclusion that I have suspected for the last 10 years, "... people most mightily used by God have always been through some tragedy. God puts them through the fire, just like the gold." You will probably agree with this assessment. You can also see the analogy of the purpose of the refiner's fire for your own life.

God allows trials into our lives to bless us in the long run. So, in the words of Beam, "God uses Satan against himself." In other words, Satan tries to steal, kill and destroy by throwing difficulties at us. God allows some of these difficulties through his "filter" to strengthen and refine our faith. The result is the "salvation of our souls."

Whatever trial you are facing, know that it is for a reason and God has His hand on the throttle and the brake. Hold on and trust Him, you're goin' somewhere good!

Scripture of the Day: *"See, I have refined you, though not as silver; I have tested you in the furnace of affliction."* (Isaiah 48:10)

Quote for the Day: "Troubles are often the tools by which God fashions us for better things." (Henry Ward Beecher, Proverbs from Plymouth Pulpit)

109. Why the Evil?

Don't you hate it when an evil person can get away with an injustice? Doesn't it seem odd that evil continues to prosper? If God is so good and powerful, why does He let sin flourish? Let Jesus answer that in His own words in Matthew 13:24-30:

Jesus told them another parable: "The kingdom of heaven is like a man who sowed good seed in his field. But while everyone was sleeping, his enemy came and sowed weeds among the wheat, and went away. When the wheat sprouted and formed heads, then the weeds also appeared. The owner's servants came to him and said, 'Sir, didn't you sow good seed in your field? Where then did the weeds come from?' 'An enemy did this,' he replied. The servants asked him, 'Do you want us to go and pull them up?' 'No,' he answered, 'because while you are pulling the weeds, you may root up the wheat with them. Let both grow together until the harvest. At that time I will tell the harvesters: First collect the weeds and tie them in bundles to be burned; then gather the wheat and bring it into my barn.'"

God can see what is going on. Good and evil are growing up together in the world around us. He will judge the earth and its inhabitants, but He is waiting for the right time.

Many people are putting off the decision to repent of their sin and trust God. Others will never turn to Him. But there are those who will come to understand the error of their ways and repent.

Have you experienced the grace and forgiveness of God yet? Are you "wheat" or a "weed?" You're on the clock.

Scripture for the Day: *"... the present heavens and earth are reserved for fire, being kept for the day of judgment and destruction of ungodly men. But do not forget this one thing, dear friends: With the Lord a day is like a thousand years, and a thousand years are like a day. The Lord is not slow in keeping his promise, as some understand slowness. He is patient with you, not wanting anyone to perish, but everyone to come to repentance."* (2 Peter 3:7-9)

110. Where's the Fan?

Recently our central air conditioner went out. You don't want that to happen in south Louisiana in August. When we built the house we made the central a/c closet door too small. That means there was no room to pull out the old coil. So for about three weeks we were without a/c on the bottom floor.

I ended up having to cut a hole under the furnace and drop the whole unit down to get the old coil out. Until we could find a new coil to fit and install, we were "sweating it out." I pulled an old box fan out of the attic and placed it in the window to draw cool air in at night. Periodically, I would move the fan to another part of the house. Sometimes I would ask Linda, "where's the fan?"

We took our air conditioning for granted. I'll bet you don't do that, right? It is in our human nature to get used to something good, take it for granted, then expect more. It seems that it is not until we lose something that we finally appreciate what we had.

Is there something in your life you are taking for granted? A car that is running good, a job, food in the fridge, a paycheck, good books on the shelves, appliances that are working, kids that are not in jail, stereo at you fingertips, friends that care, a spouse? Ok, maybe you don't have all of these, but maybe you should appreciate what you DO have.

Maybe we should take some time with God to thank Him for the blessings He has already given us, before we start our shopping list of the things we want. A thankful heart is the key to contentment. Read what happened to a man who was thankful for what Jesus gave him:

Now on his way to Jerusalem, Jesus traveled along the border between Samaria and Galilee. As he was going into a village, ten men who had leprosy met him. They stood at a distance and called out in a loud voice, "Jesus, Master, have pity on us!" When he saw them, he said, "Go, show yourselves to the priests." And as they went, they were cleansed. One of them, when he saw he was healed, came back, praising God in a loud voice. He threw himself at Jesus' feet and thanked him—and he was a Samaritan. Jesus asked, "Were not all ten cleansed? Where are the other nine? Was no one found to return and give praise to God except this foreigner?" Then he said to him, "Rise and go; your faith has made you well." (Luke 17:15-19)

Quote for the Day: "He who is not grateful for the good things he has, would not be happy with what he wishes he had." (unknown)

List what you are thankful for:

111. Making Sense of Confusion

Have you ever gone through a time that didn't make sense; then looking back with faith you understood what God was doing?

One such time for me was when I had just answered God's call to ministry and had been accepted into New Orleans Baptist Theological Seminary. (That's a post-graduate school for ministers, in case you were wondering.) I was scheduled to start class on a Tuesday. The week before I fell while fielding a ground ball in a church league softball game and broke my left forearm. It required surgery because of the crooked break. They put a plate and seven screws in it.

At the time I couldn't understand why God would allow that to happen right before I was going to do something important He had called me to do. I decided to go to class anyway. It was a good thing it was not my right arm, because I needed it to take notes and shift the Toyota Camry. I had to take pain pills the first two days of school. When I sat down in the library to study after class, I found myself reading for several hours at a time. For someone with ADHD who never sits still, that was unusual. On the third day, when I stopped taking the pain medication, I had already established a habit of long hours of study in the library. That stayed with me through three years of undergraduate work and three years of masters work.

Looking back I can see why God allowed me to break my arm and have surgery just before I went to seminary. He was settling me down so I would be able to spend long hours of study. It was a discipline I would need for that stage of my life. He was using something painful to equip me for the future He had planned for me. Even today I can sit still for hours to read or write when I take my prescription medication for ADHD. Hey, it helps me stay focused.

When you find yourself facing a situation that doesn't seem to fit in your life, stand firm in your faith. Be confident that God is in control and has a reason for taking you through this time of confusion. He will justify Himself in the long run. He will carry you through to the end, while teaching you a new lesson you will soon need. Remember that God has bigger plans for you than the little issues you are asking Him about right now.

Scripture for the Day: *"'For I know the plans I have for you,' declares the LORD, 'plans to prosper you and not to harm you, plans to give you hope and a future.'"* (Jeremiah 29:11)

112. Saints Fan

I'm a New Orleans Saints fan. I'm not really a fanatic, just a long-time advisor to such coaches as Hank Stram, Bum Phillips, Jim Mora, Mike Ditka and now Jim Haslett. Since I used to play little league for 7 years I consider myself an expert. I've sat on my sofa and called plays, shouted at refs, benched players and recovered fumbles on my living room floor. I have helped them draft players in May, cut players in August and have scanned the waiver wire for unrestricted free agents. Have the coaches ever listened to me? No. But I've never called them either. I've only contacted them by speaking at the radio and TV. What would you label me, an armchair quarterback or coach? They don't respond to me because I've never made contact with them. They don't know me. I have no relationship with Jim Haslett. Am I a part of that sport? Only as a bystander.

But in motocross racing I have relationships with many riders, parents, mechanics, shop owners and track owners. Since I used to race back in the 70's and then briefly in the 90's (also a mini-rider parent), I consider myself an expert. I have announced races, talked to parents and riders, huddled with track owners on decisions and published race reports to news outlets. Am I a part of this sport? Yes, in several capacities. Do motocross people at the local level know me? Yes.

What's the difference in my association in the two sports? In the NFL, I'm a nobody - a faceless voice in the crowd. In motocross racing, I'm a somebody - a participant. I belong. What makes the difference? RELATIONSHIP.

Are you involved in the kingdom of God? Does His Son, Jesus Christ know you, personally? Or are you just an "armchair theologian," a fan with opinions? Do you know ABOUT Jesus Christ, or do you KNOW Him personally?

It's one thing to study about the Bible, about God and learn what Jesus said and did. It's quite another to know Jesus personally because you have met Him. If the coach of the New Orleans Saints was having a party, entertaining players and other coaches, do you think I would be admitted if I showed up at the door? I don't think so. Furthermore, I wouldn't have the confidence to walk up and feel like I belonged.

What if God was holding a banquet? Would you have the confidence to walk up and be admitted? Would the host recognize you when you came to the door? Do you have a "ticket" for the kingdom of God?

If you do, rejoice. If not, here's how to get accepted into God's unending party in heaven. Realize your need for forgiveness. God is Holy and pure. All people are sinners. In our minds and hearts we have rebelled against God's perfect law. Ask God to forgive your sins. That's why Jesus died, to pay the penalty for sin. His shed blood was the payment for your rebellion. God accepts Jesus' payment because He was perfect and died as a substitute for you and me. By faith place your life in God's hands. He forgives you, cleanses your record and declares you "not guilty." He sends His Holy Spirit to live inside of you as a down payment and to help you live a pure life. Now you have power over sin and will live forever.

When God holds His judgment, your defense attorney, Jesus Christ will step forward and declare, "I know him. He gave me his life." You will be declared "not guilty" and invited to join the great banquet party of heaven for all eternity.

Thousands of years ago, people tried to know God by keeping His law. One day God sent a prophecy by Jeremiah seven centuries before the time of Christ. In this good news prediction, God promised to work in His people in a new way. Instead of knowing Him by exterior works of righteousness (keeping the law, bringing sacrificial animal and grain offerings), He would forgive them and place His Spirit within their hearts. There would be personal relationship. Read for yourself.

"This is the covenant I will make with the house of Israel after that time," declares the LORD. "I will put my law in their minds and write it on their hearts. I will be their God, and they will be my people. No longer will a man teach his neighbor, or a man his brother, saying, 'Know the LORD,' because they will all know me, from the least of them to the greatest," declares the LORD. "For I will forgive their wickedness and will remember their sins no more." (Jeremiah 31:33)

Scripture for the Day: *"Yet to all who received him, to those who believed in his name, he gave the right to become children of God—children born not of natural descent, nor of human decision or a husband's will, but born of God." (John 1:12-13)*

Quote for the Day: "Friendship is a single soul dwelling in two bodies." (Aristotle. Quoted in Diogenes Laertius, Lives and Opinions of Eminent Philosophers)

The author learning how to be a dive tender (apprentice) at Commercial Diver Training
in Houston, 1987.

113. As Green as the New Shoots of Spring

It was the winter of 1988. I had just graduated from dive school and had visions of high income, world travel and home-made respect. But I found myself working as a shop hand for Martech, a large diving company in Morgan City, Louisiana. I tried to get on as a dive tender, but there were plenty of tenders ahead of me. So I settled for working in the shop as an assistant to the maintenance mechanic to pay the bills. We re-built the dive compressors and other off-shore equipment divers used on the lay barges (laying pipelines).

My mechanical experience from wrenching my motocross bikes came in handy. I had already worked my way through dive school by making and breaking tow for a barge company on the river. (Lashing together those barges you see going down the Mississippi with steel cables) I already thought I was a pretty good deckhand the way I whipped my Buck knife out my homemade leather case like a gunslinger.

One day I was using a little gasoline motor to pump the oil out of a compressor. The motor was running so I didn't hear the shop supervisor come up behind me. While I was leaning over to check the fitting, he used a three-foot long screwdriver to ground me out against the spark plug on the pump. The shock surprised me so much I jumped a foot off the ground. The shop hands that were watching roared with laughter. The grizzled old diver said something to me I'll never forget, "Son you're as green as the new shoots of spring."

He was right. It took time to learn the dive business from the ground up. When I was finally called offshore I learned more, setting up and breaking down stations; pulling divers up and maintaining equipment. Washing out diver's wet-suits didn't fit into my dream. But I kept going out on jobs and when I was finally ready (after a couple years), I finally "broke out" as a diver.

I've seen something similar at the motocross track almost every race. A new rider invests in a motorcycle and gear. He practices a little and before his boots are broken in he thinks he's ready to race. He signs up to race with a nervous smile. He goes out to practice leaving most of his energy on the track. When the gate drops, his inexperience shows. By the second turn most of the pack is gone. If he's lucky he'll find someone else at his skill level at the back of the pack to race with before he gets tired out. When he pulls off the track of his first moto, one of two things happens.

He has accepted reality or he has an excuse. Usually it is a combination of both. He doesn't become a real contender until he has learned some lessons that can only be learned in the heat of battle with plenty of race time.

It's the same with our spiritual lives. At some point a person may decide to trust God with his life. He is excited about his new life. He has a new Bible, maybe a new church. He has new hope and new expectations, for himself and others. He sees some changes in himself and raises those expectations. If he's not careful he can become critical of others who are not doing as well as him in some areas. Then a situation arises where he fails. Reality sets in. He suffers a disappointment. He's not as spiritually strong as he thought. God is not as he thought. Doubt sets in. He's not as far along as he thought.

Has this ever happened to you? It's happened to me, more frequently than I'd like to admit. When this happens, God is forming His new life inside me. It takes time. It takes experience. Yes, it takes some failure to start getting it right. If we had perfect faith, it wouldn't be so hard. But we're human. So we are frail and mistake-prone. We go back and forth from thinking too highly of ourselves to feeling too lowly. God sends just the right dose of reality or encouragement, just when we NEED it (notice I didn't say WANT it).

If you have messed up, don't pile guilt on top of failure. You're just growing in your faith. You're learning to trust the living God, not religion. Real faith is birthed in pain. Before you can come to the new place of spiritual maturity, you must die to the old wrong ideas and habits. Before you can get in the end zone you must leave your comfort zone.

Be patient with yourself as your learn and grow. Rome wasn't built in a day. This book was not written in six months; one devotion, line upon line, page upon page, all born through my own painful trial and error of 49 years. Life is too short to judge yourself too harshly. Let yourself grow. One day it will all be over. Until then, forgive yourself, lighten up and trust God.

Scripture for the Day: *"My dear children, for whom I am again in the pains of childbirth until Christ is formed in you, how I wish I could be with you now..."* (The Apostle Paul to the church he planted in Galatia, Galatians 4:19-20)

Quote for the Day: "Why stay we on earth except to grow?" (Robert Browning, Cleon)

Michael T. Gleason's Mom watches and waits with her son for their turn to race at Fernwood MX.

Motocross Moms at Wildwood MX on race day. Kim Buratt in race gear, Kay Kirby on left and Paige Patterson sitting.

114. Raising Kids

An old story circulating on the internet is told of a little girl sitting in her Mom's lap. She looked up and saw some gray hair. "Mommie, you have some gray hairs." "Those are from the times you wouldn't listen to me, and made me fuss at you," her Mom lovingly said. Her daughter thought a moment than asked, "Then why does Grandma have a whole head full?"

If you are a parent, you have probably figured out that this is the most important and most difficult, yet joyful endeavor you will ever attempt in this life. It puts a strain on our health, finances, time, emotions and faith. Sometimes we wonder if we'll survive as we raise our kids. It is in their nature to test the limits. It is in our job description to enforce them. Clashes inevitably result. Though our children complain when we discipline them, deep down inside they are satisfied with the knowledge that we love them. They find security in boundaries.

My cousin's wife was cutting my hair this week. I asked her about their youngest child, Cole. Jennifer's face lit up when she thought about him, "Oh, he used the potty for the first time yesterday. We celebrated with candy. I called my Mom and Dad, my sister, my aunt and uncle ... " She went on and on about Cole.

A big celebration for using the potty? That's love. One day Cole will go through the "terrible two's"; start his first day of school; play in his first game; ride his first bicycle; take his first exam; catch his first fish; like his first girl-friend; express his first desire for independence; break his first curfew; get his first ticket; break his parents' heart; change jobs; get his heart broken and give Jennifer and David their first gray hairs. (We probably won't see hers since she's a hairdresser.)

But one day, if Cole is like most kids, he will return with his own family. David and Jennifer will hold their grand-child. Cole will get HIS first gray hair. Such is the cycle of life.

If you are struggling with being a parent or a child, relax. You aren't the only one dealing with the pressures of family. Keep the big picture in mind. Don't get blown away by the little battles. Raise the banner of God's love in your home and enjoy the little moments. Listen to the words of an old wise king who had seen it all:

I have seen the burden God has laid on men. He has made everything beautiful in its time. He has also set eternity in the hearts of men; yet they cannot fathom what God has done from beginning to end. I know that there is nothing better for men than to be happy and do good while they live. That everyone may eat and drink, and find satisfaction in all his toil—this is the gift of God. (Ecclesiastes 3:10-13)

Quote for the Day: "In your time; the innocence will fall away. In your time; the mission bells will toll. All along the corridors and river beds, there'll be sign, in your time. ...

And after all the dead ends and the lessons learned; after all the stars have turned to stone. They'll be peace across the great unbroken void, all benign, in your time. You'll be fine, in your time." (*In Your Time*, a song written by Bob Seger for his son Cole)

115. Right Handed

I really noticed it today. I've known it all along of course, but today I was surprised by how much I favor my right hand. I used it when I was cooking breakfast, taking vitamins, shaving and other routine activities. Then I used it when I was banging a stuck wheel off the lawnmower, unbolting the spare tire from my truck and rolling the tire into the shop. The only time I used my left hand was to help my right hand. There was nothing wrong with my left hand, it's just that it was kind of … forgotten. It was called on only when the right hand needed help.

Is your relationship with God like your right or left hand? Is He your first or last resort? Is He your constant companion and guide, or do you just "activate" Him when you can't handle something? Do you "raise your Christian flag" up front, when ethical or moral questions need answers? Or are you a "secret Christian?" Is God your leader, or do you have Him in reserve in case you need Him? Is He the engine or caboose?

When we ask Jesus into our lives, we are giving Him the controls. When we try to control things without His help we are increasing the risk of failure. If He is Lord over our lives then He is like our right hand (left for lefties). We lead with Him. We start with Him. We follow Him. We engage Him first under conflict. We keep our Christian "flags" up. Our answers to life questions come from His Word. We go to His provisions to satisfy our needs. We talk with Him every day before we get going. We trust Him first and foremost.

Are you like me? Do you INTEND to let Him lead, but get lazy and start depending on your own feelings, plans, schemes and selfish ideas? If so, how do we make Him our RIGHT hand?

Here's what I started doing today to remind me that God is first. I started using my left hand more. That does two things. First, it gets me out of my comfort zone. Second, it reminds me to let God be God in my daily routine.

Wow. I just caught a fly with my left hand! I'm on my way to a better day.

Scripture Verse for the Day: *"I have set the LORD always before me. Because he is at my right hand, I will not be shaken. Therefore my heart is glad and my tongue rejoices; my body also will rest secure..."* (Psalm 16:8-9)

Quote for the Day: "Judas heard all Christ's sermons." (Thomas Goodwin)

Cody Smiley at Gravity Alley MX in 2004, riding his new 450f in the money class.

The author at Turkey Creek MX in the early 70's after having crashed and re-entered the
race. Notice the broken rear fender.

116. Keep Your Head Up

When I am having a bad day and things aren't going my way, I have a little saying: "Keep making good decisions." It works. I just have to keep doing what is right, and my situation eventually improves. Saturday night, September 20, 2003 held two good examples of how "sticking with the plan" paid off for others.

The first example was the LSU tiger football team. They were hosting seventh-ranked Georgia at Tiger Stadium in Baton Rouge. We were listening to the game during practice at the race in Gonzales. LSU was having trouble moving the ball in the first half. They failed to get past Georgia's 46 yard-line until the final five minutes of the first half. Wide receiver Skylar Green had dropped three passes while quarterback Matt Mauck lost a fumble. Coach Nick Saban patted Mauck on the back after the fumble and said, "forget it, next time we score." To the team he said, "whatever happens, you play the next play, and you do it for 60 minutes." Georgia had penetrated LSU territory five times in the first half, but only came away with three points.

Despite the lack of success, the offensive lineman kept trying to open holes. The defense kept playing hard. The receivers kept running their routes. Finally it paid off when Mauck hit Green with a 31 yard pass on third and nine. Two plays later running back Shyrone Carey broke loose for a 21 yard touchdown. They held on to win the game, 17 -10.

Right when the game ended, about twenty miles down-river at our motocross race in Gonzales, the first class was lining up at the starting gate. A 17 year-old rider by the name of Cody Smiley was signed up to race in the money class. He had just moved up out of the novice class last month, and was not a favorite to win.

Cody got off to a poor start, watching the whole field get away from him. But he kept running his race. He kept making good decisions, even though things weren't going his way. Eventually, the leader crashed and two other riders' bikes broke down. Cody finished in second place.

The second moto it happened again. He got off to a poor start. Even a novice class rider, who was racing this class tonight, passed him. But he hung in there and rode hard. This time both leaders went down and Cody ended up winning the race!

During his post-race interview, I asked him what he'd like to say to those riders who are struggling. He answered, "just keep your head up, keep practicing, and you'll get good." That's not the whole story. Four years ago Cody watched his little sister recover from Leukemia. Two years ago he lost his mother in a car accident. Now he's won his first moto in the money class as a motocross racer.

Keep YOUR head up. Keep making good decisions. Things will change.

Scriptures of the Day: *"But as for you, be strong and do not give up, for your work will be rewarded."* (2 Chronicles 15:7)

"Let us not become weary in doing good, for at the proper time we will reap a harvest if we do not give up." (Galatians 6:9)

Quote for the Day: *"The end is not yet."* (Jesus in Matthew 24:6)

117. Simplify

Have you ever prayed about a certain issue over a period of days, then finally you understood, because the answer was right there; you just didn't see it? God may have used a family member, a friend, a song or a scripture. It just took you a few exposures to the answer before you recognized it.

This happened to me this week. I have been studying through the book of Matthew for my devotions lately. I kept coming to the same verse on different days. During the same period of time I had been praying for help in the way I was thinking. I had been in some confusion about some things. Since confusion doesn't come from God (Job 25:2; Rev. 21:4), I knew that He would help me clear it up.

Here's the verse from Matthew 6:22-24: *"The eye is the lamp of the body. If your eyes are good, your whole body will be full of light. But if your eyes are bad, your whole body will be full of darkness. If then the light within you is darkness, how great is that darkness!"*

It's not an easy verse to understand. Finally I figured out what He was trying to tell me. I have been too distracted lately with many things, some spiritual, most worldly. A few had to do with material possessions. The "eye" in the verse is a metaphor for our attitude. Our attitude, our "way of looking at the world" affects everything we think, do and say. The word for "good" means "undivided." A "divided eye" is like looking through the world with a pair of glasses with several layers of different colored lenses. Your sight would be "skewed" or "confused." If you took off those "divided" glasses and put on a set with one of rose color, you would see things through "rose-colored glasses."

So I understood that my attitude (glasses) was casting darkness and confusion into my soul. I read further in the chapter and learned how to get the right vision (glasses). Jesus said in verse 24 that *"you can't serve two masters."* He was referring to God and the world money system. If you turn your attention to one, you turn your back on the other. Jesus invited us to put our trust in Him.

In the following section (verses 25-32) He encourages us not to worry about things. Finally, in verse 33 He presents the focus (glasses) we should have, *"Seek first the Kingdom of God and His righteousness."*

So I asked Him to re-set my perspective (glasses) and the clouds of doubt and despair went away. The light of God drove out the darkness of confusion. I simplified. So I have a renewed vision (glasses) - pleasing Him. He will take care of all the rest.

Scripture for the Day: *"But seek first his kingdom and his righteousness, and all these things will be given to you as well."* (Matthew 6:33)

Quote for the Day: "There is a simplicity born of shallowness, and falsely so-called; and there is a simplicity which is the costly outcome of the discipline of mind and heart and will..." (Arthur Michael Ramsey, Archbishop of Canterbury. Quoted in James B. Simpson, The Hundredth Archbishop of Canterbury)

Nathan Davenport #7 and Blake Kennedy #806 choose different ruts in the Pro class at the AMA Championship qualifier at Gravity Alley in 2004.

First turn action at Down South MX. Chad Dubroc #226 leads Bryce Landry #294, Joseph Pizzuto #219 and Cory Rodriguez #117.

Jeremy Aitken #961 and Cody Smiley #42 commit to clear the high speed double at Holeshot MX.

118. The Real Thing

This is a typical situation for younger motocross racers who are still in school. Guys are sitting around at lunch or at recess or maybe after school. They are bragging about their exploits. It's a game of one upsmanship. You know the routine. It's male egos getting their exercise. But some are not telling the truth. Here's where real racing experience separates the racer from the poser. One young racer says something like, "I won a race Sunday. I beat Billy Sandwich AND Mark Mayonnaise. I crashed once when Hamhock 't-boned' me. But I got up and block passed him. In the 2nd moto I had to brake-check banana head. The trophy was this tall." He holds his hand near his shoulder.

"Oh yeah, I like that track," says Tommy. "One time when I raced there I got a flat, and still won the race." "Which one?" asks John. "Front, no back. Yea it was the back," replies Tommy. "What happened?" asks another boy. "The bike got squirrelly and kept sliding around. But I held on for the win," he finishes with a smile.

"I race," states Matt, a little too loudly. "Yeah, where?" Tommy tests. "Uhhh. All over. Mainly at Dirt Squirt MX," Matt replies thinking fast. "Which race?" asks John. "The uhhh mid-state race a few months ago," Matt sputters out. "There was no mid-state race there," corrects Billy racer. "We go there all the time. You don't race." The crowd of boys and a few girls look at Matt suspiciously. Matt makes his recovery, "I was out there with some friends and they told me it was a race. Anyway, I got on the track and hit the big double, you know the one in the middle?" Boys nod in agreement. "I cased it and almost went over the bars. Then made a run for the big tabletop. I cleared it the second try. Some other guys got on the track and raced with me, and I was on an 80, and they were on, like, 125's and 250's that were, you know, had kits in them. I stayed with em'." He's got their confidence, so he slows down. "I love motocross. I was probably the 2nd fastest guy there that day. I can't wait to go back."

"How about today? After school?" asks Tommy to call his bluff. "Oh, well I have homework today," answers Matt. "I'll help you," chides Mary coyly with a smile. "Yeah, we'll all go to the track, the girls can help us finish the homework in the pits, and we can ride!" announces Tommy. "I have an extra bike you can ride," nudges John. "Well, I don't think..." "What's a matter, you said you love motocross and ride all the time?" asks Jane. "I just don't have my own gear yet," states Matt. "That's ok, we share boots and helmets all the time," waves Tommy. "We'll hook you up."

They get to the track. Matt has been telling stories about racing all the way there, along with the others. When they unload and get dressed in, Tommy offers a bike to Matt. "No, you go first," Matt decides. "Ok." Tommy takes a few hot laps, looking good. John gets on the track and sails around faster and faster clearing all the jumps, railing the turns, blitzing the whoops. They come in and take off their helmets. "Here Matt, you can use my bike," John says. By now Matt is confident, because they made it look so easy. He gets on the bike, buckles his helmet, but has trouble starting it. "No gas! Don't turn the throttle to start this 4 stroke." John explains to Matt.

John starts it for Matt then hands it to him. Matt takes off, almost stalling it because he let the clutch out too fast. He gets on the track and putts along without shifting. He is sitting back on the seat and his head is bobbing with every bump. Other riders are flying by him. He swerves off to the side in front of a speeding rider behind him who looks back and yells at him.

Matt is obviously not a racer, nor a rider. He putts around a little faster. He hits a small jump and almost goes over when he loses his balance. He starts imitating the other riders by putting his foot out, but way too early for the turn. He never uses the front brake. He accelerates long after he has straightened out for the next straight-a-way, but lets off way too early and coasts to the turn. The kids are roaring with laughter. They know a goon when they see one. Matt pulls into the pits. "This track is hard!" Matt spits out. "This is the easiest track on the circuit," John corrects, shaking his head.

Matt knew the lingo, could talk a good game, maybe even ridden on a track before, but he was no motocross racer. He had watched it on TV, read about it in the magazines, maybe even been to a few races as a spectator. But he had never really experienced motocross racing as a racer. You couldn't tell back at school while they were talking about it. The only way to tell was to watch him actually get on the track and ride.

Jesus said life is like that. There are those who talk a good game of religion, but they don't KNOW Him. They know the Christian clichés and some scriptures, but don't ACT on it. They may have attended church, but they are not CONNECTED into the TRUE VINE, which is Jesus Christ Himself (John 15:1-8). We know we are connected with Jesus as our life produces good fruit.

Jesus warns us about people like that, especially if they pass themselves off as teachers. We are not to become judges who condemn other people. *"Do not judge, or you too will be judged. For in the same way you judge others, you will be judged, and with the measure you use, it will be measured to you."* (Jesus in Matt. 7:1-2)

We should, however, watch for fruit in the lives of the people we imitate or follow.

Watch out for false prophets. They come to you in sheep's clothing, but inwardly they are ferocious wolves. By their fruit you will recognize them. Do people pick grapes from thorn bushes, or figs from thistles? Likewise every good tree bears good fruit, but a bad tree bears bad fruit. (Jesus in Matt. 7:15-17)

So how do you know if you are a true believer in the Lord Jesus Christ? Listen to Jesus' continuing words in his message: *"Not everyone who says to me, 'Lord, Lord,' will enter the kingdom of heaven, but only he who* does *the will of my Father who is in heaven."* (Jesus in Matt. 7:21)

The key word is "DO". Not that doing good things gets you into heaven, but when you really trust Jesus, you will enter into a relationship of Love, and want to please him. You won't become perfect, just forgiven. Your life will begin to change as you *DO* what pleases Him.

Many people can pass themselves as Christians when there is no trouble or hardship in their lives. But the real test of faith comes when the storms of life blow. When trials and tribulations come into our lives and blow away the false gods we WERE depending on, we are forced to face reality. Do our lives fall apart under fire? Or do we depend on the God who is bigger than any trial or hardship? We can only know that in the heat of the battle.

Scripture for the Day:

*Therefore everyone who hears these words of mine and puts them into practice is like a wise man who built his house on the rock. The rain came down, the streams rose, and the winds blew and beat against that house; yet it did not fall, because it had its foundation on the rock. (*Jesus' invitation after His Sermon on the Mount" in Matt. 7:24-25)

119. Doubt Your Doubts

Are you plagued by doubts? Do you believe in God, believe His word, yet sometimes wonder? You know, "is it really true?" "Does He really know me?" "Is He really hearing my prayer?" "Is He really going to rescue me?" "Am I really a believer?"

You don't have to deal with doubts, unless you are human. Ok, all human beings raise their hands. Yep, that's us. We will ALL have doubts. Everyone else can leave the room now.

Seriously, doubts are attached to our mood swings, the circumstances we find ourselves in, what someone says, etc. So doubts WILL come to even the strongest believer. When I'm not feeling good, doubts come. When I don't get a prayer answered the way I wanted, doubts come. When I give in to my selfish nature and do or say something I shouldn't, doubts come to me. I need an anchor when my life gets rough. I need something that is changeless in a changing world. That's when I find solace in God's Word.

I need "child-like" faith. You know how young children believe what you say? That's simple trust. That's what we need to carry us during times of doubt. Our faith becomes our anchor to keep us from being blown away.

The next time you start hearing that whiny voice in your mind that leads to self-pity, discouragement, rejection, or doubt about God; battle it by saying :

"I doubt that, because my God says... (insert scripture)."

"My God has NEVER lied."

"The Bible says... (insert scripture)."

Some might argue, "But why does God let me have doubt?" Because He doesn't control our thoughts. We do. He doesn't "take every thought into captivity." We are instructed to *take every thought into captivity to the obedience of Christ."* (2 Corinthians 10:5)

Even Jesus' closest disciples had doubts. Jesus said John the Baptist was the greatest of all men, yet when John was in prison, he doubted; and he was Jesus' cousin! Thomas was known for his doubts. When the disciples were all excited because the risen Jesus had appeared to them, Thomas said, "I won't believe unless I touch his wounds for myself." Jesus came to Thomas at his point of need. He'll come to you at your point of need.

So next time you are being tempted with doubt, read the Bible. Memorize scripture. Believe it. Use it against doubt. Look around and see God at work in the lives of others. Remember when He helped you in the past. He never leaves Himself without a witness. When doubt comes - DOUBT IT! Then replace it with scriptural truth.

Scripture for the Day: *"I waited patiently for the LORD; he turned to me and heard my cry. He lifted me out of the slimy pit, out of the mud and mire; he set my feet on a rock and gave me a firm place to stand."* (Psalm 40:1-2)

Related Scriptures to fight doubt:
    Genesis 17:15-21; 18:10-14: Nothing is too hard for God.
    Matthew 11:1-6: Jesus helped remove John's doubts.
    James 1:5-8: What doubt does to your faith.
    Romans 1:20: No excuse for unbelief.
    Acts 14:15-18: God never leaves Himself without a witness.

120. Little Drummer Boy

I love Christmas time. So many people celebrating Christ's birth for so long. Nowadays it starts right after Thanksgiving. There are many different motivations and ideas about what we are celebrating, but the core message is still there for those who want to understand - the birth of the Christ-child, sent by God to save us from our sin.

The airwaves are filled with songs of hope, joy, grace and divine love. One of these such songs is "The Little Drummer Boy." Many artists have performed their unique interpretation of it. A couple of my favorites are playing on the radio as I write: Ray Charles and Bob Seger. What makes this song so popular? It's not even in the Bible - or is it? What message does this mythical story deliver that touches so many hearts? Shall I tell you, or do you want to sort through the lyrics for yourself? Ok, lyrics first. See if you arrive at the same conclusion as me. Be careful, you may have to wipe a tear of joy as you read this fictional story.

LITTLE DRUMMER BOY

Come, they told me.(pa-rum-pa-pum-pum)
A newborn king to see. (pa-rum-pa-pum-pum)
Our finest gifts we bring; (pa-rum-pa-pum-pum)
to lay before the king. (pa-[rum-pa-pum-pum x 3])
So, to honor him; (pa-rum-pa-pum-pum)
when we come.

Little baby; (pa-rum-pa-pum-pum)
I am a poor boy, too; (pa-rum-pa-pum-pum)
I have no gifts to bring; (pa-rum-pa-pum-pum)
that's fit to give a king. (pa-[rum-pa-pum-pum x 3])
Shall I play for you; (pa-rum-pa-pum-pum)
on my drum?

Mary nodded. (pa-rum-pa-pum-pum)
The ox and lamb kept time. (pa-rum-pa-pum-pum)
I played my drum for him. (pa-rum-pa-pum-pum)
I played my best for him. (pa-[rum-pa-pum-pum x 3])
Then he smiled at me; (pa-rum-pa-pum-pum)
me and my drum.

(Written by Katherine Davis, Henry Onorati and Harry Simeone)

Message of the song: We may not possess the wealth, power, or wisdom of the wise men who visited the baby Jesus with gifts. All we have is what we have. Is it good enough for the baby Jesus? Yes, Jesus says, that's all I want - your heart and service. So we give him what we have, no matter how small or trivial it may seem. It's a holy exchange between us and God. We give back to God what we have received, as an act of love. For the mythical drummer boy it was a drum. That was all he had at his disposal. God had given it to him. Now he uses it to serve God. He played "His BEST" for Him. Jesus smiled and received the gift of love.

My drum is this laptop. So to honor him, a-rap-a-tap-tap. I play my best for him a- rap-a-tap-tap. Words of truth that He has revealed to me appear on the screen. There, I feel it in my heart - the joy of giving to Him and His acceptance. Warmth moves from the keyboard, through my arms, into my spirit, then back to my mind and emotions. Now, He smiles at me, a-rap-a-tap-tap, me and my laptop.

What is your drum? Will you give your best in service to your maker? Will you allow His love to flow through you into the lives of people around you? Will you use your gifts and abilities for His glory?

And there were shepherds living out in the fields nearby, keeping watch over their flocks at night. An angel of the Lord appeared to them, and the glory of the Lord shone around them, and they were terrified. But the angel said to them, "Do not be afraid. I bring you good news of great joy that will be for all [emphasis mine] the people. Today in the town of David a Savior has been born to you; he is Christ the Lord. This will be a sign to you: You will find a baby wrapped in cloths and lying in a manger." Suddenly a great company of the heavenly host appeared with the angel, praising God and saying, "Glory to God in the highest, and on earth peace to men on whom his favor rests." When the angels had left them and gone into heaven, the shepherds said to one another, "Let's go to Bethlehem and see this thing that has happened, which the Lord has told us about." So they hurried off and found Mary and Joseph, and the baby, who was lying in the manger. When they had seen him, they spread the word concerning what had been told them about this child, and all who heard it were amazed at what the shepherds said to them. But Mary treasured up all these things and pondered them in her heart. The shepherds returned, glorifying and praising God for all the things they had heard and seen, which were just as they had been told. (Luke 2:8-20)

121. Necessary Investments

I was rebuilding the motor on a Chevy Lumina I got in a trade for my old pick-up truck. I struggled for a long time with a couple of the bolts on the a/c motor mount bracket. Finally I came to the conclusion that more leverage was needed than my ratchet could give. I went to my neighborhood auto parts store (they know me well in there), and priced a 24", ½ drive breaker bar - 20 dollars! But I needed it to remove the bolts. I finally made the plunge and bought the tool. I got it home, put the extension and 15 mm socket on it, and... presto! The bolts loosened. I justified the expense by telling myself it would be another tool I could hand down to my son one day. I resisted the temptation to put it back in the package and return it. It turned out to be a good decision, because I used it several more times before the job was over.

Fast forward two weeks. My daughter lives in Baton Rouge where she attends college. The tires on her Camaro were worn down to nubs. The 16" wheels that came on the car were a special size that, you guessed it, cost much more. Should I make the investment? Did I really have a choice? It was necessary. Like the breaker bar, I bit the bullet and made the investment. Yesterday when she pulled up for an unexpected visit I examined her new tires. I realized that the $450 was a good investment for her road safety and our peace of mind.

Sometimes we have to make a "necessary investment." We may not get the instant gratification in return, but over the long haul it will pay off. Sending kids to college, buying insurance, buying a car or house, spending time with kids (even someone else's kids), giving a favor, overlooking an insult, taking vitamins, exercising, resisting temptation, pacing yourself, reading a good book, attending church, being a peace-maker, placing the phone call, writing the note, or doing good deeds - some sacrifices are worth making.

Is there anyone or anything you should invest yourself in today? It may be a necessary investment.

Scripture for the Day: *"Give, and it will be given to you. A good measure, pressed down, shaken together and running over, will be poured into your lap. For with the measure you use, it will be measured to you."* (Jesus in Luke 6:38)

Quote for Day: *"Sow your seed in the morning, and at evening let not your hands be idle, for you do not know which will succeed, whether this or that, or whether both will do equally well."* (Ecclesiastes 11:6)

List possible future investments:

122. Resolving Personal Conflicts

Have you ever had a disagreement with someone? Have you ever just avoided them and let it fester? Have you noticed that chasm between you and them seemed to get wider; so wide that no one was able to jump across and restore the relationship? Do you want a secret to restoring the relationship? Are you tired of these questions and are ready for answers?

I stumbled across this secret years ago, and have used it many times (not as many times as I should). Rick Warren coined a word for it that he uses in his life-changing book, "The Purpose Driven Life." The word is "ventilate vertically." In other words, when you are trying to restore a damaged or broken relationship with someone, you ventilate to God first.

Here's a few sample prayers: "God I want you to prepare the heart of so and so," or "God reveal to me what I did wrong," or "God please show me what to do and say to them," or "Please restore this relationship, and show me what to do." Basically, just cry out to God how you feel. Be honest. He's big enough to take it. Just be ready to allow Him to work on your end as He works on their end. There are probably unmet needs or unrealistic expectations that caused the rift between you in the first place.

Many needs can only be met by God, not by people. So as you pray and open your heart for God's "hotfix" (to borrow an internet term), you are being prepared to talk to the other person. Here's the bonus: God is already preparing them as well. Here's the caution: they may not respond to God's preparation. Here's the chance: they may need more time to absorb and respond, even after you have extended the olive branch. But that's their freedom, their realm of responsibility. You can only work your "side of the net" and wait for them to return your serve.

Is there someone you need to reach out to today? Don't allow anger or resentment to turn into bitterness and take root - it will destroy you. Someone once said that "bitterness is the only poison we drink hoping the other person will die." Take the first step, ventilate vertically, pray. Then make contact at your first chance, whether by phone call, e-mail, card, letter or visit. Leave the rest to God. You'll be glad you did. So will those around you.

Scriptures for the day: *"God blesses those who work for peace. They will be called children of God."* (Matthew 5:9 N.L.T.)

"Do everything possible on your part to live in peace with everyone." (Romans 12:18)

123. Discovering a Man's Heart

Ladies, can I have a few moments alone with guys? Thank you.

Guys, why are you alive? What is your purpose in life? If you can answer these questions with conviction, you have found the key to happiness. We are each uniquely created. There is no one else with our DNA; our combinations of strengths, talents, knowledge, ideas, interests, abilities, experiences, tolerances, passions, circle of friends and family. Every failure or success we've had to this point was a building block for today. Whatever "lights our fire" or "fuels our interest" is an indicator of our purpose.

John Eldridge in his book, *Wild at Heart,* challenges men to recover the wildness of their heart and find their mission. He believes that, "locked away in the heart of every man are three main desires: a battle to fight, an adventure to live and a beauty to rescue. Until a man discovers these three, his life is incomplete."

Let's look at each one.

I. The Battle to Fight.

The "battle to fight" is ingrained in a boy's nature; the evidence clear as they "whack at balls," "race bicycles," "carve guns out of graham crackers," and "wrestle on the floor." It is placed deep in the heart of every male. He then must choose the time, place and reason to fight. Without this fierceness, who would have stopped Hitler, slavery, pirates, the spread of communism, smallpox, Saddam Hussein, or any other threat to our world? We still need new warriors for such threats as: AIDS, racism, illegal drugs, terrorism, crime and a host of others. Every man wants to be a hero. The recent success of blockbuster movies like *Braveheart, Saving Private Ryan*, *Gladiator* and *The Patriot* are evidence that honor is an important part of who we are. Ask a general why so many men are willing to follow him to certain death. It's not about their paycheck, blind obedience or even geography. If the cause is just, a healthy male will take the risk, for the cause and for the man on his right and his left. God made us that way.

II. An Adventure to Live.

An "adventure to live" is also ingrained in every male. Why are sports so popular? Boats? Airplanes? Motorcycles? Camping? Hunting? Fishing? Travel? As a teacher I planned all year for the "trip of the summer." One year I loaded my 700 Yamaha with camping gear, put my 13 year-old son on the back, and along with my Dad on his Goldwing, camped our way from New Orleans to Pennsylvania for two weeks. The following summer, we toured Northern California with the same camping gear, same bike, excitement and sense of purpose. The trip met a deep need in our souls.

In the movie, *Fast and Furious*, actor Vin Diesel had a famous line that explained why he drag-raced. Any racer can relate to his statement, "for 6 seconds, I am alive." The challenge of an adventure sparks our hearts to new life. For some, the adventure may be extreme sports, racing, diving, sailing, flying, exploring, while others enjoy investments, exploring the internet, playing video games, re-building cars, or old houses. Sometimes, though, this desire can become dark and turn into an extra-marital affair, dealing drugs, gang activity, or other crimes. Reality TV has shown that the desire for adventure is alive. Men yearn to be tested, to see if they have what it takes.

III. A Beauty to Rescue.

Eldridge's final point involves women. Men have an innate desire to "rescue a beauty." Romeo had his Juliet, King Arthur, Gwenevere, Robin had Maid Marian. After all, where would Indiana Jones or James Bond be without their ladies. They fought with them, and <u>for</u> them. Women have the desire to "be rescued," "fought for," or "wanted." To men, there is nothing more inspiring than a beautiful woman. She'll cause him to "slay the dragon," "storm the castle," or "take on rush hour traffic every morning." Some men may even take a shower, brush their teeth or shop for clothes to impress her.

It's not enough to "be a hero," but to "be a hero to someone," the woman he loves. Chivalry is not dead; it can't die because it is deep in the heart of every man. For some it just needs to be re-discovered, un-covered, or activated.

Conclusion

Bottom line? God has created a certain wildness in the heart of every man. Our modern culture has tried to down-play, cover-up, emasculate and ridicule masculinity. They have tried to blur the roles between the sexes, pit them against each other and confuse our children. What we need to do is turn to our creator (the one who invented sex, passion, strength, and love). He's the one who gave us the adventurous spirit, the desire to live, survive and defend. God loves to rescue us in our times of need. He's done it all throughout the Bible and history. He has placed this strength and desire in the heart of every man.

Eldridge also cautions against taking these desires too far: violence for the sake of violence, adventure into the wrong places and worshiping or abusing women. Each man must choose his battles, engage his adventure and love his woman. Older men must guide this powerful energy in teenagers whose urges sometimes far outweigh their maturity and self-control. And we don't need to just tell them to "sit down and shut up," (although there is a time and place for that, too); or it will come out in other ways. Our deepest needs can only be met by God, in His way. Once we make our peace with God, He will take us on an exciting journey where we will ultimately find ourselves.

Scripture for the Day: *"Delight yourself in the Lord, and He will give you the desires of your heart."* (Psalm 37:4)

Quote for the Day: "Man's spirit is like a kite, which rises by means of those very forces which seem to oppose its rise; the tie that joins it to the earth, the opposing winds of temptations, and the weight of earth-born affections which it carries with it into the sky." (Coventry Patmore, *The Rod, the Root and the Flower*)

Tyler Hancock in the middle of a "Heel Clicker"
over the finish line jump at Wildwood MX

Blake Thompson #933 and Kory Bond experience a little
wildness during a race at Wildwood Motocross in 2004.

Daniel "Boone" Crayton glances over at his competitors
on the finish line jump en route to victory at Holeshot MX.

124. Free Money!

The first time I saw this phrase was August 2002 in Ponca City, Oklahoma. We were in town for the National Amateur Motocross Championships held annually by the NMA. "Free Money" was on sign outside a bank. Obviously they were trying to entice customers to come inside and sign up for something. Is there really anything of value (like money) that is free? If there is we'd like to know about it, right? The answer is - yes. There are some valuable things that are free. You've heard the old saying, "the best things in life are free." Here's a few freebies most all of us can enjoy today: life, good advice, laughter, beauty, forgiveness, friendship, freedom to choose, air to breath, water to drink, rest, sight, sound, feelings, opportunities, hope, faith and love.

Our creator has given us all some free gifts. The best and longest lasting of his free gifts is available at no cost to us. It did cost Him, but He offers it to us at no charge. This gift is eternal life. It is a new kind of life that starts when you receive His Son, Jesus Christ into your heart. I'm still trying to sort out the implications of this, but I know, it was the best gift I have ever received. Here are a few benefits.

1. Forgiveness of all my past mistakes, failures and sins
2. Light of truth that fills my dark soul
3. A future filled with meaning and purpose
4. A free pass into heaven
5. A right relationship with God - His acceptance, approval, protection and family name
6. The Holy Spirit living in me as comforter, encourager and teacher
7. Power over sinful desires
8. Victory over death
9. A friend that sticks closer than a brother - Jesus
10. An on-going construction project to renovate my mind, heart and soul
11. A new love for others
12. Updates into my mind of the wisdom and meaning of life

Yes, the best thing in life is free. Jesus took the punishment for our sins when He died on the cross over 2,000 years ago. He has already paid the price for our salvation. All we have to do is receive it. Sound too good to be true? That's why many people won't receive it. Read these scriptures for yourself, and go rent *The Passion* movie by Mel Gibson. You may get a new perspective on life.

Ephesians 2:8-10; Matthew 19:25-26; Romans 3:8-23; Hebrews 7:25; Galatians 5:1; John 3:16-18.

Quote for the Day: "'It is not my good works that save me. It is not my experiences that give me peace. I rest simply and solely on the merits of Jesus Christ,' said a dying soldier on the African Veldt." ("His Merits" Quoted from John Ritchie, *500 Gospel Sermon Illustrations*)

"He is our peace." (Ephesians 2:14)

Paige Patterson and her son Chad. His Dad, Danny, used to race when he was younger, and again when he was older until the injury bug bit.

The author (right) and his son embark on a day ride together.

125. "You ARE the Chosen One"

One of the greatest men in history suffered from doubt, discouragement and depression. His name? Winston Churchill. His game? Saving England from destruction during WW II. He had been prepared for destiny through many experiences, including discouragement and failure.

He lost his family fortune in the American Stock Market crash. After years of service in high level cabinet positions, England voted him out of office in the 1930's. He took the rejection personally. He suffered with bouts of depression, calling it, another "visit from the black dog."

But when England was in the darkness of the war, they turned back to Churchill and voted him in as Prime Minister. He was the right man for the job. He was a former soldier who had come up through the ranks of the army. He had studied warfare, particularly certain battles between England and Germany. He had served as Sea Admiral, Minister of Munitions, President of the Board of Trade, Home Secretary, Chancellor of the Exchequer, Secretary of State for War, Minister of Defense, and finally Prime Minister. He was one of the few voices in leadership warning Chamberlain (then Prime Minister) not to appease Hitler in the early days of his intimidating land grab.

In the darkest part of the War, when his nation was "on the ropes," barely surviving the nightly bombing raids from the Luftwaffe, Winston Churchill made one of his famous speeches that rallied the spirit of England.

What is our policy? I will say it is to wage war, by sea, land and air, with all our might and with all the strength that God can give us… What is our aim? I can answer in one word: It is victory, victory at all costs, victory in spite of all terror, victory, however long and hard the road may be; for without victory, there is no survival." (Quoted from *Churchill, a Biography*, by Roy Jenkins). [another Roy Jenkins]

He is best known for his famous speech in which he told the world by radio that they would "Never, never, never give up," with the guttural tenacity of a bull dog.

Later Churchill was to say that "all the bad in his life, was but preparation for his hour of leadership on the world stage…." (Ibid)

Have you ever had doubts about whether you were the best person for the job? Have you ever wondered why God put you with this spouse, these kids, this family? Have you ever thought, "There are so many other people that would be better suited for this than me?" Have you felt like a failure? I have good news for you. You are not a failure. God didn't make any failures or mistakes. We Do fail, but that doesn't make us a failure. We do fall, but we <u>can</u> get back up and try again - if we want to.

YOU are the right man to be father of your children. You have the right DNA, personality, experiences, failures, emotional make-up, body type, knowledge and wisdom. God put <u>you</u> there and gave <u>you</u> those children. You may not be perfectly wise yet; you may have a lot to learn; you have room for growth - but God put <u>you</u> there. No one is better suited for your family than you; not Dr. Phil, not James Dobson, not coach Bill Parcells or Bill Belecheck, not Dr. Spock or some movie star or sports hero. <u>YOU</u> are the man for your situation.

Ladies, <u>you</u> are the woman for your family. God has put <u>you</u> together just right to be the wife and mother of those children. <u>You</u> have what they need. If you use God's resources, you will lack nothing. Even if your family traded you for Dr. Laura, Laura Bush, Opra Winfrey, Ruth Bell Graham, Celine Dione or even Joan of Arc, they could not make a better you. Be encouraged that God designed <u>you</u> specifically for your family.

Don't let careless comments, critical in-laws, know-it-all authors, air-brushed perfected models, edited talk show hosts, or big screen stars plant doubt in your mind. Don't give in to kids who are trying to manipulate you into "caving into their wishes," or "wiggling out of their consequences." Stand your ground when you are right. Know that God created you for this time, place and people. Strengthen your resolve from God's Word, and head right back into battle armed with truth. Life is short, pray hard, don't give up.

Here's some "want to" medicine for your soul. Read and absorb these truths:

• All of are imperfect and make mistakes. (Romans 3:23)
• God loves us and knows all about us, even down to the hairs on our heads. (Luke 21:18)
• God will meet our needs. (Matthew 6:25-33)
• God knew you before you were born. (Isaiah 1:4)
• God purposely placed you in this time and place in history. (Acts 17:26-27)
• You were chosen to train your children. (Gen. 1:28)

- God can bring good from the bad that happens. (Romans 8:28)
- Trials bring growth, maturity and character. (James 1:12)
- We learn and grow from suffering. (Romans 5:3-5)
- Jesus will help us in our suffering. (Hebrews 2:11-18)
- We can learn from failures. (Isaiah 42:18-25)
- Defeat can be turned into victory. (Philippians 1:15-18)
- Everyone gets depressed at times. (John 16:33)

Quote for the Day: "The day may dawn when fair play, love for one's fellow man, respect for justice and freedom, will enable tormented generations to march forth serene and triumphant from the hideous epoch in which we have to dwell. Meanwhile, never flinch, never weary, never despair." (Sir Winston Churchill as quoted in Gilbert, Winston S. Churchill, VIII)

Johnny Fuller works on Dustin Manuel's bike while the rest of the group is inside partying.

Former Pro Racer Bobby Handy invests time in a group of young racers at G2G camp.

D.J. Cortez takes the lead at Kentwood MX. He once stopped in the middle of a race at Holeshot MX, threw down his bike and went over to help another rider pinned under his bike.

126. "Brother's Keeper"

One of my heroes is Rich Mullins. This singer/songwriter has penned such beautiful praise and worship songs as "Our God is an Awesome God," "Sing Your Praise to the Lord" and "I Believe," among others. He lived what he believed. In the final years of his life, he was living under a vow of poverty with a poor Indian tribe to bring the gospel of Jesus Christ as a missionary. One of his last music videos was "Brother's Keeper," which was shot on location in that Indian village with the people he loved and lived with. Tragically, he died when a jeep overturned with him in it a short time later.

This song, "Brother's Keeper," is on my heart many times as I travel back and forth to races with the people I love most outside of my family - motocross racers. One day I'll sing it to them. This song is dedicated to those racers and families who put their beer can behind their back, or put out their cigarettes when I come walking up. Listen to the words:

Now the plumber's got a drip in his spigot, The mechanic's got a clank in his car, and the preacher's thinkin' thoughts that are wicked, and the lover's got a lonely heart. My friends ain't the way I wish they were, they are just the way they are,

(Chorus)
And I will be my brother's keeper, not the one who judges him.
I won't despise him for his weakness, I won't regard him for his strength. I won't take away his freedom, I will help him learn to stand. And I will, I will be my brother's keeper.

Now, this roof has got a few missing shingles, but at least we've got ourselves a roof, And they say that she's a fallen angel; Oh I wonder if she recalls when she last flew? There's no point in pointing fingers, Unless you're pointing to the truth.

(Chorus)
And I will be my brother's keeper, not the one who judges him.
I won't despise him for his weakness, I won't regard him for his strength. I won't take away his freedom, I will help him learn to stand. And I will, I will be my brother's keeper. (Fade)

Scripture for the Day: *"Therefore as God's chosen people, holy and dearly loved, clothe yourselves with compassion, kindness, humility, gentleness and patience. Bear with each other and forgive whatever grievances you may have against one another. Forgive as the Lord has forgiven you. And over all these virtues put on love, which binds them all together in perfect unity."* (Colossians 3:12-14)

Tanner Leger looks over at his Mom as she celebrates his finish at Holeshot MX.

127. Is the puddle half-full or half-empty?

So the big race was rained out this weekend. Many riders were looking forward to testing their skill, motorcycles and gear against the competition and the track. Now they can't - not this weekend anyway. Is it an occasion to whine, pout, or stew? Is it a lost weekend?

For those who take the position that circumstances are random and without meaning or purpose, this weekend might be a washout. But, for those who trust in a loving God who is overseeing His creation, this rain is an opportunity. The opportunity comes in the form of spending some quality down-time with our families. How about the Dad who has been working hard all week to pay for those motorcycles, parts and gear? He probably went directly from the stress of making a living, to preparing the race machinery. Maybe Mom went right from her weekday pressures, to preparing the food, clothes and other pit support. Maybe one person is trying to prepare everything. Maybe the racer has been working hard all week in school, looking forward to racing and now is disappointed. It's a rain-out. Is that bad or good?

Perhaps the rain is a blessing - not just to the environment, but to the creatures. Scientific studies have proven what God has already commanded; we need a day of rest. Our adrenal system needs to re-charge. Our brains need to re-set. Our bodies need to recuperate. Our spirits need refreshment. We need to re-orient ourselves to our maps. We need to glance at the bigger picture, even meditate on it. Our batteries need to re-charge. Who are we? Who is most important to us? What is our purpose? Why are we living? Are we on the right track to meet our life-goals? Is there anything we need to change today that will bring us back on track?

So the race has been called. Maybe that means we've been given a gift; a time to rest. Maybe even an opportunity to go to church.

The puddles outside are half-full.

Scripture for the Day: *"No one was at war with him during those years, for the Lord gave him rest."* (About King David in 2 Chronicles 14:6)

Quote for the Day: "The real equation is not Peace = satisfied feeling, but Peace = willed abandonment." (Evelyn Underhill, *The Letters of Evelyn Underhill*)

Instructor Tad Cotinie takes the students for a walk of the track to discuss lines at G2G camp in the spring of 2004.

Race Tech Mechanic Shay Racca (measuring rear suspension) gives lots of free advice to the kids.

128. Following My Lines

One Sunday morning I was riding my motorcycle through the country roads of south Louisiana on the way to a motocross race. Suddenly I noticed another motorcycle in my rear view mirror. He was following me and watching the lines I used as I negotiated the road. As I dipped inside, he dipped inside. When I turned left, he turned left. When I accelerated around a sweeping turn, so did he. He was shadowing my every move for a few miles.

Motorcycle racers know about this. Whether it is in practice or during the race, sometimes a competitor comes up behind you and "watches your lines." When you become aware of this there are several choices: One, you can use your fastest lines to try to shake the follower off your tail. Two, you can pull over and let the rider by, then follow his lines. Three, you can show the rider some false lines. Four, you can "brake check" the rider, sending a message to back off or pass. Or you can ignore him and stay within your own race. What strategy you use depends largely on the situation. For instance, is it during a race, or are we just playing? Is the rider much faster? Is he a teammate or foe? Do I want him to see my lines?

What does this have to do with parenting? Have you heard the saying, "Our children do what we do, not what we say?" They are following our lines. There are always watching, studying and learning. Though they may not choose to follow our example, we will affect their perception of the world and can influence their way of thinking. My children are now grown and I've seen them choose some of my good lines and bad. It hurts when they make bad choices - me and them. Ultimately they choose for themselves and bear the responsibilities and consequences for their choices.

Early that morning when the guy on the motorcycle was following my lines, he eventually made the pass, and with a friendly wave was gone. One day, when they are ready, our children will make the pass, and with a wave they will disappear over the next hill to find their own highways. Until then, may God give us strength and wisdom to choose our lines carefully.

Scripture for the Day: *"Sons are a heritage from the Lord, children a reward from Him. Like arrows in the hands of a warrior are sons born in one's youth. Blessed is the man whose quiver is full of them."* (Psalm 127:3-5a)

Quote for the Day: "It is easier for a father to have children than for children to have a real father." (Pope John XXIII)

List children to pray for:

129. Losing a job.

Have you ever lost your job? Whether it's your fault, the company's fault, the economy's fault or just circumstances – it happens to the best of us. Sometimes life is just not fair. To make a successful rebound we must pursue two priorities: We must put our faith in God and look for new opportunities. The first is most important because it gives us peace, stability and direction. Direction is important because not every open door is the one meant for us.

Looking around for the new opportunity is the second priority which hooks us up with our new career path. Perhaps it is time to turn a hobby or passion into a profession. If you have been dabbling in a hobby, you have gained knowledge and insight into that discipline that others can benefit from. Maybe you were being prepared for this all along. What looked like a crisis to you is really an opportunity in disguise. The Chinese word for "crisis" means "dangerous winds," (dangerous opportunity) which means the sailor can now embark on a new journey.

Billy Stranahan lost his job in 2003 as an electrical engineer. He turned a passion into a new career path while lesser men would be sitting around whining. He hooked up with Jeff Hinds of Hinds Performance Motorsports in Columbus, the oldest Kawasaki/Yamaha dealer in Ohio. They found a neglected yellow Ducati and started tinkering with it. Then they took it to the 2004 AHRMA/AMA Vintage Bike Days race at Mid-Ohio to compete with other road racers. In his own words Billy described the events leading up to the big race:

> The bike's been in a garage for about 2 ½ years. We just pulled it out of the garage about a month ago and decided we were gonna come out here and race it, so we started getting ready. We dropped the drain plug for the oil and found metal shavings in the oil, so we cracked the side cases and found a thrust washer that had exploded... before it got put up, I guess. We ended up having to replace the clutch basket and a thrust washer. We tried to get it running, but couldn't until 1:00 A.M. Friday of practice day; came out and got about 20 laps of practice on it and just got lucky with everything on it. We never changed the fork oil, shock setting. It was a street bike, not a race bike and it worked well. It's a 2000 996 Ducati.

He won Saturday's BOT (Battle of Twins) class, surprising the regular leaders. In Sunday's race he took a close second in the SOT (Sound of Thunder) class behind Paul Vitale's 25X '01 Ducati. In his next race he won the BOT Formula 1 class over 17 other riders from all over the nation. He took advantage of an opportunity and put his passion to work. His history is still being written.

Scripture for the Day: *"Be very careful, then, how you live – not as unwise but as wise, making the most of every opportunity, because the days are evil."* (Ephesians 5:16)

Quote for the Day: "The opportunity that God sends does not wake up him who is asleep." (Senegalese Proverb)

Billy Stranahan#244, choosing the outside line to pass #25x Paul Vitale at Mid-Ohio's road race in 2004.

B man (Benny Boudreaux) at Holeshot MX in 2004.

130. The "B" Man Overcomes Adversity

By: Benny's Mom, Lee Ann Whipkey

Setting: Louisville Round 3 of 5, National Amateur Arenacross Championship Series, 2004

After 715 miles on the road, we arrived in Louisville to weather reports of an ice storm to hit early the next morning! Now, being from New Orleans, none of us had ever experienced an ice storm and we were not really looking forward to it. We went to bed not knowing what to expect when we woke up. We woke up early and it was dry as a bone, but the weatherman was reporting it would hit at any minute. We scrambled and got to the arena just as the ice started to fall, and was it COLD! Thank God for indoor pits!

When B Dad went to get into the trailer, the lock was frozen. He had to beat on it a few times to knock all the ice off just to get it unlocked. We got inside where it was cozy and warm, and set up our pits. Then we went to get our pit passes.

Practice was at 8 A.M. sharp. B Man did well, taking command of the track and never looking back. Next were heat races; there were 12 in his class, so they had two heat races. B Man was in the second. He backed up his excellent practice ride by taking the holeshot and leading his heat to the checkered flag.

Then time for the main event. B Man shot off the gate like a bolt of lightening. He was just about to score himself a holeshot when – "Boom!" From out of nowhere he was hit. A rider had shot out of the pack of riders and hit B Man from behind. He was on the ground, but jumped up quickly. The referee got to him, took off his goggles, and B Dad ran out to him. You could tell B Man was upset and the referee and B Dad were talking to him. Just as the leader was about to come by and lap him, B Man jumped on his bike and took off, broken visor and all. He never got lapped, and within 5 laps, pulled himself from 12th place on the ground to 5th place at the checkered flag!

Way to go B MAN! He maintains his 1st place in the series point standings and we are looking forward to Raleigh!

Note: Benny qualified first in the 50cc 4-6 year-old division. At the final race, he complained of itching and high fever. It turned out he had chicken-pox. Despite that He went on to finish ninth in the National Championship in Las Vegas on October, 2004.

Scripture for the Day: *"In your anger, do not sin."* (Psalm 4:4)

Quote for the Day: "If you are patient in one moment of anger, you will escape a hundred days of sorrow." (Chinese Proverb)

131. "You were there"

My Father's Day Tribute

As early as I can remember; you were there. The day I entered the world in Montgomery, Alabama; when I got my first slap on the rear end – you were there. You watched with high expectations as you proudly handed out cigars while I screamed bloody murder – you were there.

You worked hard learning your craft, building our house and filling our table so I could toss spoonfuls of baby food back in your face because you were there.

We stood at attention for the camera, you in your Air Force uniform, me in my mock uniform, imitating your face, your stance and your attitude not knowing nor fearing what the world would bring, because you were there.

You helped me deal with sibling rivalry, the move to New Orleans, the first day of school, handling bullies and the first of many trials – and you were there.

When you worked late, building your business I worked hard at pushing the boundaries – and you were there. When I tried being class clown and expressing my will against the school – you were there when I got home, you and the belt, it was there, too.

When I was looking for something to do during the summer, Mom took me to little league baseball, then football, then cub scouts. I presented you with home runs, touchdowns, handicrafts and awards; you were there to watch me receive them.

When I graduated to Boy Scouts, you were there; as chaperone, leader, guide and ultimately Asst. Scoutmaster and again we shared uniforms. This time I stood almost as tall as you in the picture, but the faces still looked fearlessly into the future, because you were there. When I wanted to quit at the rank of Life, you persuaded me to earn those last few merit badges and the coveted rank of Eagle by offering your outboard motor. The motor is gone, but you and the rank are still there.

When my bicycle broke you put a wrench in my hand and showed me how to fix it. When we got motorcycles I learned how to work on gasoline combustion engines. Then you gave me tools and put me to work on that old International Scout. We went camping, trail-riding and mudding. When we got stuck I learned how to winch us out. You took me to church and I found the winch for life. When I was baptized, you were there.

When I left your tools out in the yard, or stepped over the garbage I was to take out, or argued with my sisters, you were there – with correction, instilling within me the fear of obeying the law.

When I wanted to drive your '55 Chevy hot-rod to the Prom, you wisely declined. I didn't understand it then, but I wasn't ready for the responsibility. When I finally <u>was</u> ready, my graduation present was an old station wagon from the junk yard that needed work, because you were trying to build a responsible man.

When I moved out of the house you handed me a savings account with all the car insurance money I had been paying you. It was my nest egg. I didn't deserve it, but I got it and the message.

As I grew more mature, you looked wiser. When it was time I sent a letter of apology asking for forgiveness for my arrogant independence and youthful disrespect. I came to see you had been right. You understood because at one time you were there, too. Only your Dad didn't live to see you as a grown man because he was taken while you were young. Being the father of a man was new ground to you. But you covered it well.

Through the years we worked our way through mistakes, missed opportunities, hurt feelings and misunderstandings. I'm just now beginning to see how long and difficult the task of raising teenagers and the importance of the commandment: "honor your father and mother."

Thanks Dad for enduring the long, slow, sometimes frustrating process of forging me into a man. I'll bet you never dreamed how long the battle would be when you entered parenting, but the seeds you have sown are producing fruit in the next generation.

Don't worry about your surgery this week, I'll be there.

Note: Aubrey Jenkins made a successful recovery from cancer surgery. He suggests all men over 40 get a PSA screening to catch cancer early enough to treat. At the time of this printing He is still working and helping his son and two daughters. Thank you God for answering our prayers.

The author and his Dad pose in Washington DC where he was stationed with the Air Force, serving at the Institute of Technology at Walter Reed Army Hospital. (1958)

132. Silva's Comeback Race

Like the movies *Sea biscuit*, *Rocky*, and *The Natural*, "washed-up," "has-been," "down-and-outers" have had to reach down and find the will to beat the odds and achieve victory. You know the setting; when Father Time, Mother Nature, Uncle Dire Circumstance and Aunt Fleeting Opportunity all seem to scheme against a man's dream. We've all experienced this. We yearn for the under-dog to defy the odds, silence his critics, overcome the circumstances and claw his way out of the hole to victory.

A story like this happened in May, 2004 in south Louisiana. Local rider Shannon Silva got his opportunity to make a comeback onto the national road-racing scene. Another local racer, Billy Orazio, offered two of his vintage era racing Hondas to Silva to contest the event. AHRMA (American Historic Racing Motorcycle Association) held its National Vintage series race at No Problem Raceway on May 29-30 in Belle Rose, La. Orazio, who collects vintage motorcycles and runs Orazio's Cycles north of Covington, provided Silva with a 1977 Honda MT125-R and a 1962 CB72 Honda Hawk. Both rider and bikes were looking for another shot at glory.

With cooperate sponsors looking for younger and younger talent, Silva is an old man in a young man's sport. Silva, now 40, graduated from Bonnabel High School and pursued plumbing as a career. He now operates "Tinting Technologies" in Jefferson, but his passion has always been motorcycles. He cut his teeth on the curvy roads next to the mighty Mississippi river, and periodically made the trip across the lake for some deserted country roads. "It just kind of came to me while I was riding, and I realized, 'I gotta go to the track.'" He has been racing off and on since 1986, taking the "low-budget road" in his quest for a pro road-racing career. He tints glass seven days a week to buy parts and pay entry fees. When he races he has to use "take-offs" which are used tires other racers have discarded.

He broke an ankle and compressed a vertebra in 1987 at a road race in Texas. He remembers having to drive to work with a cast and a back brace. "I had to use a stick to push in the clutch." He re-entered the sport when he saw Scott Russell race on television. "I saw Scott winning on TV and I said, 'I can beat him. I need to get back in.'"

He took advantage of his few opportunities when they came. He was a top five finisher in WERA (Western Eastern Road-racers' Association) Grand National finals in 1994. He almost won the championship at Road Atlanta, but ran out of gas only moments from victory. He finished 3rd in the National A Production, and was the Southeast Region Formula One and 750 Champ, 2nd in A Production and 3rd in B Production. When he returned to the expert class in early 95, he suffered a blown motor and had to sit out the whole year.

He captured second place at Daytona's Aprilia Cup Challenge behind Australian Jamie Stauffer in October of 2000. He has found more success in the Aprilia Cup Challenge because all racers use the same bike under strict guidelines which levels the playing field for low-budget privateers like Silva. "I've learned a lot racing the 250. Every little mistake matters. You have to concentrate on technique. You have to change your gearing 2 or 3 times a weekend, whether for practice, leading or drafting."

Silva tells about Daytona in March of 2001.

> My bike blew up; We pulled the motor and found broken power valves. I ordered the parts from Pennsylvania and went to the race hoping they would show up in time. They showed up on Thursday, but we discovered we needed more parts. Finally at 1:00 A.M. on Saturday morning we got the bike back together. I broke in the new motor while qualifying the next day. Then it started raining! I hadn't raced in the rain in years, but went on to win and picked up a new sponsor for the rest of the year.

In 2002 he came as close as one turn from winning the championship before crashing while attempting a pass with only a few laps left. He picked up his bike to salvage third for the year in the series championship. The following year at Daytona he had trouble with the transmission jumping out of gear and the forks sticking. "I finally started 'short-shifting' to keep it from jumping out of gear. Before the last race my mechanic said, 'the bike is not able to win, take 2nd place money and let's go home.' I got on the bike and forgot about that and just raced. I just knew I could win. I ended up crashing out of 2nd as we were reeling in the leader."

The odds were against him. Silva has sacrificed owning his own home for an opportunity at pro racing. He had no money, no time to train, no time to rest, and no time to practice. But with Billy's bikes, a home town crowd, some rusty experience and a racer's heart, he won five out of five classes. A few months later he went up to Mid-Ohio to the big National event and won the 125 class on Orazio's '77 MT 125 Honda.

Scripture for the Day: *"... and by persevering produce a good crop."* (Luke 8:15b)

Quote for the Day: "Some men may succeed because they are destined to, but most men succeed because they are determined to." (unknown)

New Orleans area racer Shannon Silva made a successful comeback at the AHRMA 2004 series race at No Problem Raceway. He won five out of five races. He is pictured in front of Billy Orazio's 1962 CB72 Honda Hawk.

133. My 3300 mile Attitude Adjustment

Have you ever felt bored, tired of your surroundings, in need of some change? Have you ever been stuck in a routine you can't tolerate any longer? Have you ever thought of just running away, fleeing the country, taking on a new adventure, testing yourself against a new foe? In July of 2004, I packed my camping gear and debit card and hit the road for a little "attitude adjustment."

One BMW ad reads, "Become that distant spec on the horizon," so that's what I did. I buzzed off on my 1999 F650 BMW. I had a tank bag with personal gear in front with a see through map bag on top. I tossed a pair of Tour Master saddlebags across the seat filled with clothes and camping gear. On the passenger seat rode a small ice chest, flanked on either side by my sleeping bag, backpacker mattress, tent and chair. How did I justify this trip? It would be business. As a moto-journalist I would be getting stories on my voice recorder, camera and note-pad. How did I alleviate the fears of my family? I rode up to Ohio with the Orazio Race Team from Covington. Billy Orazio, Shannon the racer and George the mechanic/chef rode up in Billy's truck. They made a space in the trailer among the race bikes for my Beemer in case I got tired or broke. I never needed it, that is until Canada.

We played cat-and-mouse up the Interstate corridor until about 2:30 A.M. where we took our first and only hotel just north of Nashville. By 8:30 A.M. we were under way. I had to stop every 130 miles for fuel and refreshment. Already the guys were asking to take a turn on my bike. Thursday afternoon we arrived at the famous AMA Hall of Fame motorcycle museum in Pickerington, Ohio. Billy was dropping off a bike from his Vintage collection for an upcoming motocross display. I had 30 minutes to snap a few pictures before they closed for the day. Shannon was getting antsy with his big race just a day away and asked to ride my bike the last leg to the Mid-Ohio Sports Car Course. I finally relented and took a turn in the truck with the guys. Shannon amused us as he tried to ride the white line on the shoulder the next ten miles. "He's tuning up for tomorrow," Billy defended, as I started getting nervous.

We pulled into the big Mid-Ohio Race Car Course before sunset Thursday but had to wait in a long line to get in. We were up early for Friday's practice sessions. Shannon had only one race on these two vintage Hondas and had never raced this course. He cut chunks of seconds off his lap times as he learned the course. The Mid-Ohio Race Car Course is a 2.4 mile permanent race course which is also home to car racing and AMA Superbike competition. Shannon made the most of his opportunity to race this major national event by winning the Formula 125 class over last year's champ Greg Steinbeck, both on 1977 Honda MT125's. In the 250 class Silva was trying to find a way around second place rider Jonathan White on his '66 Ducati. Top seeded champion David Roper was leading the first five laps on his '66 Aeromacchi when the trouble started. Silva's '62 Honda CB 250 locked up at over 100 mph. Silva went down and skidded across the infield. He walked away with bruised ribs and a skinned elbow. The next day they allowed him to ride the MT 125 in the class and he won.

As for me I was overwhelmed by the big event. Every kind of motorcycle from every era was present. Manufacturers and Vendors filled the midway. Motorcycle Hall of Famers signed autographs, raced and gave seminars. Motorcycle shops from 45 states filled over 30 acres for the largest swap meet in the country. The stunt rider from the James Bond movie, Jean Pierre Goy was entertaining. I just took pictures and rode my bike around… looking, absorbing, learning. I couldn't get press credentials, but Billy pulled some strings and got me in the media tower. Sunday morning I was designated a corner worker trainee and I had a close-up spot for photography.

On Sunday, the triumphant Orazio race team started for home while I headed north looking for adventure and cooler air. I got unseasonably cool air at my first campground just south of Detroit on Lake Eerie. The next day I crossed the Canadian border and spent three days in Ontario, but that's another story. I came back home through New York, Pennsylvania, Kentucky and Alabama. So I made it home on the eve of my 48th birthday with too many pictures and stories to tell here... and somewhere along the 3300 mile, ten day trek I got my new attitude.

Scripture for the Day: *"You were taught, with regard to your former way of life, to put off your old self, which is being corrupted by its deceitful desires; to be made new in the attitude of your minds and to put on the new self, created to be like God in true righteousness and holiness."* (Ephesians 4:22-23)

Quote for the Day: "All some people need to make them happy is a change – and most of the time that's all a baby needs." (Unknown)

134. My Trek into Canada

On Sunday, the triumphant Orazio race team started for home while I headed north looking for adventure and cooler air. I got to ride through cities I'd only seen on Monday night Football: Cincinnati, Cleveland and Detroit. I got unseasonably cool air at my first campground on Lake Erie. I was at the halfway point of my Louisiana to Canada trek and my trusty steed, "Silver" hadn't let me down yet, in any sense of the word. After crossing the border into Ontario, Canada, I toured the northern coast.

One night, while I was camping on Lake Huron, a young man driving a campground truck stopped by to admire my bike and gear. After asking all the usual questions, he mentioned that a really good motorcycle mechanic had a shop just down the road. I told him I probably wouldn't need him, but took the shop name and number just in case. The next morning, my bike wouldn't start – the next morning! God was at work answering my prayer for a safe trip. I loaded my gear, push-started my bike and rode down to the campground headquarters to call this mechanic. The campground worker made the call, gave me directions and I was on my way.

A few miles, excuse me, kilometers later I pulled up to a large, modern, metal building. The doors were closed as the sun was blazing straight up in the sky. Even though there was nothing but corn fields all around, the skid marks on the pavement gave away the secret of the business – performance motorcycles.

As I stepped off my bike a tall young Canadian came out with hand extended. His close-cropped blond hair and boyish good looks were a far cry from the usual tattooed, greasy, long-haired, bearded mechanics one usually associates with a bike shop. "Hi, I'm Donald." "I'm Roy Jenkins and I've got a problem with my Beemer." "Let's have a look. You'll have to take off the gear and seat," he continued, staying a step ahead of me.

He went back in to get a voltmeter and I unloaded my whole bike, making a pile bigger than my motorcycle. His diagnosis was quick and firm, "your battery is dry. It's shot. You'll need another one." "Do you have any in stock?" "I think so." After checking his stock, he discovered that he didn't. "I'll have to order one from Quebec." When he saw the look on my face, he quickly countered with, "don't worry, it's not far from here." "Oh yeh, we're in Canada," I mumbled dumbly. "Meanwhile you can wheel your bike in out of the sun and do some maintenance."

As I wheeled my bike inside, the shop was alive with activity. Platinum Powersports consists of the usual cycle shop ingredients: 8 work stations, tools, 3 mechanics, parts bins, waiting area, gear, apparel and accessories display. I was drawn to the largest publications rack I have ever seen in a motorcycle shop. After leafing through a few magazines, I discovered a technical column entitled, "technically speaking," written by none other than, Donald Broadfoot.

A little while later he found a place for me to spend the night while I waited for my new battery. We tinkered on bikes, talked and tinkered on bikes. Then he asked, "Have you ever gone faster than 100mph on a bike?" "Uhhh, sure, once or twice," I replied, a bit surprised by the question. "What's the fastest bike you've ever ridden?" I thought of my motocross races of the past, then realized he meant on the street. "Besides my 1100 Shadow, I guess a Suzuki Bandit." He thought a moment then announced, "We're goin' into town for supper," with a grin that had a slight trace of, "I know something you don't."

We got suited up and I looked around at the bikes on the floor. "Which bike are you gonna' loan me?" I asked. "Who said anything about loaners? Come see." He backed a big blue Honda CBR out into the driveway. "This is Honda's fastest production bike," he explained proudly. "The XX Super Blackbird is named after the SR71 air-force jet." I examined the aftermarket pipe as I put my helmet on. "I've done a little hop-up to it," he explained coyly, "It makes 142 hp at the rear wheel." He fired it up and let it idle while he donned his leathers. He gave me a chilling instruction as I cautiously swung a leg over the passenger seat, "Put your hands up on the fuel tank when we brake so ya don't crush me." With that we flipped down our visors and rolled out.

As we turned onto the deserted country highway he looked over his shoulder and said, "I'm just gonna warm up the tires." Then he went straight for the ditch. My fingers curled hard under the luggage rack. He whipped it round for the other side of the highway, and he zigged back and forth about 8 times, straightened up, then cut loose the ponies. They ran like they were late for supper. He applied just enough throttle to keep the front wheel on the ground as he climbed through the gears. I struggled for a peek over his shoulder and was shocked to see the speedometer needle touch 245! That was kilometers, not miles per hour, but it still sent me into EPM (emergency prayer mode). He backed off the throttle when a pickup truck appeared on the next hill in our lane. I was wondering if he was going to pass, but he braked hard and my hands went to the tank to brace. We almost did a stoppie as the back end started to rise beneath me. Good thing he stopped because another bike went flying by going the other way.

"This thing does a wheelie in 3rd gear at over 100 mph," he said over his shoulder in the calm of the slow speed. "I believe you," I said in fear.

After a few miles he reached back and put my hand on the throttle. I wound the bike up feeling no noticeable power band. When I asked about it later he said, "I'm always in 6th gear when I let people do that, so they don't loop us." Did I mention he's a motorcycle safety instructor?

We stopped at Katie's Place, a little restaurant just outside of Clinton, Ontario. When the waitress saw Donald a strange smile came over her face that remained while we placed our order. She kept saying, "You're a bad boy." As soon as she walked away, I asked, "Why is she looking at you like that?" He smiled and said, "Cause she knows I'm the one that burned the smiley faces in the parking lots in town during the parades."

Donald has the volatile combination of youth, knowledge of bikes and need for speed. At only 29 years old he has already operated Platinum Powersports for 8 years. He has a ton of technical data in his keen mind, along with the uncanny ability to recall it at a moment's notice. He road races when he can, stays in shape by playing hockey every week, runs his motorcycle shop, writes his articles and still finds time to farm his 200 acres with his Mom and sister.

While strapping our helmets for the ride home he said, "Be sure to lean on the inside." I just nodded. As soon as we turned onto deserted highway, he let the Blackbird fly. The gentle hills of the Canadian farmland had just the right amount of curves for two-wheel cutlery. As we ducked down inside a right-hander I leaned forward and watched the blur of the white shoulder line inches beneath my boot. Back and forth we went as the sun was setting on the horizon.

When we got back to the shop I still had my supper and my legs weren't shaking – too bad. "Addicting, huh?" He gloated as he removed his helmet. "How fast were we goin' in the turns?" He quickly calculated kilometers to miles for me and quipped, "130 miles per hour." I went into my "addicted to adrenaline" speech until he lost interest. He pulled out a track-prepped CBR600F4 that had been laid down once or twice. "You wanna ride?" "Of course." He started the bike and gave me his prep speech as we pulled on our gloves. I followed him out to the end of the gravel road where he stopped. We noticed the flashing lights a quarter mile down the highway. One of Canadian's finest was giving a ticket. Donald assessed the situation and raised his visor, "let's go put em' back up. We're not going out now." "But…" I grudgingly turned and followed him back to the shop. Did I mention that he's a hockey player? Sadly we put our toys away for the night. The next day my battery arrived at 11:00, and by noon I was on my way to Niagara Falls. Thanks Donald, for the Canadian hospitality. But you still owe me a ride on the 600. Thanks for not overdoing it – too much. Did I mention I'm going to write a story about you?

Later that evening while gazing down at the violent cascade of water of the Niagara River into the famous Falls, I got a sense of my own insignificance against the vastness of God's creation. If this is so powerful and majestic, just think of what God is like. I walked away with new inspiration to serve the God that is powerful enough to make Niagara Falls, but concerned enough about me to love me.

I eased back across the border into New York and started the trip south. I mostly stayed on the Interstates to burn the miles, saving time and money. I still enjoyed some great scenery, especially in Kentucky where I camped again. I arrived home with a new appreciation for life and what God has given me, such as air-conditioning, shelter, a soft bed, a refrigerator full of food and my family, especially my wife.

Scripture for the Day: *"But let all who take refuge in you be glad; let them sing for joy. Spread your protection over them, that those who love your name may rejoice in you. For surely, O Lord, you bless the righteous; you surround them with your favor as with a shield."* (Psalm 5:11-12)

Quote for the Day: "He traveled in order to come home." (William Trevor, *Matilda's England*)

Canadian motorcycle mechanic Donald Broadfoot on his tricked out Honda CBRXX Super Blackbird. Here he stops to pose after our ride back to his farm/motorcycle shop.

The author's bike at the Canadian border near Port Huron in July, 2004.

135. Mr. Persistent in the NFL

I am such a fan of the NFL, so much so that it guided my tour when I left Mid-Ohio and headed north on my motorcycle trek in July. I deliberately charted a course to Cincinnati, Cleveland, Detroit and back through Pittsburg to see the skylines I'd seen on Monday Night Football. The Interstates inevitably brought me past a major body of water, over a bridge, through the center of town and the stadiums where Al Michaels, Frank Gifford, Howard Cosell, (whoops, I just dated myself)... I mean John Madden would announce the game. If you've watched Monday Night Football, you've seen those city skylines after returning from a commercial break. When they pan over The Meadowlands, Soldier Field, Paul Brown Stadium, Three Rivers Stadium, Pro Player Stadium and others I would try to imagine the city from its skyline.

Monday night, October 4, I was watching the Kansas City Chiefs play the Baltimore Ravens in Baltimore. As a New Orleans Saints fan I imagined on several occasions, "I hope the Saints players saw that good play." Anyway, besides the running of Priest Homes, I was impressed with the quick release and decision making of Trent Green. During a break they played a special piece on the Kansas City Quarterback. He was originally drafted by San Diego, spent time at Washington, then ended up with Dick Vermeil in Kansas City. Did you know he sat on the bench for 85 straight games before he threw his first pass in an NFL game? 85!

Can you imagine him at game 17, sitting there in his pads, helmet next to him, holding a ball, wondering if he would go in soon? How about game 29? By game 48 he must have considered himself a permanent bench warmer. Self-doubt must have plagued him. How did he keep showing up at training camps? But you say, the money; he was well paid. Yes, but his dream was to <u>Play</u> the game, not to <u>Watch</u> the game. While in Washington, he said he learned the most by listening on the headset as offensive genius Norv Turner called the plays. By game 72 I wonder if he had developed a habit of resignation to an attitude of not being good enough to play. But he kept his dream alive. He paid his dues. He showed up and worked. Then at game 85 he got his first playing time, and now he leads one of the most potent offenses of the 2004 season.

I think it's fair to say he earned his spot and he's ready. The price he paid by all the studying, watching, learning, maturing and waiting means he won't lose the job easily. He paid his dues, he belongs. In the little promo, Green is shown with a big smile and naming himself, Mr. Persistent.

In the Bible David the shepherd boy was anointed king by the prophet Samuel, but that didn't put him in the starting line-up. He didn't go right to the throne. He ran for his life from King Saul, hiding in caves for almost 13 years! What was God up to? He was preparing him.

When the time was right and David came to the throne, he was well prepared for the most difficult job, leading God's people. Don't forget about Moses' 40 years of preparation on the back side of a desert before being called back to Egypt to lead God's people to freedom. The Apostle Paul spent years in preparation before starting his mission journeys. Even Jesus didn't start his earthly ministry until He was 30.

If you have trusted God with your life, He has put a calling, a plan, and a purpose on your life. But you may not be in that position yet. It may take years of preparation. Don't give up. Don't go off course. Don't be distracted. Be faithful. He'll put you there when you are ready. Meanwhile, do your best to serve Him where you are.

Scripture of the Day: *"'No eye has seen, no ear has heard, no mind has conceived what God has prepared for those who love Him' – but God has revealed it to us by His Spirit. The Spirit searches all things, even the deep things of God."* (1 Corinthians 2:9-10)

Quote for the Day: "If at first you don't succeed, try, try again." (William Edward Hickson, *Try and Try Again*)

136. Redeeming Old Motorcycles

There are as many ways to enjoy motorcycles as there are people who enjoy them. One way is the restoration project. This is especially rewarding for those of us who have fond memories of certain motorcycles as a kid. When I was 14 years old I wanted a motorcycle so bad I could taste it, but alas, my Dad would have none of it. He had just crashed his old Maico under a bus on a rainy night and walked away from motorcycling, for good, or so he thought.

Enter my cousins in Covington. Every summer I would visit with them for a week, and the Stonecyphers had something I couldn't have – a Honda Trail 70 motorcycle. One lazy summer afternoon we snuck away to Garrett Honda and drooled over the new bikes. Honda had just developed an off-road model called the SL70 Motosport that came in Summer Yellow, Aquarius Blue and Light Ruby Red. It was love at first sight. I took home a brochure of a yellow SL70 and pinned it to my wall. It was my motivation to keep the dream alive. My Dad finally relented and allowed me to buy a mini-bike, which led to a Honda CL90, later a Kawasaki 100, then on to Pentons for racing off-road.

Now I live in Covington, too, but I never got my SL70. The faded brochure is still in my son's room somewhere. The high fenders, the muscular tank, the semi-knobby tires and upswept pipe ignited a fire in my heart that still burns today.

In May of 2004 while announcing the AHRMA vintage race at No Problem Raceway, I saw an SL350 go by near the front of the pack. I made it a point to meet the rider and was surprised to find out that he had built his bike, piece by piece from junkyards and spare parts! Scott Turner, from Fort Walton Beach, Florida, pulled out his photo album and drew a crowd of like-minded admirers. I saw him again at Mid-Ohio on yet another creation bike as he was visiting Billy Orazio's pit. I asked him about his bike and he cast an "aww... shucks, everybody does this" smile, then began to tell me about his "Junkyard Honda" with growing pride:

> This one is built from parts I found at the junk yard. I just put it together and made it look good. It has 17" alloy rims, a little megaphone, fiberglass tank and tail section. The tank I found at a swap meet and I kinda built the bike around it... I made the seat... from a little creation that popped up in my mind. The motor is about a 72, but the rest of the bike comes from other years. I found a CB front end at a swap meet and put it on. The shocks I got at Mid-Ohio two years ago.

Here comes the best part. He spent under 500 dollars on the whole bike, 300 of which was the paint job. Scott went on to explain:

I told my buddy, "I just want a blue and silver tank," and he came up with the paint scheme. I spent the other money on the Cheng-Shin tires which were about 20 bucks apiece. The rims I swapped stuff for, the spokes cost me about 10 bucks. I found a piston for it, and had to buy a gasket set, and new grips. The rest is just out of the junk yard. I like to build vintage road-racers for the street.

God is in the business of reclaiming old lives from the junk piles. Since he created us he can re-make us according to what we were designed to be. No matter how broken you are, how much rust you have, how worn out you feel, how used you are or how lost you are, just put yourself in His hands.

Pray this prayer: "Father, I know you love me. Please forgive me for my past sins and I release and forgive those who have done me wrong. I know that Jesus already paid for my sin at the cross and I yield myself to you, dying to my old self. Come into my life and re-make me according to your plan. I make you my Lord and Master and will now live for you, in Jesus name, amen."

Scriptures for the Day:
"I have come to seek and to save what was lost." (Jesus in Luke 19:10)

"In Him [Jesus] we have redemption through His blood." (Ephesians 1:7)

"Since you call on a Father who judges each man's work impartially, live your lives as strangers here in reverent fear. For you know that it was not with perishable things such as silver or gold that you were redeemed from the empty way of life handed down to you from your forefathers, but with the precious blood of Christ, a lamb without blemish or defect. He was chosen before the creation of the world, but was revealed in these last times for your sake. Through Him you believe in God, who raised Him from the dead and glorified Him, and so your faith and hope are in God." (1 Peter 1:17-21)

Floridian Scott Turner and his 70's era Junkyard Honda

Pennsylvanian Karl Bungerz on his restored 1966 R69S BMW

137. The Great Escape

Questions – How can an 87 year-old invalid enjoy the rich imagery of a market in Morocco? How can a man languishing in prison chuckle over the misfortunes of a traveler who lost his passport while traversing the streets of Bombay? What about a middle aged housewife taking an afternoon break from her endless chores, get a glimpse of a majestic sunset over the Andes from the seat of a motorcycle? Consider a single guy who has been framing houses all day see a Grizzly bear for the first time on a desolate dirt road in the Yukon against the backdrop of the Northern Lights. A businessman, who has been manning the phone, processing numbers and tracking sales, now finds himself tracking a trail, processing obstacles and manning the controls of a motorcycle through a Bolivian jungle. How can these miracles occur?

Reading. More specifically – adventure touring. While many seek escape through alcohol and drug abuse, let me offer a better alternative – reading adventure stories. It's legal, safe, leaves no guilt and costs less money. Although movies, plays and some TV channels offer up their versions of escape; with books and magazines I can plop down in my favorite chair at my own convenience and disappear for hours to parts unknown.

Some people like romance novels, others art, poetry, sports or science fiction. While I can appreciate those genres, the one that captures my imagination and carries my interest is the solo traveler. Give me the true stories that were born and bred for adversity, discovery and adventure. Combine nature and people, history and geography, politics and religion. I want to see what gear the traveler used, and what resources he used to solve problems. Blend machinery, curiosity, ingenuity and an open mind, and let's see how far it takes him. Let's discover those other cultures and uncover their mysteries while riding village to village on a motorcycle. Whether it's Triston Jones or Robin Lee Graham circumnavigating the world on their little sailboats in the spirit of Kon Tiki; or Ted Simon, Robert Fulton, or Helge Pederson camping their way across the globe, something magical happens in the reader's mind.

While some are called to travel and record, others benefit without the risk. I enjoy both. I've logged thousands of miles of motorcycle camping, and a few hundred miles in a small sailboat. But that takes time and money. Reading is free.

But you say, I can't afford all those books. Ever heard of the LIBRARY? It's not just for research papers. What about the internet? Now we have the whole world at our fingertips. But there's no replacement for firsthand adventure, then, second hand – the book that chronicled the trip.

Let me suggest some classic adventure travel books. For the sailors, check out:
- *Kon Tiki* by Thor Heyerdahl
- *My Old man and the Sea* by David and Daniel Hayes
- *The Incredible Voyage* by Tristan Jones
- *Dove* by Robin Lee Graham

For World tours by motorcycle read:
- *Jupiter's Travels* by Ted Simon
- *One Man Caravan* by Robert Fulton, Jr.
- *10 Years on Two Wheels* by Helge Pederson

There are many others worth reading and most of these have sequels. Ok, now you're saying, "That's book overload. Just give me one." For sailors, especially younger readers, start with *Dove*. This 16 year old sailed for 5 years and 33,000 miles in 1965. He grows up right before your eyes, finding love and starting a family.

For motorcycle adventure, the most imaginative writer is Ted Simon who opens his heart and mind to the reader while doing some growing up of his own. He traveled for 4 years around the world on a Triumph twin.

The most popular book of all time is the Bible. It was written on three different continents, by over 40 different authors. They were as diverse as kings, peasants, fishermen, lawyers, doctors, farmers, soldiers, tax collectors, prophets and shepherds. It was written from palaces, prisons, remote areas in the wilderness, islands and cities over a period of over 2500 years. Yet it all fits together like a glove, as if one person wrote it. It was inspired by one individual – God's Holy Spirit. It's God's love letter to you. That's why I'm writing this book, so you'll read His book.

"But I don't have time to read books," you whine. Hey, turn off the TV for a night. You might discover new worlds.

Scripture for the Day: *"Afterward, Joshua read all the words of the law – the blessings and the curses – just as it is written in the Book of the Law."* (Joshua 8:34)

Quote for the Day: "Reading is to the mind what exercise is to the body." (Richard Steele, The Tatler)

The author's 1984 700 Yamaha Maxim in front of a wall of ice in Northern California.

(from left) The author's son on the Maxim and Dad on his old Gold Wing, about to leave Covington, La. on the Pennsylvania trip.

138. Shared Adventure

A shared adventure can be good for relationships, especially guys. In the summer of '97 my 13 year-old son accompanied my Dad and I on a motorcycle trip. My Dad rode his aging Gold Wing while Kyle and I went two-up on my '84 Yamaha Maxim. What a sight we were as we said goodbye to the girls at the Shoney's in Covington that bright summer morning. My bike was loaded down with a fairing, two sets of saddlebags, a tank bag, canoe bag and a tool pouch. Old and new camping gear scraped together from our attic were carefully combined with our clothes and strapped aboard. With most of the causeway commuters safely at work the "Beverly Hillbilly motorcycle show" had room to ease into the east bound lane of I-12.

On the sixth day we arrived at one of our most anticipated destinations. Known affectionately to bikers as Deals' Gap, this mountain pass connects Tennessee and North Carolina and is one of America's best-known motorcycle roads. The "Crossroads of Time" motorcycle campground is located on Hwy. 129 where you can find rental cabins, campsites, fuel and a store. This is the base camp for "The Dragon," the 11 mile mountain road filled with 318 curves, scenic overlooks, pristine wilderness and smooth asphalt. We set up our tents near a stream, unloaded our bikes, and then jumped on the dragon, an adrenaline-pumping, eye-popping, two-wheeled ballet. With the right combination of balance, throttle and brakes we felt the foot-pegs dragging on many of the twisty switch-backs. But this road is like a potato chip, you can't stop at one. As soon as you finish one round, you stretch your legs, make eye contact with the other riders, smile; and then everyone mounts up for another run.

After a few days of playing road racer, we were ready to continue our tour. As motorcycle adventurers know, the first few days of a tour can make you sore, but by day four your body gets in shape and you can really ride. We rode from early morning to well after dark, carving the Blue Ridge Parkway. The only drawback to the scenic route was the slow pace, but the payoff was grand: sweeping vistas, fresh evergreen scents and wind in our faces.

Just north of Virginia Beach my bike started cutting out, and died at the worse possible time and place – the left hand lane of I-29 rush hour traffic, raining, with darkness setting in. We were forced to pull off where there was no shoulder near a bridge. After a prayer, the bike roared back to life as if nothing had happened. We continued on to the Shenandoah state forest under clearing skies and an extraordinary sunset singing, "I can see clearly now, the rain is gone...."

We set up camp at 3000 ft among the cool mountain clouds. The next morning we awoke to a gentle rain tapping on the tent. As soon as the sun emerged, so did we for a hike on the Appalachian Trail. Later, as we were comfortably back on the bike winding through scenic Skyline Drive I tapped Kyle's knee and pointed to a Black bear leading her two cubs along the road. A few miles further down the road an eight point buck crossed in front of us.

Interstate 81 took us from Maryland into West Virginia across the historic Potomac River. It was the clearest, brightest day I can ever remember. When we got to the state line, Kyle played a game of jumping back and forth at the Pennsylvania line so he could say he'd "been to Pennsylvania 30 times." The next few days were spent with my old diving buddy, Wally Diaczenko, recounting salvage jobs and hunting stories. We shot skeet, played laser tag and just goofed off with our sons whose energetic horseplay reminded us of our youth.

After a few days of re-living old times and enjoying the present, it was time to face the future. We began the long journey home on Sunday evening armed with a fresh tank of gas, two day old pizza and contented hearts. Just north of Covington, Virginia we pulled over at a crowded overlook for a break. There we happened upon one of the most enchanting spots of the whole trip. A picturesque waterfall cascaded 300 feet into the mysterious mist below. We grabbed a snack and hiked down the steep trail, descending into a maze of caverns, pools and bubbling brooks. The cool air and amazing beauty held us spellbound as we edged closer to the heart of this miraculous setting. We enjoyed lunch on a dry rock to the sounds of the waterfall, engrossed in God's creative work. Kyle broke the silence with an observation, "this is an ace, beating a two in a card game," his eyes still wide in wonder.

We re-traced our journey back through Atlanta, where I had worked as a van driver for the media during the Summer Olympic games of '94. We toured the TV station and Centennial Square before turning for home. We splurged for our first hotel on our last night in Meridian, Ms. to clean up for the last leg of our journey. After 15 days, 3000 miles, 11 states and three mountain ranges we gained more than good memories. The bond between Grandpa, Dad and son were strengthened by the shared adventure.

Scripture of the Day: *"He will turn the hearts of the fathers to the children, and the hearts of the children to their fathers; or else I will strike the land with a curse."* (Malachi 4:6, the last sentence in the Old Testament)

Quote for the Day: "The waterfall sings, 'I find my song when I find my freedom.'" (Rabindranath Tagore, Stray Birds)

Blake Kennedy sails the finish line jump at River's Edge MX in Jan. 2005

85 class race at Gravity Alley MX in 2005

139. Addicted to Adrenaline?

I know what it means to look forward to the next "adrenaline fix." Whether it is racing, touring, trail-riding or cruising, you moto-heads know what I'm talking about. The thrill of twisting the throttle and feeling the kick in the butt; watching the ground go by inches from your boots; outmaneuvering cars through traffic; smelling the aromas of the food cooking in the restaurants as you cruise down the boulevard all tickle the senses. Then there's the warmth of the sun on your nose as you zip down the interstate; the sense of independence as you roll into the campground with your gear strapped to your bike. Or if you're racing motocross, the thrill of passing a rider in the air and looking at him, feeling that super charge of adrenaline when the gate drops, or slamming into a berm. Motorcycle riding stimulates our senses. We live for it, we work all week for it, and we spend our money and sacrifice for it. Whatever your "It" is; whatever you call "It"- "It" comes with a price.

My "It" was motocross racing, then touring and camping on my motorcycles. It was my high, my fun, my adventure. I noticed when I retired a couple years ago from racing (for the second and final time) that I started experiencing some depression. A lot of things go into the mix, but I found something interesting for motorcycle riders in Dr. Archibald Hart's book, *Unmasking Male Depression*. Without going into too much detail here, let me give you a few high points from his book.

Some of the classic signs of depression are: intense sadness, dejection, little pleasure from anything, loss of sense of humor, don't feel or can't give love. But more specifically in men look for: grumpiness, irritability, moodiness, sulking, overt anger, anxiety, agitation, preoccupation with work, or OTHER DISTRACTIONS. (motorcycling?)

The reason I capped the last sign is because I believe many men use "It" to medicate or cover their depression. I'm not saying all fun hobbies are linked to depression, but an unhealthy dependence on one could be. The key word for healthy living is balance. Dr. Hart contends that men tend to live in denial or refuse treatment. (Hey, I don't even like stopping to ask for directions, much less telling some man I need help with my life.)

In his book he includes a male depression inventory you can take to see if you may be dealing with depression. He also talks about treatment, masks of male depression, clinical depression (2 years or more), post-adrenaline depression (which I have dealt with), mid-life blues, strategies for coping with depression, over attachment to things, analyzing losses, how testosterone works, depression and sex, healthy fathering, and even a chapter for your wife to read about living with you.

For us post-40 men, he gives some good advice about "necessary losses."

- Sexual prowess will decline.
- The disappointment of unfulfilled dreams.
- The failure/success dilemma. He says depression haunts every failure. His advice? "Get your priorities straight. Success is relative. What is failure to you may be success to someone else." Also, "in God's economy, there is no such thing as failure, only forced growth." Think about it.
- Marriage isn't always the heaven it promised.
- When children disappoint.
- Coping with job disappointment.
- Coping with relationship disappointment.

Ok, I got carried away with depression. I did that for a reason. I believe there are many men reading this who are depressed, but will never look for help. Hopefully they will investigate further, turn it over to God, and allow Him to bring healing, get professional help, make changes, whatever. But they must do something to avoid the spiral downward into destruction of family, job, or even their very lives.

Back to adrenaline junkies. How do you know if you are one? I gave a condensed form of this article at a rider's meeting devotion before a motocross race in January. When I asked the riders to raise their hands if they thought they were addicted to adrenaline, guess how many raised their hands? If you said almost all, you were right! Later, a couple friends (former pro racers) came up to the tower while I was announcing the race and asked to see the list of symptoms. They said they were experiencing almost all of them.

What is this adrenaline stuff? It is chemical within the body and is directly related to STRESS. So we get it at work AND during the weekend! It is an "emergency chemical" released by the body for emergency situations (flight or fight). Dr. Hart states that "adrenaline is extremely energizing and also provides a sense of elation and exhilaration – and therein lies our problem. High stress, caused by excessively high adrenaline is extremely pleasurable and becomes addicting."

Listen to his symptoms of post-adrenaline depression:

- Intense depression of short duration (3 days to a week), which occurs every few months, following a period of high demand
- Unusual difficulty in getting your energy going in the morning. Often you increase your consumption of coffee to get a jump-start
- Being overcome by great tiredness or exhaustion whenever "you let yourself down," so you have to keep your activity going at all costs for fear that if you stop, you will crash (which you do)
- High irritability, which you cannot control and which is sparked with the slightest incident
- Feelings of panic, which are triggered by physical activity or exercise
- A profound sense of negativity with a bleak outlook
- A low grade depression where you just want to lie around, have no interest in anything, and no ability to start anything

Here are some of Dr. Hart's milder and less serious symptoms:

- Occasional muscle tension, resulting in sore neck, shoulders, and back, as well as common tension headaches
- Occasion insomnia, where it is difficult to get to sleep or awake early and can't get back to sleep
- Feelings of fatigue - especially awaking tired in the morning
- Loss of enthusiasm for you job or hobbies
- Spiritual lethargy, a feeling of boredom with your church, other believers or God
- Low grade feeling of being down, moody, or even slightly depressed
- If you can find something exciting to do - buy something, for example, you feel better

All right moto-heads, I know just what you are thinking on the last one. You buy something for your bike during the week to tide you over until the next ride. Ask me how I know? I have more spending money since I quit racing. I wonder why? It is important to remember that most people have several of those symptoms as part of our high-speed lifestyle. But if you are experiencing many of those symptoms to the point of interference with living, you may need to get some counseling from a professional.

In conclusion let me leave you with some good news. There are many good anti-depressants on the market that your doctor can prescribe. The newer ones have less side-effects. The medication can help you while you change your thinking or habits toward a more balanced life (that of course, still includes motorcycles).

Another thing that has really helped me is living according to the manufacturer, God. In his ten commandments, he commands, not suggests, that we take a day of rest once a week. The Bible is a very practical book for living. If you take a day to rest from your work (not racing), your adrenal system can recharge. Your stress level will go down. Your body can rebound. You can be reminded about the most important things of life that you have been working for: your own peace of mind, your family, your relationship with God, etc.

For me, I can take a cruise on my bike and rest, but it is not enough. I enjoy worshiping with other believers and being in God's presence. I want to hear from Him, by reading the Bible, listening to my pastor or other Bible teachers. This re-charges my batteries. Since I am usually at a race on Sunday, I must find another time to do this. You must find your way in this issue of dealing with stress and adrenaline addiction. But please, motoheads, at the very least - take a day to REST!

Scripture of the Day: *"Remember the Sabbath Day to keep it Holy. Six days you shall labor and do all your work, but the seventh day is a Sabbath to the Lord your God... for in six days the Lord made the heavens and the earth, the sea, and all that is in them, but He rested on the seventh day."* (Exodus 20:8-10a, 11)

The author takes a rest from commercial diving jobs in the Gulf.

Stuntman Jean-Pierre Goy performs at Mid-Ohio in 2004

140. Motorcycle Stuntman

Modern movies are riding the coattails of motorcycle popularity in our country. Movies like *Mission Impossible II*, which introduced the masses to such tricks as the "stoppie;" *Tomorrow Never Dies* where Bond jumps the roofs of Saigon on a big BMW road bike, then slides under the helicopter to hook the death cable; Vin Diesel starred in two, *The Fast and Furious* and *XXX*. Even Motocross racing has enjoyed exposure with Disney's *Motocrossed*. When you add *Biker Boyz*, *Terminator II*, *Supercross, the Movie*, and *Seabiscuit*... Wait, no, that was a horse. Anyway, motorcycling is being accepted more and more into the mainstream of American entertainment.

Are those real stunts? Or is it just computer generated trickery? And who are those guys that do the stunts? For the most part they ARE real stunts. I caught up with Jean Pierre Goy when I was at Mid-Ohio in 2004. Goy takes his tricks to major motorcycle events and performs the stunts for the big screen as well. I wandered into his show and watched breathlessly as his show slowly gained momentum. He started with a few short wheelies and bunt-outs. Then he went through the gears, wide-open down the asphalt on his orange BMW F650CS, eyes wide open, a look of panic on his face, horn blaring and appeared to be headed for us out of control. Though we were separated by a police barricade, it looked for a few seconds like tragedy, blood, and some major lawsuits. As the crowd stepped back in fear, he managed to stop his bike inches from the last barricade and with a maniacal laugh spun the bike around the other way.

The show got impressive - wheelies, one footed wheelies, one-handed/ one footed wheelies, stoppies; he went through a progressive display of balance and throttle control. Now I see a lot of skillful stopping and jumping every week on race tracks, but this was beyond the norm. When he did a stoppie (a front wheel wheelie using the front brake for balance), it was long, balanced and turning. The rear wheel wheelies were straight up in the air, and he could take it anywhere he wanted. Then he parked the 650 and brought out a big 800 pound BMW K1200LT, complete with hard luggage. He called someone out of the audience and wheelied with them on it.

Later I stopped by his pit and just had to ask him a couple questions. First, "Are you the stuntman from MI2 that did the long stoppie?" Goy: "No, jeoiucneooijng; khjojdlkjsjlsjlkj, sljdodiljgjlkfj." "What?" I couldn't understand his French/English. He repeated twice more. Then it sounded more like this: "No, I not do the MI2, but vwhill do ze MI3," holding up

295

three fingers. "I see. You were the stuntman on Tomorrow Never Dies that jumped the roofs?" I asked. "Jhesss, Jhesss," he nodded. "Good job out there," I said as his lunch was being served and I was being served notice that my bike was parked in the wrong place.

After this show he will leave for Berlin where he will be filming *Mission Impossible III*, on a Triumph. He didn't know yet what kind of stunts he'll be doing. Goy got his start riding Trials at the age of 18, which requires tremendous balance and hand/eye/foot coordination. He did 200 test jumps in preparation for the James Bond movie stunt, then three jumps with stacked boxes to break his fall, then the final jump, without the planned security cable (like the one used in Terminator II). He credits his success to significant preparation and planning, even to the exact millimeter to make the stunt work, safely.

Goy is the current record holder for the longest wheelie. He wheelied through a town (somewhere in France I think) for 100 miles, turning down streets and entertaining the crowd lining his route. The only bit of cheating he did was strap himself to the bike to take the weight off his arms. His secret? Practice, practice, practice.

That's also one of the keys to living a successful life. You can know all about motorcycles and how they work, but if you don't get on one and ride the wheelie the way you're supposed to, you'll just embarrass yourself, or get hurt.

It's the same with life. You can know how to live right, know the Bible, know about God, but until you get on with him, let Jesus into your life, live the way He says, and practice it each day, you will crash and burn, bringing pain and embarrassment into your life.

Scripture of the Day: *"Do not merely listen to the word, and so deceive yourselves. Do what it says. Anyone who listens to the word but does not do what is says is like a man who looks at his face in a mirror and, after looking at himself, goes away and immediately forgets what he looks like. But the man who looks intently into the perfect law that gives freedom and continues to do this, not forgetting what he has heard, but doing it, will be blessed in what he does."* (James 1:22-25)

Quote for the Day: "The world we live in is old-fashioned. It still judges a man by what he does." (Unknown)

Checkered Flag comes out for #537 Mike Parker at the AHRMA Vintage Road Race at No Problem Raceway in Belle Rose, La. in 2004

141. Victory for the Taking

Do circumstances sometimes discourage you? Do you find yourself in a state of defeat and hopelessness? Are you suffering from feelings of loss? Is fear knocking at your door because the situation isn't working out? It happens to me, too. I'm struggling with this devotion right now. I look outside and see that my motorcycle is still sitting in the driveway all apart waiting on parts. How are the bills going to be paid? Are my aches and pains going to go away? Will my children succeed? These questions could go on and on if we let our thinking wander along behind our feelings. How do we turn it around?

There was a situation in the Bible when the Israelites were facing an overwhelming obstacle that stood in their way from entering the land God promised them. Jericho was smack dab in their way just across the Jordan River. This enemy city had walls so thick that it was said chariots raced on top. People actually lived in the walls. The ex-slaves were no match for the well-armed warriors in that major fortress. So Joshua, the leader, went to God with the problem. They had just celebrated the Passover meal and searched their own hearts for sin, presenting themselves as a nation to God. Now something unusual happened starting in Joshua 5:13-14:

> *Now when Joshua was near Jericho, he looked up and saw a man standing in front of him with a drawn sword in his hand. Joshua went up to him and asked "Are you for us or for our enemies?" "Neither," he replied, "but as commander of the army of the Lord I have now come." Then Joshua fell facedown to the ground in reverence, and asked him, "What message does my Lord have for his servant?"*

The pre-incarnate Christ had appeared to Joshua to give instructions. Notice that first, Joshua had to get on God's side, submit to God's plan, and not just assume God would bless his plan. We are guilty of that sometimes, just praying and asking God to bless out plans, then we are confused when they fail.

Further instructions were to let God be the commander, not Joshua. Joshua had to give up control of the situation. We need to let God take control. Let Him operate from His higher perspective. The battle is His, not ours, if we are His children in faith and are willing to obey.

The instructions went on for them to march around the city seven times, then on the seventh time, shout, for the Lord had already given them the city. When the Israelites did that, as told, the walls fell down and they took the city.

There's another lesson for us. We are to act obediently to God for as long as it takes with, prayer, Bible study, worship and church attendance. God will do two things: Break down the enemy's defenses and prepare and strengthen our faith to gain the victory.

But you say, "Couldn't God just have handed the enemy over to them without all that trouble?" Yes, but they wouldn't have built enough faith through obedience and preparation to hold the victory. In other words, God is making you strong enough to gain permanent victory over whatever you are dealing with, so it won't come right back to enslave you again.

Faith + Obedience + Time + Right Decisions = Success

Remember that the battle is God's. Let Him do it.

142. Sell Your Life

The Alamo is one of my favorite stories in history. The determination, bravery and will to fight of the men who defended the territory of Texas from Santa Anna's overwhelming army will forever be remembered as an important legacy of the American spirit.

I was watching a 2004 remake of the movie starring Dennis Quad as Sam Houston, Billy Bob Thornton as Jim Bowie and Patrick Wilson as Lt. Colonel William Travis. It had come to the point where Colonel Travis realized that no reinforcements were coming and the 200 men would have to defend the Alamo against the Mexican army. Crockett told Travis the men needed to hear from him. Travis didn't know what to say, but assembled the men and made the speech. He started by expressing his fear that no reinforcements would be coming to help. He went on to challenge the men to remember what they were fighting for and gave them one more chance to leave before the final battle. He told them they would "show the world what patriots were made of," and in so doing, "deal a crippling blow" to their enemy. He ended his challenge by stating that "if you stay and fight with me, in the Alamo; we will SELL OUR LIVES DEARLY."

Lt. Colonel Travis looked them in the eyes, paused, and then walked away, leaving them in their moment of decision. Some chose to save their lives and they left. Others chose to save Texas and the new nation and stayed to fight, knowing they would not survive the battle. This sacrifice rallied Americans to their aid, and later a group led by Sam Houston defeated Santa Anna's army and freedom was purchased for the new state of Texas.

The great missionary, Jim Elliot said, "He is no fool, who would give what he cannot keep to buy what he can never lose." Elliot was killed for his faith by the very Indians that God called him to bring the gospel. Later his very murderers came to faith in Christ and much of the tribe experienced the forgiveness of sins and the benefits of knowing God personally, inheriting eternal life.

This is what Jesus did for me. He SOLD HIS LIFE in this world, to purchase eternal life in the next for me. Now I have SOLD MY LIFE in this world for an eternal life with Him. Just like Jesus, I sold my temporary life for eternal life. Why? Because He did it for me. I value something bigger and better and permanent more than that which is small and temporary.

Are you living for the moment, for selfish indulgence, for something temporary and small? Or do you have the bigger, more permanent picture in mind? If you are willing to give your life to your creator, He'll give it back to you forever and grant you the privileges of sonship in His eternal kingdom. But it takes a decision, a sacrifice, and a death to selfish plans in exchange for a larger divine plan. Just like this book is somehow part of God's divine plan for my life, I keep writing until I am done.

Scripture for the Day: *"If anyone would come after me, he must deny himself and take up his cross daily and follow me. For whoever wants to save his life will lose it, but whoever loses his life for me will save it. What good is it for a man to gain the whole world and yet lose or forfeit his very self?"* (Luke 9:23-25)

143. Motocross Racer's Prayer

Heavenly Father, I have another race this weekend and again I need your help.

Help me prepare my bike properly, leaving no parts or fasteners unsecured.

Give me the foresight to pack the right gear, tools and parts; leaving nothing important behind.

Protect me on the road, guide me to the track, make me a blessing in the pits; that I might leave no good word or deed undone.

Grant me sleep, heal my body, refresh my spirit, cleanse my mind and forgive my sins; that I will carry no burden to the starting line.

Bring me safely through the first turn; so I will neither receive nor inflict any race-ending crashes.

Keep my bike from missing gears on the jump faces, washing out in the turns, going sideways or endo-ing; so I will not suffer any dismounts or injuries during the race.

Guide me as I calculate my landings, choose the right lines, time the whoops and master the track; leaving no doubts I raced my best.

Carry me smoothly to the finish line, reminding me that I am a winner for engaging the battle no matter where I placed; keeping the right attitude all the way home.

Bestow on me the wisdom to race no longer than I should; that when I hang up my gear for good, you will preserve my health for life after racing.

Impart to me the same passion for you that I had for racing, the same compassion for people I had for trophies; that I may help train the next generation to become champions, leaving no one behind.

And I thank you for Jesus, who gave His blood to qualify me to stand victoriously on the great podium in heaven. You have forgiven my sin, cancelled my debt, removed my guilt and set me free. Your perfect love overcomes my fears, renews my faith and fills me with hope; because you Oh Lord, have given me … Yourself.

(R.J.)

144. My Story

How I Became a Christian

I grew up in a typical middle-class family in the 60's. My Dad had his own business selling post cards and gifts to tourist shops in New Orleans. My Mom kept the home until we got older. We attended a Baptist church where I heard the Bible preached. At twelve I made a decision to trust Jesus Christ as my savior. But I began to turn from my faith when I encountered problems at school and home. After school I would spend hours riding my Kawasaki 100, then later my Penton 125 with friends down by the canal. The more troubles I had with my parents, the more I withdrew into dirt bikes. By the time I was 17 my parents divorced and I had joined a motocross racing team. I converted an old van to haul two bikes, tools, gear and a bed. My friends and I would go to races and spend the night.

I always worked hard and had spending money. But I also began smoking marijuana and getting drunk. I started winning races, so I quit smoking cigarettes and started training seriously. My dream was to become a pro motocross racer.

One day at a race in Waggaman, my reckless lifestyle caught up with me. After the first moto I reached into the ice chest and grabbed a beer. I drank a few more to cool down. A friend lit a joint and I took a few puffs. Then I went out and raced the second moto. I made a mis-calculation on a dangerous section of track. I was accelerating out of a 60 foot ravine when my bike looped. I was going about 40 mph and was 15 feet up in the air when I had to step off the bike. I can still remember seeing my bike land on its wheels and roll into the crowd that parted before it. I landed sideways on my right ankle and tumbled head over heels down the track.

I remember the ambulance ride and the emergency room. The ER staff cut my expensive leather race pants against my wishes. When I was on the x-ray table, the technician turned my foot and my leg just stayed straight because all the bones in my ankle were crushed. I had to bite my wallet because of the pain.

I had broken bones before, but this was different. The doctors told me I'd never walk again. My Mom rallied prayer support. A specialist was called in to re-build my ankle with screws. I spent my 18th year in and out of the hospital. I lived that whole year on crutches. Fortunately I kept my job as a counter salesman at a refrigeration supply house, but had to move back in with my mother. I lost my dream of becoming a pro motocross racer — but I still didn't turn back to God.

Years passed and I became a commercial oil-field diver, met a lovely lady and got married. Linda and I bought a small camp and some land on the Tangipahoa River. We planned to build a new home over-looking the river. But the infamous flood of '83 came while Linda was pregnant with our first child. We got flooded out of our camp and the river washed away our septic tank, gas tank, water well, vegetable garden and 1/3 of our 2 acres of land. If you stepped off our back porch you would fall 25 feet down into the new river channel. Soon afterward, the oil-field went into a slump and I lost my job.

A few months later my daughter, Lacey, was born very sick. She had a mysterious infection and a 50/50 chance to survive. Linda wasn't allowed to hold her so she became scared. I'll never forget my first look at Lacey through the glass window of the father's waiting area. That little screaming, pre-mature baby was attached to an IV, monitor wires and oxygen in the incubator. Still, I didn't shed a tear.

After the first two days I was allowed to scrub down, don a mask and gloves and hold her in intensive care. They told me someone needed to start "bonding" with the baby and her mother was too sick. I would hold her and talk to her and tell her not to cry. I would pray for her, but in a casual, shallow way because it was all I knew to do. Still my heart remained hard.

The local church started praying for us. Although they had come out to visit us, we told them we weren't interested. For some reason they were still interested in us. The doctors didn't know what Lacey had, so they just gave her ampicillin. Three days later they isolated the infection. Guess what the cure was? Ampicillin.

Looking back I can see that God was at work, answering someone's prayer, working out his will. Finally, after two weeks Linda and Lacey re-gained their health and returned home - what was left of it. We had to move in with someone else in town until our house could be re-built and moved away from the edge of the riverbank. The bridge had washed out, so we had to drive several miles out of the way then hike down a trail for a few miles to get to the river. Finally we crossed the river in a little flat-boat to get to our home. I would go there to work on it every day.

The months passed, God miraculously sent some money to move the house and we moved back in, but my heart remained unmoved. I was still living my life apart from God. Money was hard to come by as I was still unemployed. I was struggling with tremendous feelings of guilt because I wasn't supporting our struggling young family.

One day, while Linda and Lacey were gone, I drove my old International Scout into town to make a withdrawal from my dwindling checking account. When I got back home I couldn't find the twenty dollar bill. So I drove back to the bank and asked the teller if she'd given me the money with the slip. She looked at me like I was crazy.

I drove back home and walked in the door. I muttered angrily to myself, "You know, it's come to the point when I can't even drive a twenty dollar bill home!" I just lost control. I started breaking furniture, tossing chairs around and having a temper tantrum. Anger turned to grief. I fell onto the floor, face down and started sobbing. Finally, after all the tragedy and problems, my heart broke before God. After a while, I said to God, "There's not much left to my life, but what's left, you can have." In that moment I could feel God reach down and pull my frustration, anger, despair, and worry off of me. It was like pulling up a tree by the roots. Suddenly I felt an unexplainable peace come over me. It was as if God had been right there all those years, waiting for me to surrender to His will.

In those moments I made a new commitment to Him. I decided to "do" what was in the Bible, not just "read" it. I took the family to the church that ministered to us in our time of need. After hearing God's Word, Linda made a decision to ask Jesus into her heart. We started a new life that has been abundant, secure and meaningful. Although problems still come, we now have the answer. Though we still have our disagreements, we are still on the same team. God's peace, provision and purpose have filled our lives. Soon after joining that church I got a business opportunity that led me on a new path. Years later, God has called me into ministry and I attended Seminary for six years, eventually graduating with a Master of Divinity in Pastoral Ministries with a major in Biblical Studies. I pastored a church for three years, then taught Junior High Bible at a Christian school for seven years, but eventually God led me to go back to the motocross racing community with the good news of His love, forgiveness and truth. Jesus said, *"You will know the truth and the truth will set you free."* (John 8:32) *"I am the way, the truth and the life. No one comes to the Father except through me."* (John 14:6)

There's no greater satisfaction than finding what you were created for, then doing it! Now He is taking the truth to new people through my speaking and writing. Today our children Lacey and Kyle are strong and healthy. Lacey is in college and Kyle is working in the offshore oil field. They are trying to find their own way in life. We still have problems, but God is always there to strengthen us and answer our prayers.

For God to be God, you have to just... let Him be God of your life. Don't just believe in Him - <u>trust</u> Him. Jesus died for our sins so we could be made right with God by faith. Jesus paid the price to "buy us back" from our life of sin. He has overcome death and evil for us. We can have this victory and live forever with Him if we are willing to yield to Him.

"Yet to all who received him, to those who believed in his name, he gave the right to become children of God—children born not of natural descent, nor of human decision or a husband's will, but born of God." (John 1:12-13)

R.J. 7/20/05

Our old camp on the Tangipahoa River in Amite, La. after the flood of '83, pictured here in its new location, still unfinished, during a very rare snow.

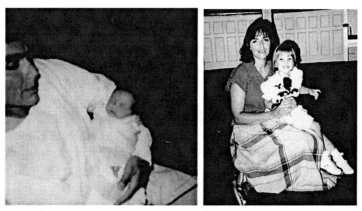

Lacey bonding with Dad at 2 days old. My wife Linda with Lacey on Mother's day (Which happens to be Lacey's birthday, too)

145. Self Esteem from the Pen of a Teenager

By: Lacey Jenkins, Dec. 3, 2000

Low self esteem. Where does this come from? Contrary to how it seems, low self-esteem does not come from a belief that I am "not good enough." Low self-esteem, for me, comes because of the opposite: "I do not believe I am weak." I cannot convince myself I need help. I believe in the American pioneer: strong, unconquerable, unstoppable, fearless... all of the above.

I cannot persuade myself that Christ's gruesome death is necessary. I have been told so. I know that I owe God a great debt. But, I also desperately feel a burden to try and pay that debt. Kinda like when someone gives you a Christmas present that you didn't expect a gift from, so you race around to find a gift for them in return?

I have not yet fully realized the extent of my weakness, because I have not, I cannot bear to read about the extravagant price that was paid. Instead, I try to repay Christ for dying for me, I try to "be good" but I will not take the help He offers. To use Him to pay my debt to Him would be to increase the debt, right? And yet, all my striving to pay the debt fails. Instead of finding myself a better person, I only discover more weaknesses, more failures to measure up; which depresses me.

That is low self-esteem. It comes from me being too proud to admit that I was ever terrible enough to need such redemption as the death of my Maker. I feel that Christ over-paid my bail, that there was some mistake made. How could I have ever been bad enough to require that great sacrifice: an innocent person slaughtered for me?

So, as my hard work comes to nothing, as I drive myself in circles to make myself good, I have yet served a purpose: my failures assemble and say to me, "You are indeed, in need of Christ's sacrifice. You never knew it, but now you do." The sacrifice was ENOUGH, not too much. I WAS terrible enough to need his sacrifice.

And once I realized this, shame filled me. I wish I could go back in time and say to this dear God: "Don't! Don't die for me! Can you not see I am worthless? I deserve nothing but death." I sentence myself to death and worse. I refuse Christ's gift again, this time because my debt is too great. No amount of goodness on His part should be able to cancel my sin

(there's a root there that says I am bigger than any God, so my badness will outweigh His goodness. I put myself over Him.)

Yet... I can't accept death. My soul groans for relief from the inner war I wage. And so, out of exhaustion, I fall down before my Christ and scream my pain to His ear. I cry for His grace. I beg to be freed of the chains I put on myself. And He frees me. The bliss of the first moment of freedom is even surpassed by days of peace, awake and sleeping. I am filled with joy.

I'll bet my family can track when I'm having quiet times because I'm ALWAYS singing and talking and hugging and giving back-scratches =). In these times, I'm so sure of His love, and I love Him back and want to love Him more.

Every once in a while, I attempt to take up my chains again. And the whole process repeats. Eventually, I grow depressed at my lack of faith. I leave His presence so often. I stray. How can He want me back after so many journeys away from Him? If my friends left me that often, and acted to me as I act to Him, I would drop them as quickly as possible. Cold shoulder. Will He do the same for me?

But this He has told me: "My dear Bride, I miss you and long for you with all my heart. I cannot wait for the day when we will be together."

So THAT is why He takes me back. He LOVES me. I am a part of His Bride, the Church. For His Bride, Christ will do anything. Christ will always welcome His beloved home again. No matter what. Because He is good.

The closest parallel I can see in the world is a man who is in love with a woman. No matter what he hears about her, no matter what she says to him, no matter what she does to him, he loves her deeply, and all she has to do is call his name, and he will catch the first flight to where she is and pick her up tenderly, saying, "Come dear, there's a meal waiting for us at home."

When I think of this story, I can hand my guilt right back to Satan where it came from and return to my Lord. God knows I'm not perfect. He would never let a mistake come between us. I would. But He wouldn't, and He's the only one that matters. I change. He doesn't.

How does this tie to self-esteem? Simple. My self-esteem is soaring when I spend time with God. Because I know that my worth is based on Christ, and what He did. So it's not based on me. Nothing I could or would ever do can possibly change my worth. And nothing anyone does to me will change my worth. Because God doesn't change, and what He did will never change.

I hope this helps someone.
Lacey Jean Jenkins

The author's daughter, Lacey Jean Jenkins in contemplation.

146. Yelling at God

Roy's note: I thought you might enjoy reading Lacey's e-mail she sent me after I asked her to proof read my first rough draft of this book while she was in from college one weekend. You'll get a glimpse into her own heart as she writes a thought-provoking devotion. Following are her words:

I would like to entitle this email: Yelling at God: Only a Good Idea if you're Very Close to Him. I actually don't have much to say. I was paging through my father's new book (the rough draft) when the thought hit me. Dad actually went really smart on me, this time. I am going to write down the conversation, and please don't be too hard on me for the immature tone of thoughts... I'm studying Adolescent Literature because that's the age group I'm going to teach. That means a LOT of reading the thoughts of teens. So here goes.

Dad: I finished the new book.
Me: *looks at him, vaguely*
Dad: You should read it, maybe proofread it?
Me: *nods, while thinking "Hey how about you proofread my papers? Like, all 87 of them. Then we can be even."*
Dad: You're in it. I put in something you wrote.
Me: ....

Later...
   Lacey waits till all family is asleep, then tiptoes to where the book is lying, and grabs it Like I said, Dad went smart on me. Laziness, foiled!
   So I'm paging through this huge binder, looking for whatever it is I wrote. I realize how big it is, and know the only way I'll be able to proofread it is to steal it for a couple of weeks. I read ONE devotion and it left me thoughtful. This is a pleasant thought. He probably won't want to give it up for that long. But I kinda wish he would. It might be good for me.
   I finally arrive at what I wrote. Surprise! It's on low self-esteem. For someone who has that figured out, shouldn't I be immune to it by now? Anyhow, I read through it and was surprised. It mentioned "scream at God" and I realized that I had done that just last night. How much of my time is spent growling/yelling/glaring at God? How much time, otherwise? Lots, and none, are the respective answers. This isn't as bad as it seems. I

don't spend much time talking to anyone. I spend all of my time in class, asleep, reading, or writing for class.

Anyway. The piece that my dad put in that book hit me below the belt. It talked about when I was happy, and it claimed that the times when I was happy directly corresponded with the times when I was talking to God. You know, you have a friend and you say "I'm not speaking to them anymore"? I don't mean just talking to Him, I meant just spending time with Him.

It must look pretty dumb to whoever is in the throne room with God. Girl storms in, tears streaming down her face, "I gave up my friends for you! Well, where are my new ones? You're supposed to provide them! I hate you! I can't be happy living life against your principles. I wasn't given a choice at all!" Girl storms out. Months later, Girl walks in again, "WHY ARE YOU DOING THIS TO ME? Where are my blessings? I thought you would take care of me!" Girl falls to knees crying. God tries to speak, tries to explain, but Girl left her earpiece on the shelf (Bible), and can't hear. Girl finishes crying, and leaves just as upset as when she came in.

I can just see it now. Archangel Michael looks at God and asks, "Is she always like this?" And God smiled sadly, and like a true parent says, "Lately. I'm hoping it's just a phase." He pauses, then adds, "I left her some special notes, aside from the usual letters. It's up to her to catch the hints." Michael nods and murmurs "So mote it be." The phrase ripples around the room as the other members catch it and pass it on, and God nods. Love always hopes, always perseveres.

Lacey

Psalm 97:11: *"Light shines on the godly, and joy on those who do right."*

Topical Index of Devotions

Forgiveness: 1, 4, 17, 27, 45, 46, 56, 66, 77, 83, 104, 106, 107, 112, 113, 122, 124, 130, 136, 144, 145.

Future: 9, 29, 48, 58, 65, 70, 71, 72, 77, 82, 84, 90, 91, 94, 99, 106, 109, 111, 112, 113, 114, 117, 121, 123, 124, 125, 129, 131, 132, 135, 136, 141, 142.

God

    Shepherd/Leader: 14, 36, 42, 47, 48, 49, 52, 74, 98, 102, 111, 112, 113, 115, 117, 120, 125, 129, 141, 145, 146.

    His Love: 28, 45, 72, 81, 91, 95, 120, 124, 136, 142, 144, 145, 146.

    His Power: 2, 6, 27, 31, 32, 40, 42, 46, 48, 50, 56, 67, 68, 75, 76, 77, 93, 100, 136, 141, 144.

    Presence: 8, 27, 30, 38, 47, 67, 68, 75, 76, 78, 92, 102, 107, 112, 115, 118, 144, 145, 146.

    Promises: 6, 27, 40, 61, 72, 73, 76, 79, 109, 112, 121, 124, 136.

    Protection: 38, 47, 61, 63, 92, 103, 122, 134, 141, 144.

    His Requirements: 6, 26, 39, 53, 54, 56, 59, 89, 90, 91, 104, 110, 118, 122, 126, 139, 140, 142.

    Understanding Him and His Plans: 5, 23, 24, 25, 39, 41, 42, 43, 47, 51, 52, 58, 62, 63, 64, 70, 71, 82, 84, 95, 101, 102, 107, 108, 109, 111, 113, 117, 121, 123, 124, 126, 136, 145, 146.

Greatness: 3, 20, 22, 33, 50, 58, 60, 65, 80, 85, 97, 108, 120, 121, 123, 125, 126, 132, 135, 141, 142.

Guidance: 9, 27, 29, 36, 37, 40, 48, 52, 54, 67, 85, 92, 98, 105, 115, 117, 121, 122, 123, 125, 128, 131, 143, 146.

Habits: 20, 65, 80, 93, 94, 97, 103, 115, 116, 119, 128, 135, 137, 139, 140, 145.

Health/Healing: 27, 39, 44, 55, 58, 65, 67, 69, 70, 79, 80, 84, 92, 93, 96, 99, 108, 117, 123, 133, 137, 138, 139, 144, 145, 146.

Hope: 17, 29, 61, 63, 67, 69, 70, 75, 77, 78, 82, 99, 101, 102, 106, 108, 109, 111, 114, 116, 119, 121, 124, 125, 127, 129, 132, 135, 136, 139, 145.

Humility: 3, 62, 64, 83, 86, 88, 97, 110, 115, 126, 135, 145.

Joy: 6, 15, 27, 29, 55, 57, 61, 69, 82, 84, 108, 110, 120, 121, 123, 124, 127, 132.

Laziness: 20, 50, 115, 118, 123, 125, 129, 140.

Love: 26, 28, 58, 66, 74, 80, 81, 83, 85, 86, 99, 105, 114, 120, 122, 123, 126, 131, 136, 142, 145.

Motivation: 25, 59, 74, 81, 83, 99, 115, 116, 120, 121, 123, 125, 130, 132, 133, 135.

Obedience: 26, 47, 51, 52, 53, 57, 59, 64, 72, 73, 76, 89, 90, 93, 94, 95, 100, 101, 102, 113, 115, 118, 119, 120, 140, 141, 142, 144.

Pain: 30, 47, 56, 64, 66, 71, 77, 79, 82, 84, 89, 96, 99, 101, 108, 111. 144, 146.

Parents: 21, 58, 70, 74, 80, 83, 85, 86, 87, 88, 90, 99, 105, 114, 121, 123, 125, 128, 130, 131, 138, 139, 141, 144.

Patience: 23, 38, 39, 42, 43, 47, 48, 59, 62, 63, 66, 67, 70, 78, 87, 97, 99, 109, 113, 114, 116, 135, 138, 141.

Perseverance: 1, 22, 37, 38, 43, 47, 49, 50, 62, 70, 71, 76, 78, 84, 89, 97, 99, 101, 108, 109, 113, 114, 116, 129, 130, 131, 132, 135, 141.

Prayer: 12, 27, 40, 44, 67, 79, 92, 93, 94, 98, 101, 117, 119, 122, 134, 141, 143, 144, 145, 146.

Preparation: 2, 12, 47, 63, 84, 93, 100, 101, 108, 111, 113, 116, 121, 125, 131, 132, 135, 140, 141.

Relationships with Others: 58, 60, 61, 66, 72, 74, 80, 81, 83, 85, 86, 88, 90, 94, 95, 97, 104, 105, 106, 121, 122, 123, 125, 126, 131, 138, 139, 143, 146.

Repentance: 28, 45, 56, 72, 91, 104, 106, 107, 112, 118, 142, 144.

The Resurrection: 17, 67, 71, 76, 109, 124, 142.

Respect: 58, 60, 74, 80, 83, 85, 86, 88, 97, 122, 123, 126, 138.

Salvation: 4, 18, 24, 28, 56, 71, 76, 91, 109, 112, 120, 124, 136, 142, 144.

Sin: 4, 28, 31, 32, 44, 45, 50, 53, 56, 72, 76, 90, 91, 93, 100, 103, 106, 107, 109, 112, 119, 124, 130, 136, 144, 145.

Spiritual Warfare/Satan: 13, 17, 31, 32, 42, 54, 67, 72, 90, 91, 92, 93, 100, 103, 108, 109, 113, 118, 119, 122, 141, 145.

Strength: 7, 31, 43, 59, 67, 68, 76, 77, 78, 82, 92, 93, 97, 101, 102, 115, 116, 119, 123, 125, 139, 141, 142, 143, 145.

Suffering: 1, 7, 31, 47, 48, 56, 62, 64, 70, 73, 76, 77, 79, 82, 84, 89, 99, 101, 108, 111, 129, 132, 135, 136, 144, 146.

Surprises: 12, 48, 72, 73, 82, 94, 111, 113, 116, 129, 130, 134, 144.

Temptation: 2, 13, 31, 32, 56, 60, 72, 93, 100, 103, 104, 109, 119, 130.

Testing: 5, 18, 26, 30, 32, 33, 39, 42, 59, 67, 84, 89, 100, 101, 108, 113, 118, 129, 135, 144, 146.

Trials/Trouble/Problems: 1, 2, 12, 19, 22, 30, 31, 32, 36, 37, 38, 41, 42, 47, 56, 62, 64, 68, 70, 77, 78, 79, 82, 84, 89, 92, 99, 100, 101, 102, 106, 108, 111, 113, 114, 116, 122, 129, 130, 132, 135, 136, 139, 141, 142, 144, 145, 146.

Trust: 9, 23, 38, 39, 52, 57, 59, 62, 67, 68, 73, 75, 76, 77, 82, 91, 92, 95, 102, 108, 111, 112, 115, 116, 119, 121, 125, 131, 140, 141, 142, 143, 146.

Victory: 17, 18, 30, 31, 32, 50, 53, 56, 61, 64, 67, 71, 76, 79, 82, 91, 92, 93, 94, 97, 99, 100, 101, 102, 112, 113, 116, 119, 121, 123, 125, 129, 130, 132, 133, 135, 136, 139, 140, 141, 142, 143, 144, 145, 146.

Vision: 9, 24, 25, 29, 48, 52, 59, 63, 90, 97, 103, 106, 110, 111, 116, 117, 121, 123, 125, 127, 131, 132, 135, 137, 140, 145, 146.

Wisdom: 11, 39, 52, 54, 60, 65, 69, 71, 80, 85, 94, 97, 101, 110, 114, 118, 121, 123, 125, 128, 131, 137, 139, 142.

Worry: 19, 30, 38, 47, 55, 57, 59, 75, 78, 79, 82, 92, 93, 101, 103, 106, 109, 110, 117, 119, 127, 129, 144.

This is what the Lord says:
"Let not the wise man boast of his wisdom
Or the strong man boast of his strength
Or the rich man boast of his riches,
But let him who boasts boast about this;
That he understands and knows me,
That I am the Lord, who exercises kindness,
justice and righteousness on earth,
For in these I delight,"
Declares the Lord.

(Jeremiah 9:23-24)

Printed in the United States
126504LV00003B/116/A